Political Illiberalism

Political Illiberalism

A Defense of Freedom

Peter L. P. Simpson

Routledge
Taylor & Francis Group

NEW YORK AND LONDON

First published 2015 by Transaction Publishers

First published in paperback 2018
by Routledge
711 Third Avenue, New York, NY 10017

and by Routledge
2 Park Square, Milton Park, Abingdon, Oxon OX14 4RN

Routledge is an imprint of the Taylor & Francis Group, an informa business

© 2018 Taylor & Francis

The right of Peter L. P. Simpson to be identified as author of this work has been asserted by him in accordance with sections 77 and 78 of the Copyright, Designs and Patents Act 1988.

All rights reserved. No part of this book may be reprinted or reproduced or utilised in any form or by any electronic, mechanical, or other means, now known or hereafter invented, including photocopying and recording, or in any information storage or retrieval system, without permission in writing from the publishers.

Trademark notice: Product or corporate names may be trademarks or registered trademarks, and are used only for identification and explanation without intent to infringe.

Library of Congress Cataloging-in-Publication Data
A catalog record has been requested for this book

ISBN: 978-1-4128-5574-7 (hbk)
ISBN: 978-1-4128-6522-7 (pbk)
ISBN: 978-1-315-12666-1 (ebk)

Typeset in WarnockPro

To the free and the brave,
wherever they may be

Contents

Introduction

The title of this book, *Political Illiberalism,* should sufficiently indicate its point and at least some of its contents. The title is a play on Rawls' book *Political Liberalism,* and the point is to give an account of political phenomena and to present a political theory opposed to what Rawls has presented in that and other writings (particularly *Theory of Justice*). Chapters One and Two of the present book are polemical, not by way of direct analysis and critique of Rawls, but rather by way of deconstructing the story about liberalism that Rawls and others have assumed or put forward. That story bears little resemblance either to the facts of history or to the actual workings of liberal states. Chapter Three does directly analyze and confront liberalism by challenging its view of liberty and by outlining a different and better-founded view.

The claim is controversial, for it has become virtually axiomatic in the modern world that freedom is only possible under modern arrangements and that it hardly existed before. The axiom darkens counsel. We cannot know where freedom exists unless we know what freedom is. Chapter Three expressly raises that question. It prepares the way for the rest of the book, which presents an alternative account of political phenomena and political theory that, while polemically called political illiberalism, is a truer account of political liberty than liberalism has put forward. The essence of this alternative account, in opposition to the one given by Rawls and his followers, states that politics is and must be about comprehensive visions of the good; and that a politics that is not about such visions and their promotion, as the Rawlsian is not, is fundamentally flawed. Liberal theory and practice need to be replaced. The titles and sections of the chapters from the contents will give a fair sense of what the replacement should be.

Integral to this argument is the claim, presented in the first chapters, that the modern state is, in its essentials, indistinguishable from despotism. This fact and the anti-state form of genuinely human politics are thence shown and argued in the following chapters, but particularly—as regard the American context—in Chapters Two and Eight, from what happened in the United States during the period when the Articles of Confederation were abolished and replaced by the Constitution. What the Federalists said about both of these constitutional arrangements was exposed by the Anti-Federalists at the time as false. The US Constitution did not save the American Union from imminent collapse, but opened the way instead to the collapse of freedom. The Constitution may, not unfairly, be described as a coup d'état, an oligarchic coup d'état. The fact had become evident already by the time of John Adams' presidency, if not already by the end of Washington's. Were it not for Jefferson's victory in the presidential election of 1800, the country might well have fallen into civil war then and there. But Jefferson's victory only delayed the inevitable, which came soon enough under Lincoln, whose centralizing of power followed the earlier example of Adams and Hamilton, first secretary of the treasury under Washington.

Centralizing despotism, however, is not inevitable and has not been the norm through most of human history. There is hope, and there are alternatives—provided we deconstruct the story of liberalism and of the state that the story promotes. The cornerstone of liberalism, and its strongest support, is the claim that politics should not be about the comprehensive good; whereas, on the contrary, such good is what politics should be about, from first to last. This point is defended throughout the present book, and especially from Chapter Four onward. That chapter and Chapter Five present the fundamentals of the idea as derived from human nature, with particular attention to the role and power of religion. Chapters Six to Nine apply and illustrate the fundamentals, using the political thought of Aristotle and the examples of the United States, of the Roman empires, and of some modern practice. The final chapter, Chapter Ten, concludes with some reflections on certain particular issues of morals in the political context of the comprehensive good.

The message and conclusion of the book may be expressed fairly simply. The modern state is despotism, and to seek for liberty within it is illusory. Human politics requires the devolution of authority to local communities on the one hand and a proper distinction between spiritual and temporal powers on the other. Neither of these desiderata exists in modern liberalism or the modern state. Human liberty and the human good can be found only in different political arrangements.

Note: Some of this material has appeared before in various published articles. It has, however, all been revised and reworked for proper inclusion in the unified theme and argument of this book. Gratitude must nevertheless be given to the following for permission to make use again of the cited articles:

"Liberalism: Political Success, Moral Failure?" *Journal of Social Philosophy* 21 (1990): 46–54.

"Political Authority and Moral Education." *Public Affairs Quarterly* 9 (1995): 47–62.

"Deus e Sócrates sobre os Males do Governo." *Hypnos* 15 (Sao Paolo, Brazil, 2005): 13–24.

"Representative Democracy's Feet of Clay." *Die Fragile Demokratie—The Fragility of Democracy*, ed. Anton Rauscher (Soziale Orientierung Band 19, Duncker & Humblot, Berlin, 2007): 277–290.

"Global Religious Education." *Philosophy of Education in the Era of Globalization*, ed. Raley & Preyer (Routledge, New York 2010): 212–225.

"Toleration Today and in Medieval Christendom (or How Medieval Christendom Got it Right)." *Toleranz und Menschenwuerde—Tolerance and Human Dignity*, ed. Anton Rauscher (Soziale Orientierung Band 21, Duncker & Humblot, Berlin, 2011): 283–293.

"Transcending Justice: Pope John Paul II and Just War." *Journal of Religious Ethics* 39 (2011): 286–298.

"A Corruption of Oligarchs." *On Oligarchy: Ancient Lessons for Modern Politics*, ed. David Edward Tabachnik and Toivo Koivukoski (University of Toronto Press, Toronto, 2011): 70–89.

"Property the Basis of Freedom against the State." *Das Eigentum als eine Bedingung der Freiheit—Property as a Condition of Liberty*, ed. Anton Rauscher (Soziale Orientierung Band 22, Duncker & Humblot, Berlin, 2013): 241–250.

"Aristotle (on Government)." *A Companion to Ancient Greek Government*, ed. Hans Beck (Wiley-Blackwell, 2013): 105–118.

1

Liberalism in Practice

The Official Story about Liberalism

Liberalism is a doctrine about the state and society and their inter-relations, and in particular about the interrelations between the state and the thinking and desires of those who make up society. As such the doctrine of liberalism is intrinsically tied to the idea of the state. Here lies a first fact about liberalism that needs to be more carefully noticed, for the assumption is typically made that the state is the organ of political power in communities, and that what disagreement concerns is not whether there should be states but what form these states should take. The assumption is further typically made that the state is the political power wherever and whatever the power is, so that the state is a universal phenomenon found (if in different forms) as much in the ancient and medieval worlds as in the present one. Little argument is forthcoming on behalf of these assumptions, but they are by no means self-evident. Indeed, as will be argued shortly, there is good reason to think them false.

As for liberalism itself, it is thought to be a distinctively new and modern way of confronting and answering questions about the state, namely about what power the state should have, what things it should preserve, protect, and promote, and on what grounds or with what justification. For according to the liberal claim, prior to the modern world, there was no liberalism, but there were states. These states were all in principle illiberal, in the sense that they taught and imposed on society a distinctive view of the good life, and more often than not a distinctively religious view of the good life. Those who disagreed with this view or religion imposed by the state had to be resisted or expelled or incarcerated or killed. The premodern and illiberal state therefore led inevitably to war, and above all to religious war. The wars that followed the Protestant Reformation in Europe furnish a standard example of the fact, but the earlier history of Europe in particular

1

during the ancient and medieval eras is said to be similar in kind, if not always in degree.

There are still today non-liberal or illiberal states in the world, as in particular communist states like North Korea, and Islamic states like those in the Middle East and Far East. Moreover, the wars these states produce are not only against dissidents within them but also against the liberal states of the West. For liberal states do not do what these illiberal states say should be done: namely to impose the true religion, or the true account of the good life, on society. The imposition takes the form principally of restrictive legislation whereby those who reject the true religion or true doctrine are denied rights and privileges equal to the ones enjoyed by those who accept that religion or doctrine; or they are subject to various kinds of coercion to make them embrace the state's imposed truth. Illiberalism, therefore, is intolerant, discriminatory, and coercively repressive, and even if it does not always provoke open war, it always denies to the oppressed members of society the pursuit of their own happiness in their own way. In the end, it makes everyone miserable, because even if it does not deny the true believers happiness (for the true believers have a state that supports and promotes true believers), it does deny them freedom. For no believer is permitted, for any reason (and least of all because of sincere conviction) to become an unbeliever or to act against the rules of the true belief. Those who do so are condemned as heretics and enemies of God, or of the state, or both. Classic examples are the banishment of such unbelievers to the Soviet gulags by the communists, or the beheadings of them by Islamic sharia courts, or the burnings of them at the stake by Catholic grand inquisitors or Protestant witch hunters.

Such are the results of illiberalism in politics. Modern liberalism is the solution to this state of affairs, because it removes the cause. It separates the state and its coercive authority from questions of the true religion or the true doctrine. These questions it leaves to the free choice of individuals within society. All it requires, and all it needs its coercive force to do, is to prevent individuals, not from living the good life they want, but from imposing their vision of the good life, or the true doctrine, on others by force. All are rather to be left free to pursue whatever life and beliefs they choose, provided only that they allow to all others the same freedom. The state's job is to provide the necessary conditions for this free pursuit of happiness by all, and for this purpose alone may its coercive force be legitimately used.

The Mythical Character of This Story

This story about liberalism (thus schematically stated), about its rise and its superiority to illiberalism, is almost entirely mythical. It is a colorful story so universally taught and so universally believed that few are able, or able very easily, to see through its colors to question its truth. The myth has become a sort of instinctive state of the public mind, whereby people are caught up into the belief that liberalism, or something analogous to it, is the only acceptable doctrine about political life. This belief, however, generates a paradox on the one hand and insinuates a falsehood on the other.

The paradox is that while liberalism claims to free people from the oppression of states that impose on everyone the one true doctrine espoused by the state, liberalism itself imposes on everyone such a doctrine: namely liberalism itself.[1] Liberal theorists have long been offering solutions to this paradox. Whether they have succeeded in theory is questionable.[2] Whether they or any others have succeeded in practice seems plain to view. They have not. All those in professedly liberal states who, for whatever reason, do not accept the liberal doctrine, or are suspected of not doing so, become enemies of the state. They must at the very least be watched carefully, and if their unbelief in any way proceeds to attack against the liberal state and its interests at home or abroad, they must be hunted down and rendered harmless. The liberal state has proved itself as ruthless against its opponents as any illiberal state is supposed to have done.

The falsehood is that the liberal state, contrary to the myth, is not a solution to some longstanding political problem. It is rather the invention of a new problem that before hardly existed. For the state is not a timeless human phenomenon whose history can be traced far into the past. On the contrary, it is almost entirely an invention of liberalism itself, first in theory by theorists and then progressively in practice by men of power and influence who, whether sincerely or insincerely, embraced the theory. This claim, which may seem more startling than the paradox, needs extended explication and analysis.

The Idea of the State

The first question to ask, for it is key to correct analysis, is what is meant by the state. An answer to this question is provided by Max Weber, the founder of modern sociology, who in a perceptive insight seems to have got to the heart of the matter. Here is the apposite quotation:

> Today the relation between the state and violence is an especially intimate one. In the past, the most varied institutions . . . have known the use of physical force as quite normal. Today, however, we have to say that a state is a human community that (successfully) claims the *monopoly of the legitimate use of physical force* within a given territory.[3]

By the state, then, is meant that special organization of political power that takes to itself a monopoly of coercion; that is, of the use of force to impose obedience to laws and policies. Note too, then, the novelty of this idea, for what Weber brings to our attention in this quotation is the difference between what existed before and what exists now. Before the modern emergence of the state, no institutional structure had a monopoly on coercive enforcement. The power to coerce has, of course, always existed and always been part of communal human life. Weber is not saying anything new by associating force with politics. What is new in his analysis, and in the state he is analyzing, is how this force relates to politics. In the past the power to coerce was not concentrated at any one point but diffused through the mass of the population. The nearest approach to the state in premodern times (though Weber does not mention the fact) was tyranny, where one man or a few did possess something close to a monopoly of coercion over everyone in a given area. For this reason was it typically called a tyranny: instead of all the citizens sharing control, only one or a very few did. Even kingships were not tyrannies in this sense, since kings ruled through powers of coercion diffused in the general mass.

One sign of the accuracy of Weber's definition is the absence of organized police forces in the premodern world. The police force is the institutional locus of the state's ordinary coercive power and holds a place analogous to that held in the past by the armed guard of the tyrant. The functions we now depute exclusively to the police were performed previously by the citizens, who relied on themselves and their relatives and friends for the enforcement of rights and for defense and protection. Another sign is the professional armies that exist in our modern states. What we call a professional army used to be called a standing army, and standing armies were considered a threat to peace and liberty. They constituted a permanent power of violence in the hands of the rulers, one that the rulers could use to impose on the people whatever they wished and whenever they wished it. Liberty and peace were to be secured, not by such permanent forces of coercion, but by occasional armies, composed of the people themselves, which rulers could only muster at such times and for such purposes as the people might approve of and willingly pay for, and which, when the time and purpose passed, naturally disbanded themselves.

The liberal state is not of this kind. It is comprehensively coercive. The very self-assertions of liberalism indicate the fact. For liberalism claims for itself a comprehensive neutrality. It says that it is able to reconcile all the visions of the good life and all religions into a harmonious community. For it espouses no comprehensive vision but secures instead the conditions under which all visions can live in peace. It secures, that is, the conditions where all are able to pursue the vision they prefer without interfering with or preventing anyone else who pursues a different vision. Comprehensive coercion is claimed by the state in the name of such peace and freedom. Only if no one may forcibly impose his vision on others are all free to pursue in peace the vision they prefer. Freedom is the freedom to pursue one's own comprehensive vision. Comprehensive coercion is the means to guarantee the freedom.

This feature of the liberal state points to certain key questions raised by liberalism: is freedom the freedom to pursue one's own vision of the good, and as guaranteed by the comprehensive power of the state? If so, why? If not, why not, and what is freedom instead? These questions need a separate treatment and will have to be dealt with directly later (in Chapter Three). Here it is sufficient to note that liberalism's freedom and the claimed neutrality of the liberal state between rival visions of the good are more apparent than real. Nevertheless, the appearance in question remains stubbornly attached to liberalism, especially among its supporters, and not surprisingly. Liberalism does in fact offer people, or many people, freedom to live life in their own way. Illiberal regimes, on the other hand, old and new, impose on their people some one vision of the good life and forbid or restrict the pursuit of any other. The good life, or some vision of the good life, is the principle and goal of illiberal regimes, and according to the liberal reading of history, nothing has thrown nations into more turmoil, strife, and war than disagreement over the good life. For to disagree about the good life and to try to pursue some different and opposed vision of the good is to attack the being of the existing regime, and so to become, in thought if not in fact, a subversive or a traitor. Liberalism avoids this consequence, not because it does not require agreement (all regimes require agreement if they are to be communities at all), but because it does not require agreement about the good life. By an ingenious trick that we owe to Hobbes, it requires only agreement to disagree about the good life. (Such is the essence of Hobbesian peace, to be discussed shortly under the state of nature doctrine.)

The agreement to disagree is a reflexive agreement, not a direct one. It is concerned not with some good life or vision of the good life, but instead with the attitude one may take up toward visions of the good life. That attitude must be one of tolerance toward other and different visions. Such a requirement is no mean or trivial one. It forces moderation and humility on every pursuit of the good. Forcing one's good on others, or pursuing a good that includes within itself the forced denial of others' good, is, for liberalism, the great evil.

Liberalism is, therefore, in one sense neutral and uncontroversial, but in another sense it is the reverse (here we return to the paradox). Liberalism is neutral and uncontroversial because it regards all the visions of the good life as equal and does not choose or judge between them. It is controversial because it demands that none pursue their vision of the good life to the forced suppression of any other vision. This demand is controversial because in the light of one vision of the good, the other visions are, or always threaten to become, an offense and a stumbling block, and require to be marginalized or suppressed if the true vision, the true good, is to prevail. Liberalism, by contrast, declares that no tolerable good requires the forced suppression of any other tolerable good. No good, it says, is worth fighting all the others to the death for. No good warrants extremism and fanaticism in its pursuit.

But what liberalism calls fanaticism, the followers of the true good call zeal; what it calls extremism, they call piety; what it calls tolerance, they call halfheartedness or even treachery. Liberalism has to root out this "zeal" and "piety" if it is to secure the peace on which its freedom is based. It has to war against all the particular visions of the good life and tame them and make them harmless. Otherwise it cannot work. Liberalism can only offer the freedom that is its badge and pride because it first imposes its own form of peace. This peace is non-negotiable and absolutely required. It is not something one is free to choose or not to choose. Liberalism may proclaim openly how it sets the people free; it keeps hidden how it also at the same time binds them.

The hiddenness of this constraint at the center of liberalism can be traced still in contemporary writers. The recent Rawlsian account of liberalism rests itself on a notion of a neutral core of morality, or of an overlapping consensus between rival visions of the good, which all such visions are supposed to be able to accept and live by.[4] This core or consensus is supposed to be neutral and overlapping because it takes those moral convictions that are common to rival visions and tries to make them a sufficient basis for peaceful coexistence. The core-morality lays down conditions of respect and tolerance that, while permitting each person to pursue their vision as they wish, forbids them so to pursue it that they forcibly prevent others from pursuing other visions.

This core is indeed neutral in the way described: it does not favor one vision of the good life over any other. But it is thus neutral only because it imposes on them toleration of their rivals. This toleration is not natural to these visions; indeed it is alien to them. By themselves they reject it. The core-morality that is abstracted from them to justify toleration is distorted in being so abstracted. For while respect and toleration of others can indeed be found in them, it is respect and toleration of those who share and honor the true good, or who at least are willing to live peaceably in a community dominated and formed by a good that they themselves do not accept (the way, for instance, that Christians and Jews have lived in Islamic nations or Jews and Muslims in Christian ones). Those who openly deny and dishonor the true good, because they assert and honor some other good, are at best misguided and at worst evil. It might not always be necessary to suppress them by force (although assuredly sometimes it is), but it will always be necessary to guard against them. They might, perhaps, be allowed to live, but they cannot be allowed equal respect, or equal privileges and protection under the law. Liberalism, by contrast, therefore is neutral in regard to each of the rival visions of the good life, not in the sense that it defends them all equally, but in the sense that it attacks them all equally. It rips from each their claim and right to make themselves the exclusive and only good.

Liberalism thus allows the many visions of the good to be, but it does not allow them to be alone. It forces them to tolerate each other, or in short to tolerate what they consider wrong or evil. There are many people and nations in the world who would rather risk losing themselves and the good than tolerate evil. Such people and such nations are the natural enemies of liberalism. For them liberalism is no salvation but a dire loss, no harbinger of peace but a herald of war. They see beneath its velvet glove the iron fist. Proponents of liberalism speak always and eloquently of the velvet glove; they keep a judicious silence about the iron fist. The bolder of them, indeed, might even deny it, while the less self-conscious might be wholly unaware of it. But the opponents of liberalism feel it only too keenly. One has only to think of the groups and individuals in the world (especially, it would appear, in the Middle East) who have a passionate hatred for the liberal West. People in the West might call them mad fanatics, but they call themselves servants of God.

One should not be surprised at this consequence, or indeed at liberalism's iron fist. For here precisely lies the cause of liberalism's proclaimed success. The many rival visions of the good cannot exist together in their natural or illiberal state, it says; on the contrary, they thus generate only conflict. Peace can only arise in such a state if one of these visions is victorious and removes and banishes all the others. But such a peace only brings joy to the victors; it brings misery to everyone else. Liberal peace is not of this sort. It brings joy to all and misery to none, because its victory is the victory of all. Or so the myth goes.

Notice, however, the Weberian character of this liberal peace. The peace can only be secured if the political authority has a monopoly on coercion, or only if none of the visions that liberalism keeps from breaking the peace possesses by itself the power to coerce. For if one or more of these visions did have such power, and especially if they had it by legitimate right, the peace would end as soon as any vision started using its power to coerce other and rival visions. Liberalism, thus, in its very idea, requires the emergence of the state as Weber defined it, and before liberalism, or before the modern world (as Weber indicated in the quotation given above), the state did not exist.

There are two pieces of evidence in particular that help confirm this fact: the state of nature doctrine invented by Thomas Hobbes and the Protestant Reformation.

The State of Nature Doctrine

The state of nature doctrine has two main features that deserve special notice: it treats human beings as isolated units, and it treats political power as indivisibly single. In the state of nature, people are thought of as moved by individual goods that divide and bring them into conflict. Individuals as such could happily unite if the goods they pursued were joint goods that required joint pursuit and joint possession. They might not unite, but they would live in peace, if the goods they pursued were not mutually exclusive. They would unavoidably come into conflict if one individual could not pursue his goods without preventing other individuals from pursuing theirs. Human goods would, in this case, divide and set at odds; they would not unite. Such is what happens in the state of nature, whether immediately, as in Hobbes' version, or progressively, as in Locke's and Rousseau's, or by idealized construction, as in Kant's and Rawls.[5]

Attached to this idea of the divisive character of human goods is also the idea of the equality of all individuals. That all human beings, qua human, are equal is an old idea. What is new in the state of nature doctrine is that the desires of all human beings are equal too.[6] Earlier doctrines taught that some goods were intrinsically superior and that those who pursued these goods were superior in character (though not in nature) to those who did not. This inequality of character naturally carried over into inequality of social and political status. Such inequality can find no justification in the state of nature doctrine. What replaces it is the thing we now call liberalism. For if, first, goods do not unite but divide people, and if, second, all desires are equal, then the solution for keeping a peace that is equal for all is that each only pursue his goods to the extent and in the way that all others can also pursue theirs.

There is another way of keeping peace. One individual could dominate everyone else and pursue his goods at their expense. This solution is the very unequal peace of the tyrant. In practice there can be no such tyrant; he is only possible in idea. No mere man could manage to be sufficiently strong and clever to keep everyone else in subjection. But while an all-powerful tyrant is impossible, an all-powerful tyranny is not. In fact, as Hobbes saw, such a tyranny is necessary, for liberalism is intrinsically unstable. It requires people to refrain from doing what, according to the theory, they by nature most want to do: namely to pursue to the full their individual visions of the good. Admittedly anyone who made this attempt would come into conflict with those around him and frustrate himself as much as them. But the temptation to do what one really wants must always be strong, and so, since the fear of the war of all against all is not enough to deter everyone all the time (or to deter the strong and clever much of the time), it needs to be backed up by the fear of the state. The state fulfills the role of the all-powerful tyrant and imposes, by brute force, liberal tolerance on chronically intolerant individuals. At any rate, so goes the theory, which, be it noted, subordinates all visions of the good, whether expressly religious or not, to the state and its coercing force.

The state as so conceived is the state of Weber's definition. No state could do the job required if there were other powers of coercion around that could rightly oppose it, for the war of nature that the state was set up to stop would thus merely be perpetuated. The state must, by necessity as well as by the right of liberal doctrine, be a single, comprehensive power that brooks no rival. In particular it must brook no religious rival. The state can, to be sure, allow religions or comprehensive visions of the good to exist, but only on two conditions: that they give up any claim to their own coercive power and that they accept the principles of liberal tolerance, especially as regards other religions and comprehensive visions. Otherwise the state must, in the name of liberal peace, suppress religion as ruthlessly as it suppresses any other opponent.

The state has to take to itself, therefore, a supremacy not just of power but also of teaching. It must impose on all religions and comprehensive visions the overriding belief of liberal tolerance and must forbid them the right to teach any doctrine that is incompatible with its own doctrine of liberalism. The state cannot, therefore, be neutral between religions, for it could be neutral while also being on a par with religions. To do its job, however, the state has to be superior to religions. It must dictate to them, if they are to be tolerated, both what they may publicly do and what they may publicly teach. For instance, it cannot tolerate a religion whose practices and teachings deny the authority claimed by the rulers or the rights accorded by them to other state-sanctioned religions. Yet all religions have to do this sort of thing from time to time, since it is of the essence of what a religion is (as also of what some other comprehensive visions are) that it have authority to interpret the will of the gods to men, especially about the proper forms of worship and about resistance to impious rulers. The state, therefore, in order to retain its monopoly of control, must take to itself a role and an authority that in all previous ages had been denied to everyone except priests.

The Protestant Reformation

Prior to the famous revolution called the Protestant Reformation, the religious authorities in human communities generally held a power equal and sometimes superior to that of the political authorities. The political authorities could not conduct the ordinary business of ruling, to say nothing of the extraordinary business of waging war, without the sanction of the priests and the performance of the due prayers and sacrifices. We are nowadays inclined to say that in the premodern world, there was no separation of church and state. But this assertion is inaccurate. In premodern times there *was* such a separation, or there was a separation of the religious from the political power. For both powers were *powers*; that is, sources of control within and over people's lives. Moreover, these powers were independent of each other, or, if conflict arose, the religious power took precedence. For after all, if there are gods, men are dependent on them and not they on men. The gods can be influenced by men through prayers and sacrifices, but they cannot be ruled by men. In the end, men's lives and fortunes are dependent on the will of the gods. Woe betide any merely human or political power, therefore, that would defy the gods or ignore their earthly ministers.

Such convictions are found not only in the pagan world of the Greeks and Romans (whereof their poetry and their histories bear eloquent witness), and not only in the pagan world of other ancient peoples, but also in the theistic world of the Jews, the Christians, and the Muslims. The Old and New Testaments and the Qur'an, together with the post-scriptural histories of all three religions, bear as eloquent witness here as do the pagan writings. It is medieval Christendom, however, that probably gives us the most articulated version of the theory. The independence of the two powers and their duty of mutual support became crystallized in Pope Gelasius' famous doctrine of the two swords, where what is to be noticed is less that the swords were *two* than that they were both *swords*.[7] The spiritual power had as much its own coercive laws as did the temporal, and each fought to prevent its own force and authority from being absorbed by the other. Since they were two, neither could have, let alone claim to have, a monopoly of coercion. Indeed, neither had a monopoly within its own sphere, for feudalism, with its pervasive system of reciprocal rights and duties, checked the power of the kings through the nobles and the power of these through the vassals and peasants, while the doctrine of apostolic succession endowed the bishops with an authority that neither derived from the pope nor ordinarily depended, for its continuance, on his sufferance.

This state of affairs could only end, and a monopoly of coercion could only be secured by the political power, when the idea that religion and the gods were superior to politics and human rule ceased to have so tight a hold over men's minds. In Europe the first step in this process was taken with the Protestant revolt from Rome. That revolt was not just a revolt against priests as the authoritative teachers of religion but also, of necessity, a revolt against the Church as an independent power in men's lives. Protestants only succeeded at the time in escaping the power of Rome and of the emperor, and only continued to succeed thereafter, because they made alliance with rival political powers and won from them both protection and support. This *de facto* dependence within Protestantism of the religious on the political power became, as was perhaps inevitable in light of the struggle that had existed between the two up to that point, an absorption of the religious power into the political. No coercive power was left on the religious side, and the political power took over the monopoly of it. A key stage was reached at the end of the religious wars that the Protestant revolt precipitated when, first by the Peace of Augsburg in 1555 and then by the Peace of Westphalia in 1648, the principle was adopted of *"cuius regio eius religio"* or "whose the region, his the religion." It meant that whoever held the political power in a given region was to determine also what religion that region should follow. A neater expression of the doctrine that the political power has control over religion would be hard to find.

The main ingredient in this growth of monopolistic power was what can only be called the apotheosis of the state. Religion, even pagan religion, prevented such apotheosis because it taught the subordination of all human things to the divine. This subordination prevented men from believing that anything human could be the best or most powerful thing to which total obedience might be due. But, with the abolition of religion as a center of power and authority independent of the state, such belief became increasingly actual. It found striking expression in the remark of Hegel that the state (not the church) is "the march of God in the world."[8] To believe that oxen or other beasts are gods, or even that the sun and moon and stars are, as the pagans did, was indeed foolish, but at least it kept alive the truth that the divine must be other than man and not under his control. An extreme of folly is only reached when, as in Hegel's remark, man and the works of man are identified with the divine.

So much should serve to falsify the alleged separation of church and state in the modern world. One does not separate the religious and the political merely by denying political power to religion or merely by denying ruling status to priests. One does so by denying divine power to the political. But to endow the political with what was previously reserved to religion is not separation of church and state; it is absorption of the church by the state. In medieval Christendom (as also in other religious civilizations) there was a true separation of the political and the religious powers, for both possessed control and authority, and each could resist the other. But the reason was that there was no state, or no monopoly of coercive power, in medieval Christendom.

One might argue in response that the emergence of the state, or the political power's having a monopoly on coercion, is a good thing. It puts a stop to war and oppression. But this claim is false in both its parts. The liberal state is only non-oppressive in the sense of oppression that liberalism itself defines, which is a self-serving way to discuss oppression. Few systems are oppressive by their own definition of oppression. If the absence of oppression is to be a way to judge between systems, we need a definition of oppression that does not beg the question from the start. A true definition of oppression depends on a true account of the human good and how it is to be achieved. Disputes about oppression are thus derivative from disputes about the good, and if liberalism is wrong on this point, it will be wrong about oppression too.[9]

The monopolistic state has not served to stop war either. It has created a war unparalleled in human history for capacity to inflict death and destruction, namely total war.[10] The world wars of the twentieth century are the supreme examples. Where the political power is only one among several powers, and where power is diffused through many different orders of society, a total mobilization of society for war is near impossible. No power has the monopoly of control over society to bring about a total mobilization of it, and that all the separate powers should agree to cooperate for this purpose, or to do so for long, cannot be credited. The diffusion of power, not the concentration of it into the state, would alone prevent total war. For the world wars were as much a function of mobilization as of weaponry. The state power commandeered the whole society, with all its material and mental resources, for the effort of destroying the enemy. The sophisticated weaponry, and its availability in huge quantities, was made possible by this mobilization. Modern nuclear weapons have taken death and destruction to an extreme even beyond total war. But if anything can stop their use, it will not be the monopolistic state (which will use these weapons if it thinks it must, as the United States did in 1945). Perhaps a renewed reverence for God might do it.

One cannot even say that it was the totalitarian and not the liberal version of the state that caused total war. In the world wars of the twentieth century that were fought between liberal and totalitarian states, the liberal states caused at least as much death and destruction as the totalitarian ones, and these liberal states also pursued war when the totalitarian ones would have preferred peace. Hitler, for instance, while he wanted to conquer the Slavic peoples to the east (and at least to neutralize France), did not want to fight Britain or the United States.[11] The German dictator wanted his own empire, but alongside and not against those of Britain and the United States. That Britain and the United States fought, and for total enemy capitulation too, was the decision of these liberal states. And if it is replied that they had to fight to save liberalism, this response only shows that liberal states will fight for themselves and what they believe in, like every other political system. So how, then, is liberalism better as regards war, since all systems will fight when they think they must? The only difference seems to be that liberalism will fight total wars, while most of these other systems will not be able to, which is an argument against liberalism and the state, not for them. In light of such facts, one will be hard pressed to see how humanity has gained from the emergence of liberalism and the state. Yet the liberal myth requires us to make this supposition.

Two Kinds of Liberalism

However, to be more precise, there are two kinds of liberalism, which may be characterized as the liberalism espoused by the theorists on the one hand, and that espoused by the politicians and the men of power and influence on the other. The former may also be associated with the Lockean version of the liberal state, and the latter with the Hobbesian one. For while Locke adopted Hobbes' fundamental political stance, that politics should not be about pursuing some one supreme or final good the same for all (as previous political thought, apart from that of Machiavelli, had done),[12] he rejected the absoluteness of Hobbes' solution. For Hobbes had argued, as was indicated above in discussing his state of nature doctrine, that the power of the state had to be unlimited and all-encompassing if it was to do its job of ending the war of all against all, or of one comprehensive vision against another. Locke, by contrast, argued that this cure was worse than the disease and that, while a state was necessary to secure peace, the state should be limited in its range and its objects. The power of coercion it possessed did have to be without rival, but this power should not extend as far as Hobbes wanted it to. It would be sufficient instead if this power were limited to definite and identifiable objects and if outside that range people were left free to act as they would.

Locke's vision reaches one of its classic concrete expressions in the Bill of Rights added as amendments to the United States Constitution. His vision is also the one that theorists typically endorse, in general if not in all details. The prevailing theoretical view is that, while there should be a state and while its job should be to provide the conditions for people to pursue their own vision of the good life, a wide range of independent and free action should be left to individuals and

14

communities to decide as they will. Differences arise among theorists about how extensive the freedom should be and how much power the state should have, and over what things it should range and by what justification. But all are agreed that there should be some limits, and that the state and its coercion should only go so far and no further.

Practical men, however, the politicians and others with power and influence, tend rather to the Hobbesian vision of the state. They seem more impressed by the difficulties of maintaining peace and by the recalcitrance and the secret, or not so secret, passion for subversion that, as they suppose, is always going to be found among the people. For the people, in their view, are more Hobbesian in character than Lockean. The people are always itching for more and will always try to get more, even at the expense of peace, if they are not constantly kept in fear by the all-powerful state. To counter this ineradicable tendency to subversion in men, and to counter this threat to peace and to the survival of the state, the state's coercive power, even if limited in ordinary circumstances, cannot be limited in extraordinary ones. In extraordinary circumstances there can, in principle, be no limit to the state's coercion. Otherwise, if people's passions are allowed free play, the mayhem of Hobbes' war of all against all will inevitably ensue. Practical men and politicians, therefore, are always seeking ways to expand the state and its coercion, not to hold it back or limit it. The massive increase in surveillance and in the invasion of privacy, even by professedly liberal states, is a striking confirmation of the fact. Whatever the theorists may say or wish, the state, in practice or in the hands of practical men, has an inevitable tendency to expand without limit. Moreover, because the state, by its monopoly of coercion, is able to command and mobilize all the resources of the society or nation, it has the *power* to expand without limit.

The result, and the truth behind liberalism's pleasing myth, is that what liberalism has produced is not an unheralded peace and freedom, but instead an unheralded despotism. There is nothing left that can hinder or halt the progress of the state to total control and total coercion over everyone and everything. This total control and coercion fall, moreover, into the hands of a very few individuals, namely the few politicians at the height of power in the several states and those few who, behind the scenes, may for one reason or another sway or control them.

The state, then, is both something new in human history and at the same time something old. What is old in it is despotism and the passion for despotism that have always existed among men and whose elimination or restraint has exercised the minds of political thinkers throughout the ages. What is new in it is the ability of this despotism, precisely because of liberal doctrine or the liberal myth, to become total and to embrace not only all matters but also all people and to reduce them without mercy to its thrall. Despotisms in the past were always limited, at least in geographical extent, so that some possibility of escape nevertheless remained. In the present day, the world itself is its geographical extent, for the state now is everywhere; and we have lost, because of liberalism's all-pervading myth, even the idea of there being any serious political arrangement that is not a state. The possibility of escape has been, or likely soon will be, entirely cut off.

Notes

1. Collins (2006: 15, 31–35, 169), Furman (1997), Kalb (2008), Schooyans (1997), Talisse (2005: 59–61).
2. Talisse (2009: 11–41). For direct discussion see Chapter Three below.
3. "Politics as a Vocation," in Gerth & C. Wright Mills (1965:2). Emphasis added.
4. Rawls (1993: Lecture IV).
5. The sources are Hobbes' *Leviathan*, Locke's *Second Treatise of Government*, Rousseau's *Social Contract*, Kant's *Universal History* and *Perpetual Peace*, and Rawls' *Theory of Justice*. For critiques of this view of the individual, or of the "unencumbered self" as it is sometimes called, see in particular the essays by multiple authors collected in Sandel (1984). Also Bates (2014).
6. Cf. Kalb (2008), ch. 2.
7. Set forth in his letter *Duo Sunt* of 494 to the emperor Athanasius, although the phrase "two swords" (from *Luke* 22 v.38 "Behold, here are two swords") is used for this purpose by Pope Boniface VIII (following St. Bernard's *De Consideratione*) in his bull *Unam Sanctam* of 1302.
8. Georg W. F. Hegel, *Philosophy of Right*, §258.
9. For a proper discussion of this question and of toleration generally, see Chapters Three and Five below.
10. The human *wish* to visit total destruction on one's enemy did not first arise in the modern world of the state. Some primitive tribes no doubt wiped out opposing tribes, or tried to, and there is the more striking example of the Mongols ravaging Asia and Europe. But the *capacity* to realize the wish by mobilizing huge masses of people in the service of total war does seem to be a feature peculiar to the monopolistic state, notwithstanding the controversial thesis of Pinker (2012) about the decline of violence in the modern world.
11. Hitler made these points clear in *Mein Kampf* and also, and more clearly, in the so-called *Zweites Buch*, written later but never published at the time. It was discovered after the war and published first in the 1960s.
12. For some of the details, see the supplement in Simpson (2011).

2

Historical Illustrations

Illustration from Ancient Texts

The argument given so far about liberalism's myth may seem too bizarre to be believable. Surely political power regularly took the form of what we call the state, even if the term is new. What is the evidence that things were ever different? Well, a first retort is that Weber, who must be presumed to have known what he was talking about, considered the state to be something new. A second retort is that, as just argued, to the extent the state is not new, it is indistinguishable from what previous generations called despotism or tyranny, and these previous generations thought there were, and often also enjoyed, very different forms of rule. A third retort is to give some examples of these different forms. Here several will be given, first from the more distant past of the Old Testament and Plato's *Republic*, and second from more recent history.

The example from the Old Testament is best given by two quotations, the first from the book of Judges and the second from the first book of Samuel (or alternatively the first book of Kings).[1] First from Judges:

> And the children of Israel did evil in the sight of the Lord and forgot the Lord their God and served Baalim and Astaroth. Therefore the anger of the Lord was hot against Israel, and he sold them into the hand of Chushan Rishathaim king of Mesopotamia. And the children of Israel served Chushan Rishathaim eight years. And when the children of Israel cried unto the Lord, the Lord raised up a deliverer to the children of Israel, who delivered them, even Othniel, the son of Kenaz [chapter 3, verses 7–9].
>
> In those days there was no king in Israel: every man did that which was right in his own eyes [chapter 21, verse 25].

Second from Samuel:

> The thing displeased Samuel, when they said, Give us a king to judge us. And Samuel prayed unto the Lord. And the Lord said unto Samuel, Hearken unto the voice of the people in all that they say unto thee: for they have not rejected thee, but they have rejected me, that I should not reign over them. According to the works which they have done since the day that I brought them up out of Egypt even unto this day, wherewith they have forsaken me, and served other gods, so do they also unto thee. Now therefore hearken unto their voice; howbeit yet protest solemnly unto them, and show them the manner of the king that shall reign over them.
>
> And Samuel told all the words of the Lord unto the people that asked of him a king. And he said, This will be the manner of the king that shall reign over you: He will take your sons, and appoint them for himself, for his chariots, and to be his horsemen; and some shall run before his chariots. And he will appoint him captains over thousands, and captains over fifties; and will set them to ear his ground, and to reap his harvest, and to make his instruments of war, and instruments of his chariots. And he will take your daughters to be confectionaries, and to be cooks, and to be bakers. And he will take your fields, and your vineyards, and your oliveyards, even the best of them, and give them to his servants. And he will take the tenth of your seed, and of your vineyards, and give to his officers, and to his servants. And he will take your manservants, and your maidservants, and your goodliest young men, and your asses, and put them to his work. He will take the tenth of your sheep: and ye shall be his servants. And ye shall cry out in that day because of your king which ye shall have chosen you; and the Lord will not hear you in that day.
>
> Nevertheless the people refused to obey the voice of Samuel, and they said, Nay; but we will have a king over us; that we also may be like all the nations; and that our king may judge us, and go out before us, and fight our battles [chapter 8, verses 6–20].

The second set of quotations comes from the second book of Plato's *Republic*:[2]

> Let us then consider, first of all, what will be their way of life, now that we have thus established them. Will they not produce corn, and wine, and clothes, and shoes, and build houses for themselves? And when they are housed, they will work, in summer, commonly, stripped and barefoot, but in winter substantially clothed and shod. They will feed on barley-meal and flour of wheat, baking and kneading them, making noble cakes and loaves; these they will serve up on a mat of reeds or on clean leaves, themselves reclining the while upon beds

strewn with yew or myrtle. And they and their children will feast, drinking of the wine which they have made, wearing garlands on their heads, and hymning the praises of the gods, in happy converse with one another. And they will take care that their families do not exceed their means; having an eye to poverty or war.

But, said Glaucon, interposing, you have not given them a relish to their meal.

True, I replied, I had forgotten; of course they must have a relish-salt, and olives, and cheese, and they will boil roots and herbs such as country people prepare; for a dessert we shall give them figs, and peas, and beans; and they will roast myrtle-berries and acorns at the fire, drinking in moderation. And with such a diet they may be expected to live in peace and health to a good old age, and bequeath a similar life to their children after them.

Yes, Socrates, he said, and if you were providing for a city of pigs, how else would you feed the beasts?

But what would you have, Glaucon? I replied.

Why, he said, you should give them the ordinary conveniences of life. People who are to be comfortable are accustomed to lie on sofas, and dine off tables, and they should have sauces and sweets in the modern style.

Yes, I said, now I understand: the question which you would have me consider is, not only how a city, but how a luxurious city is created; and possibly there is no harm in this, for in such a city we shall be more likely to see how justice and injustice originate. In my opinion the true and healthy constitution of the city is the one which I have described. But if you wish also to see a city at fever heat, I have no objection. For I suspect that many will not be satisfied with the simpler way of life [372a5–373a2]

[. . .]

True, he said.

Then we must enlarge our borders; for the original healthy city is no longer sufficient. Now will the city have to fill and swell with a multitude of callings which are not required by any natural want [373b1–4].

[. . .]

Certainly.

And the country which was enough to support the original inhabitants will be too small now, and not enough?

Quite true.

Then a slice of our neighbors' land will be wanted by us for pasture and tillage, and they will want a slice of ours, if, like ourselves, they exceed the limit of necessity, and give themselves up to the unlimited accumulation of wealth?

That, Socrates, will be inevitable.

And so we shall go to war, Glaucon. Shall we not?

Most certainly, he replied.

Then without determining as yet whether war does good or harm, thus much we may affirm, that now we have discovered war to be derived from causes which are also the causes of almost all the evils in Cities, private as well as public.

Undoubtedly.

And our City must once more enlarge; and this time there will be nothing short of a whole army, which will have to go out and fight with the invaders for all that we have, as well as for the things and persons whom we were describing above.

Why? he said; are they not capable of defending themselves?

No, I said; not if we were right in the principle which was acknowledged by all of us when we were framing the City: the principle, as you will remember, was that one man cannot practice many arts with success.

Very true, he said. [373d3–374a7].

[. . .]

Then it will be our duty to select, if we can, natures which are fitted for the task of guarding the city?

It will [374e6–9].

God's Rule over Israel

These passages need some exposition and analysis in order to draw out their implications for present purposes. First consider, then, the passages from the Old Testament.

The evils that God says the kings of Israel will commit against the people are basically twofold, those to do with war and those to do with luxury, and we may well suppose that God, like Socrates, sees the two as causally connected. Luxury will require fighting, and fighting will require luxury. For if the king is to be a permanent leader in war, as the people of Israel want, he must be released from all other burdens, and in particular from the burdens of providing life's necessities. Hence he will need lots of servants to farm his fields, to prepare his food, to make and clean his clothing, to build his dwellings, to relax and divert him after military exertions, and so forth. Moreover, all these necessities will have to be provided on a more extensive and splendid scale for the king than for anyone else, since his preeminence will otherwise not be sufficiently evident to awe the people into obedience. The same will be true as regards enemies, since a key element of success in war is keeping one's enemies fearful and diffident, which can hardly be done if one lacks evident displays of power and wealth. Conversely, just as his need to be at leisure for fighting will require the king to live in luxury, so his need for luxury will require him to be always at leisure to fight. For how will he get people to be his servants unless he can take them at will from the sons and daughters of his subjects? And how will he take them at will unless he can coerce them? And how will he coerce them unless he has the leisure and the resources to fight and defeat them? Thus, while his need for an army forces him to want luxury, so his need for luxury forces him to want an army. Not only do his needs for luxury and fighting thus feed off each other, but his need for fighting must also be extended to include his own people, and not just foreigners, among the objects of attack. In short, the kind of king the children of Israel desire is indistinguishable from a tyrant.

But why this result? Tyrants are, after all, not inevitable. There are surely ways of organizing rule such that the ruler is not a tyrant. Where, then, have the children of Israel gone wrong? What in their desire has led them astray? To answer this question, we must return to the time of Judges when, as yet, "there was no king in Israel" and "every man did that which was right in his own eyes." The crucial phrase here is "that which was right in his own eyes," for what did each man see as right? The answer is that it depended on the man. Some men saw as right that which was really right: namely, and above all, the law as given by God through Moses. Other men saw as right what was really wrong: namely, and above all, what was contrary to that law. Still other men no doubt saw a mixture of these two, seeing some really right things as right and other really right things as wrong. In addition, the numbers in each of these groups would change across time, with the majority sometimes being in one and sometimes in the other. In fact, the differing fates suffered by the children of Israel under the judges varied according to whether the majority were following the law or rejecting it. The typical pattern goes as follows:

At the beginning the children of Israel are following the law, and because they are, they occupy the Promised Land in prosperity and peace. This occupation does, to be sure, require a war of progressive conquest, but this war, led first by the law-abiding Joshua, is successful and the subsequent possession secure. Later stages of the war and later stages of possession are, however, not so happy. The reason is that the children of Israel, once successful in getting some of the land, forget the example of their leaders and ignore the law, living instead according to the shameful and idolatrous practices of the people whose land they have occupied. As a result, God in his anger withdraws his protection and lets them fall into the oppressive hands of their enemies.

The children of Israel, thus subjected to loss and suffering, repent of their past deeds and cry to God for help. God hears them, sends them a judge as leader, and restores them to their former happiness. When the judge dies, however, the children of Israel go back to their evil ways and suffer the same fate all over again: they are defeated and oppressed by their enemies, they repent and cry to God for help, God sends them another judge, they are rescued and restored, they return after a while to their evil ways, and they again suffer defeat and slavery.

These alternating periods of prosperity and peace, on the one hand, and of defeat and oppression, on the other, vary in length; but it appears that they do so according to how long the respective judge lives and gets the people to obey the law, or according to how long the children of Israel can endure their suffering before they repent. At all events, we should certainly conclude that if the children of Israel had willingly followed the law, they would neither have suffered defeat and oppression nor had need of judges to lead them. By seeing, each for himself, the rightness of the law and following it, they would have been sufficient both to live nobly as God wished and to be free of enemies. The fact that they achieved neither, except under the judges, is due to their own fault. One might have thought, then, that they would eventually learn their lesson and, wholly giving themselves to God and the law, enjoy interrupted freedom and peace without need of judges or kings. God himself would rule as their king, not, as he was forced to do, by setting up some human surrogate as judge, but directly through the revealed law living in their hearts and minds. Such rule by God, however, was the one thing the children of Israel refused. Except when suffering pain and loss, they preferred to commit any crime rather than follow God and his law.

Indeed, by penetrating further into the psyche of the children of Israel as the scriptures reveal it, we may say that what they wanted was to combine peace and prosperity with crime and idolatry rather than to have one without the other. This combination, of course, was and always is impossible (though an appearance of it can endure for a time). But the children of Israel were not then prepared to give up on the attempt. Their desire for a king was, in fact, their next way of trying, *per impossibile*, to realize it. For the king they wanted was someone who would be a permanent judge over them, and who would thus not only be a defense against enemies, as the earlier judges were, but who would also, unlike these other judges, be permanently at hand and would not need to be sent for by some special act of God. Hence the children of Israel would not need to repent of their evil ways to have a judge to save them. The judge, in the person of the king, would always be there for them, quite regardless of their obedience or disobedience to God's law. For this reason God says to the prophet Samuel that, in asking for a king, the children of Israel have rejected not Samuel but God. For they have rejected what God chose for them, namely obedience to God's law as their source of peace and prosperity, and they want instead to have peace and prosperity through a human means, an earthly and a permanent king.

The folly of this desire is evident. It is the settled teaching of reason that peace and prosperity are the results of virtue and not of vice. It is also the settled teaching of the Bible that the children of Israel were the chosen people of God only because they were supposed to be, through their obedience to God's law, an example and source of virtue for all men. They were, that is to say, not chosen as a matter of some playful whim. They were chosen for a purpose. Abandoning this purpose, as the children of Israel wished, was not just a crime against virtue; it was a crime against God and indeed against their fellow man. They were abandoning their God-appointed task to be a source of blessing for others. Not surprisingly, therefore, God only consents to give them a king who will, by his tyrannical power, be a scourge and an avenger of their sins, not a peacemaker. Indeed, it could not be otherwise. Vice, by its very nature, cannot avoid drawing its own vengeance with it. For it is already by itself a corruption of nature, and what is corrupt must soon perish, whether by its own inner putrefaction or by its incapacity to resist external attack. Such is, in fact, what happened to the children of Israel. Sometimes, to be sure, their kings were good, as was especially the case with David. But not only were good kings rare, they were, even as good, possessed of arbitrary power and could do as they pleased with whomever they pleased (the striking instance of which in David's case was how he dealt with Bathsheba and her husband).

In summary, then, what God wanted for the children of Israel was that he should be their king, not by the exercise of external and human rule, but by the exercise of his own wisdom directly informing them from within. The children of Israel would thus have had no human ruler over them, but instead each would have ruled over himself. They would have ruled not only in perfect freedom, but also in perfect justice and peace, because they would have ruled according to the law imprinted on their hearts by God. So when the Bible says that "in those days there was no king in Israel: every man did that which was right in his own eyes," the sense is not that there was always a mindless and destructive free-for-all (of the sort Hobbes imagined for his state of nature), but that there was, at least sometimes, a prosperous peace under the inspiration of divine wisdom through the revealed law of Moses. The great tragedy of the children of Israel is that, for the greater part of their history, they refused to follow the law and so were subjected first to the tyranny of their crimes, then to the tyranny of their kings, and finally to the tyranny of their enemies (Assyrians, Babylonians, Greeks, Romans). It was all so contrary to what God was offering and wanting them so longingly to enjoy.

Socrates' City of Pigs

When we turn to Socrates', or rather Glaucon's, city of pigs, we find something similar to what we find in the Bible. It is noteworthy, to begin with, that Socrates asserts that this city, the city of pigs, is the best city, or, as he puts it, "in my opinion the true and healthy constitution of the city is the one which I have described." Nowhere in *The Republic* does Socrates withdraw this judgment. What, then, are we to think of the city that he actually sets up in the remaining books of the dialogue, with its luxury, its army of auxiliaries, its communism of wives and children, its philosopher kings, and so forth? Is this city, which we have all grown to love and hate, not really Socrates' best city after all? This conclusion seems to be the one we should reach if we are to follow Socrates' actual words. But perhaps there is more here than immediately meets the eye.

We can begin with a puzzle noted by Aristotle, that the healthy city, the city of pigs, not only fails to include any armed force, but also fails to include any rulers or judges. A city, however, cannot exist without some people deliberating and judging about common affairs (Aristotle, *Politics*, 6(4)4.1291a22–30). In the feverish city, this defect is supplied by the philosopher kings, as the defect of the army is supplied by the auxiliaries. Now, according to Socrates, the healthy city will not need an army, since it will not be engaged in attacking neighbors to secure more land, more *Lebensraum*, for itself. Nor will it need an army to defend itself against neighbors, since, as Socrates may be supposing, all neighboring cities will also be healthy cities and not luxurious ones. At any rate, such seems to be the implication of Socrates' claim that the origin of war lies in the desire for luxury. For if we think away the desire for luxury, both in Socrates' city and in all neighboring cities, war will not arise, and hence the healthy city will have no need of an army. But whether it needs an army or not, will it not need deliberators and judges to direct common affairs?

On this point we need to consider more carefully what Socrates actually says about the way of life of the healthy city and its denizens.

> And they and their children will feast, drinking of the wine which they have made, wearing garlands on their heads, and hymning the praises of the gods, in happy converse with one another. And they will take care that their families do not exceed their means; having an eye to poverty or war.

The phrases to note here are "they and their children will feast . . . hymning the praises of the gods, in happy converse with one another" and "they will take care that their families do not exceed their means." Evidently, then, all these people, introduced initially by Socrates as engaged in the several arts ministering to human needs, have sufficient knowledge of divine things and of education that they can hymn the gods and rule their families. Whence comes this knowledge, if all they are supposed to be is artisans? Clearly we must suppose that Socrates intended them to be more than mere artisans. However, he does not get the chance to explain this point, because he is diverted by Glaucon into talking of the luxurious city instead. Now, while the luxurious city is said to reveal the origin of war (namely human greed), it is not said to reveal the origin of rule. Such rule, as we see, must already exist in the healthy city, though war does not exist there. Socrates does allow, nevertheless, that the luxurious city will more likely reveal to us the origin of justice. *We* shall more likely see justice in the luxurious city, he says, than in the healthy one. It is for this reason, perhaps, that he does not seem very disturbed by Glaucon's intervention, nor by the diversion of the luxurious city. Still, what the luxurious city reveals about justice will be only what the healthy city could reveal if we were able to see it. The only thing that the luxurious city reveals that the healthy city does not is the origin of war and, indeed, of evils generally.

Turning, then, to the luxurious city, we find that justice is there discovered to be each doing his own job and not interfering in the jobs of others (433b3–434d1). Now, such a definition of justice is only informative to the extent that we know what our own job is and what is not our own but another's. In the luxurious city, this knowledge is achieved through the division of the city into three classes according to the grades of souls. So each one knows what he has to do from knowing which class he is in, and thus each knows how to be just. The lower two classes, however, while they know which class they are in, do not know the reason for this division but simply follow the instructions of the first class, the philosophers. The philosophers give them, to be sure, a simulacrum of the reason through the myth of the metals, but this myth, while symbolically true, is literally false and even literally foolish (for how could souls be composed of metal?). The lower two classes can be just, we must accordingly conclude, and the higher of them, the auxiliaries, can be brave, but neither can be wise. Wisdom is the prerogative, and the job, of the philosophers alone.

The luxurious city thus reveals to us what justice is, but also, at the same time, it reveals to us the origin of justice. This origin is in fact nothing other than the principle on the basis of which the healthy city, the city of pigs, was founded, namely the principle of one man, one art or skill (433a1–b1). The origin of justice is the origin of the city. The city and justice begin together (cf. Aristotle, *Politics*, 1.2.1253a37–39). War, by contrast, begins not with the city, but instead with disease in the city. By nature, we may say, the city is not warlike. Armies and fighting are unnatural. But if the healthy city does not need an army, does it need philosophers? The healthy city needs justice, of course, since justice is its foundation. So this question becomes whether the healthy city needs philosophy in order to be just, and that question is, in its turn, the question whether it is possible to be just as well as ignorant and foolish at the same time. The luxurious city reveals that while individuals in the city can be just and ignorant (namely the lower two classes), the city as a whole cannot be. For, without the philosophers, the rest of the city will not be able to determine who belongs where or should do which job, and so will not be able to be just. The same is evidently true of the healthy city. But there are no classes in the healthy city such as one finds in the luxurious city. Everyone there is an artisan, sharing his products with others and judging what is best for his family. In the healthy city, so to say, "there is no king and every man does what is right in his own eyes."

We are back with the Book of Judges. But just as in that book, the law, as imprinted on each one's heart and mind by divine revelation, is what rules and ensures, if it is followed, that what is right in each one's eyes will be what is right according to the law; so in the healthy city, the principle of justice, on which the whole city is built, must be understood as informing the hearts and minds of all. The people and the city must consciously live out one and the same principle, and the people must accordingly be wise because they are just and just because they are wise. The people, in other words, must, by the nature of the case, all be philosophers (cf. Aristotle, *Politics*, 4(7)15.1334a22–34), or philosophers enough to know, independently of political structures, what justice is and to act on it. The city teaches them through its principle of justice, as God teaches the children of Israel through the revealed law. Notice, too, that the people in the healthy city live, in material terms, very like the way the auxiliaries and the philosophers are supposed to live in the luxurious city. Neither one has or enjoys any of the luxury (which is confined to the artisan and farming class in the luxurious city). Glaucon's brother, Adeimantus, makes this complaint about the luxurious city: that the guardians will not after all be happy, because they are deprived of the luxuries. Socrates, instead of accommodating Adeimantus as he earlier accommodated Glaucon, replies first that the point of the city is to make the whole city happy, not its parts, and second that the guardians will anyway be happy (419a1–420c4). Indeed, as he later explains, they will be seven hundred and twenty nine times happier than any tyrant (587b14–588a11).

The striking result is that Socrates, despite allowing Glaucon to lead him on a detour, has brought the discussion back to where it was, with the healthy city. Socrates could, therefore, have got to where he ends up without the detour; that is, without the luxury and the war that it engenders. Right in the healthy city we could have found justice and philosophers and the philosophic way of life. The philosopher kings of the luxurious city are really the citizens of the healthy city, living in material simplicity but with philosophical understanding. Thus the luxurious city ends up being ruled in effect by the healthy city. By the same token, there is no rule in the healthy city, for the philosophers in the luxurious city, while they rule everyone else, do not rule each other. So there can be no rule of one by another (save of children by parents) in the healthy city. Instead, like the children of Israel (or rather like the way God wanted the children of Israel to be), they are ruled by the wisdom present in each of them. But since there are no lower classes in the healthy city, and instead everyone belongs to one and the same class, there will be no one for anyone else to rule over, and so no rule—or no human rule, for there will certainly be divine rule through the wisdom that is present in each. Everyone in the healthy city is a self-sufficient philosopher, sharing all in common with all and each. And this same thing is what God wanted to be the case among the children of Israel, and which was actually the case among them, if only fitfully, in the time of the judges. It was never the case among the Greeks, of course, and Socrates openly concedes that his best city is a model laid up in heaven and not a reality on earth (592b1–5). It is only a reality on earth to the extent that given individuals, namely philosophers, model themselves on it. But under the law of God, it was more; it was an actual reality in Israel.

In sum, therefore, the failure of God's experiment with Israel and the unrealizability of Socrates' healthy city are to be traced to the same cause: human greed, or a love of the material self that amounts to contempt of God (*amor sui usque ad contemptum Dei*, to quote St. Augustine, *De civ. Dei* 14, 28). Such is what, in the person of Glaucon, leads to the end of the healthy city and the beginning of the luxurious city, and what, in the person of the disobedient children of Israel, leads to the end of the judges and the beginning of the kings.

What then is the message here? Simply the following: that the best human government is no human government, or no rule by one set of men, whether elected or not, over other sets of men. All actual human governments, or all governments that involve coercion of some men by others (as opposed to all men ruling themselves by inherent wisdom), originate in evil—the evil of material greed—and ultimately end in evil—the evil of tyranny (see the rake's progress of regimes from bad to worse in book nine of *The Republic*). Of course, as both Socrates and God insinuate, this tyranny, though evil, is what greedy materialists deserve. For since they have foresworn to rule themselves willingly through acquired or revealed wisdom, they will be ruled unwillingly by the imperious greed of the tyrant-king. Refusing to live free through wisdom, they will live imprisoned through compulsion. Thus they will not even enjoy the greed for which they gave up their freedom, or only enjoy it fitfully at the whim of their tyrants. These tyrants too will enjoy precarious and short-lived rule, since they will be forever envied, and forever threatened, by younger tyrants who want to take their place (the story of David and his son Absalom nicely illustrates the point).

Things have not changed much from the time of Socrates and the children of Israel to our own. We clamor for excessive luxuries as much as Glaucon did, and for a powerful ruler to protect us in our luxuries as much as the children of Israel did. Nowadays, though, these luxuries are called government-controlled social welfare and government-controlled equal rights and government-controlled alternative life-styles, and these rulers are called presidents and prime ministers. But the government control is the same old coercion, and presidents and prime ministers are the same old tyrants or despots. The one thing we moderns do not want is exactly what Glaucon and the children of Israel did not want: the freedom of self-rule through un-greedy wisdom.

Contemporary History: Despotic Oligarchy

The above conclusions may again seem tendentious or bizarre, or true in ancient story but not in real life. The skepticism is unjustified. Some tribes still today live without any state apparatus (so-called stateless societies such as one allegedly finds in parts of Africa, the Pacific Islands, and South America), and while they lack the trappings of modern civilized life, they also lack the threat of irresistible tyranny.[3] It is arguable that, at least in this respect, they are better off than we. Further, the existence of stateless societies, or societies with a minimum of centralized coercive force, can be illustrated from the United States both in the colonial period (for Britain's rule was, for the most part, very hands-off) and in the period of the Articles of Confederation. The Articles are a striking confirmation of how easily and how well free institutions can exist. The change from the Articles to the US Constitution is a striking confirmation of how easily free institutions can be destroyed.

To begin with, then, consider that the Articles are a controlled delegation of powers of the several states to a central alliance (it is called a "League of Friendship"). Notable features are that effective power and sovereignty rest with the states; that states send a committee of delegates to Congress (at least two and no more than seven); that these delegates are appointed annually; that they can be recalled at any time; that no one may be a delegate for more than three years in any six; that the delegates are maintained by their respective state; that delegates have no individual vote, but only a single vote as the delegation of their state; that there is no army in peacetime, whether for Congress or the states; that the states maintain, equip, and command their own contingents for the general army; that the committee that sits when Congress is in recess consists of one delegate from each state and that no one can serve as its president for more than one year in any three; that the agreement of nine out of the thirteen states is required for deciding questions of major import; and that Congress has no permanent supreme judiciary, but instead convenes, by a process of delegation and lot, a panel of judges to hear and settle disputes.[4] The Articles thus do not set up a national government, nor do they provide means for anyone to make a career as a national politician. Rather they go out of their way to exclude the possibility of both. Everything is done to keep effective authority and power in the hands of the states.

The Constitution, by contrast, does the opposite, setting up a permanent national government where individuals, albeit individuals from the several states, have a share as individuals in rule and in the rewards of rule. These individuals are elected by the people or appointed by the states for periods of two or four or six years, and there is no right of recall, nor are these individuals maintained by their states. There is an elected president, a standing army, and a permanent judiciary. None of these things is funded or maintained by the states, but instead by a national treasury that is itself funded through taxation levied directly on individuals and no longer on states. The powers of Congress, president, and judiciary are also all greatly extended so as to be, in principle or at least in cases of emergency, unlimited within the national sphere.[5]

The Constitution, therefore, makes two different changes at the same time: from a league to a national government and from a congress of delegates to a congress of individuals whose collective power, because it is the coercive power of the state and because *in extremis* it is unlimited, amounts to autocracy or despotism. That these individuals should further be designated as *oligarchs* (in idea if not always in fact) and their collective power as oligarchic despotism is shown by the role played in the Constitution by election.

Election is always of some people by some people, but everything depends on who chooses whom and how. The fundamental options (to follow Aristotle) are that all may choose from all or from some or from both; or some may choose from all or from some or from both; or all and some may choose from all or from some or from both. When all choose from all, the election may be called democratic; when some from some, oligarchic; when mixed, aristocratic or political.[6] Under the United States Constitution as first proposed, only representatives were chosen by all from some (by all the citizens of the respective state from proposed candidates). The election of president and senators was by some from all or from some (by the electoral college or by the state legislatures from whomever they might wish). The election of the president, however, quickly became in fact by all from some (by all the citizens of all the states from the proposed candidates), but it took over a hundred years before, by the Seventeenth Amendment of 1913, federal senators came to be elected by all the citizens of the respective state. The same practice prevails in state and local elections, so that all elections are now by all from some, namely by all the citizens of the relevant constituency from the candidates named on the ballot.[7]

One might conclude from this analysis that the system of elections in the United States would, by this classification, count as aristocratic or political. With respect to form, it may be so. With respect to practice, it is not. For an element of political sophistry here intervenes, since there are at least two ways of understanding what is meant by election. We mean by elections choosing between candidates whose names are on the ballot and who have, before the election, been going about soliciting people for their votes. Others, by contrast, have meant choosing from among candidates who are not named on any ballot and who have not been going about soliciting votes. Aristotle, for instance, opposes soliciting for votes, because it encourages vice and crime. At any rate, he says:

> [I]t is also not right that anyone who is going to be judged worthy of office should himself have to ask for it. If a man is worthy of office, he should rule whether he wants to or not. . . . [N]o one would ask to rule who was not in love with honor, yet men commit most of their crimes from love of honor or money.[8]

And again:

> Regimes also undergo change without faction . . . as in Heraia because of vote-getting; for elections were being won by those campaigning for votes and so they had the officials chosen by lot instead.[9]

Aristotle's point is clear. Those should rule who are worthy of it, but electioneering ensures that the unworthy, the ambitious and greedy and criminal, rule instead, and it does so for two reasons: first because those who would stoop to campaign for election are mainly the ambitious and greedy, and second because where campaigning for election is allowed, those who campaign, win; while those who do not, lose. We might note also another remark of Aristotle's: that the ambitious and greedy will inevitably use office to make money.[10] Indeed, if we go by revelations of political money-grubbing over the years, we may well be astonished not merely by the effrontery but by the enormity of the thefts that modern politicians conceive and carry out and get away with.

Nowadays election campaigns are inseparable from elections, and we cannot imagine one without the other. The result is that candidates, in order to win or retain office, must first and indeed only become successful in campaigning. Success in campaigning is a function of several things but principally of what we call name recognition and image; that is to say, of the candidate being known to the electorate and of his public persona being approved by them. How does a candidate get to be known and approved by the electorate, especially by an electorate numbering in the millions (as is invariably the case today)? The answer is to be or to become an oligarch. By oligarchs is meant, as Aristotle explains, those who are rich and have the privileges that naturally accompany riches, as good birth and family, education, personal accomplishment, wealthy and powerful friends, public prominence, and the like.[11] Such things do not guarantee election, but without them election is well-nigh impossible. Those who do not have them must somehow acquire them, or acquire friends who have them, in order to be successful in winning office. The following facts should suffice to prove the point.

The first fact is that elections for office must inevitably favor the privileged few. Elections are won by number of votes cast in one's favor, and no one can receive many votes who is not known and admired by many. The features that attract attention and give renown are wealth, high social class, prominent family, conspicuous achievement, striking physical beauty, and the like. To possess some or other of these marks brings one notice and so puts one among the notables, as they may rightly be called. The notables are, of their nature, the known, and the marks they are known by are, of their nature, among things admirable. The notables need not be the best, or the wisest, or the most just, but they cannot avoid being the most electable. A second fact is that the more numerous the voters, the fewer will be the notables who are likely to win any great number of votes. Among a few hundred or a few thousand, there are many, even of a moderate standing, who could enjoy a known reputation; among a hundred thousand, likely none of them will; among a million, let alone the over three hundred million who live in the United States, only the outstandingly extraordinary would do so. Many cast votes; an extreme minority receives them. All choose; from whom they choose are very few. A third and closely related fact is that election campaigns are expensive and require leisure from necessities so that one may spend all or most of one's time seeking votes. Only the wealthy and privileged or those supported and maintained by the wealthy and privileged can afford either the money or the time. The middle class and the mass of the poor can afford neither. A fourth fact is that elections are never just a matter of casting votes for whomever one wills, for there is also the advance selection of candidates. When it comes time for the people to choose their representatives, the existing representatives along with their friends and paid retainers (the political parties and their agents) have already determined the candidates for whom alone the people may vote. Most often the existing representative is the chief of these candidates and the favorite to win again. Sometimes the people, or a limited part of them, are also given a say in this determining of candidates (as in the primary elections). But not always do they have such a say, and even when they do, they have no say in determining who will compete to be a candidate (there are no primary elections for primary elections). Those who compete to be candidates are self-chosen, if they are already among the wealthy notables, or also chosen by those who are prominent and powerful in the political parties. At no point are the people encouraged to choose whomever they wish. The eligible candidates are carefully selected for them beforehand.

Such facts have become true of politics in the United States because of the United States Constitution. They did not and could not become true of it under the Articles of Confederation. Such facts also prove the United States to be a centralized oligarchy, as is evident from the following list of oligarchic features, all of which can be seen to apply to the United States:

1) All the offices are chosen from some, namely the rich and privileged and their protégés.
2) These some are always the rulers (as a class if not as individuals), while the poor and unprivileged are always ruled.
3) No offices are chosen by lot.
4) High property qualifications are, *de facto* if not *de jure*, required for office.
5) The same individuals, by being repeatedly reelected, occupy the same office often or always.
6) All the offices are of long duration (none lasts only a year).
7) The same class or their protégés also become the judges and lawyers and decide questions of law, even controlling, to a large extent, the composition of juries; certainly this class and the elected officials control the most important cases, as those to do with the giving of accounts and with the regime and private contracts.
8) There is no popular assembly, and the people as such control nothing.

Not all these features were necessarily realized at once (as in particular the choosing of senators, which, as already noted, has only been by popular election since 1913). But the chief oligarchic features were there from the beginning. Moreover, some of these features are achieved by what may be called oligarchic sophistry, as item 4, since the requirement of high property qualifications for office is not a matter of law but of the nature of election campaigns. Only the wealthy could afford the expense or the time or could secure the number of supporters to win election or even, indeed, to get their name on the ballot. In the United States, then, all are permitted to run for office but only the wealthy could afford to do so or have any serious chance of winning. That one may be an oligarch, not by one's own personal wealth, but through membership in a party whose candidate for a given election one has managed to become, makes no difference. The candidate inherits, as it were, the wealth and support and time of the party for the purposes of winning the election.

Such political parties and their oligarchic character were well known, for instance, to Aristotle. He calls them political clubs, and thus describes their role in election campaigns:

> Oligarchies are . . . changed from within, as through the rivalry of demagogues . . . when those in the oligarchy are demagogues to the crowd, as the regime guardians were in Larissa, for instance, because it was the crowd that elected them. The same is true of all oligarchies where those who provide the rulers are not those who elect to office, but the offices are filled from high property qualifications or from political clubs, and those possessed of heavy arms or the populace do the electing.[12]

This passage describes almost to the letter the practice of election to office in our own day. We call it representative democracy, and pride ourselves on the discovery of representation, holding it to be something of which the ancients were ignorant.[13] But Aristotle knew of it. He refrained, however, from calling it either representation or democracy. He called it, as just indicated, demagogic oligarchy. What we term representative democracy,[14] and what we praise as a way to extend democracy to vastly greater numbers of people than ancient democracies ever conceived of, he would call oligarchic sophistry. It is a trick to make people believe they share rule, when in fact they do not. We should, then, according to Aristotle, pride ourselves, if pride be the right word, not on discovering universal democracy, but instead on discovering universal sophistry.

The general oligarchic character of American politics under the Constitution, and its inevitable tending to despotic control from the center, is now true of virtually every nation on earth (the exceptions are tyrannies or military despotisms, which, if anything, just exaggerate the worst elements of oligarchy). These changes in political action came about in the case of the United States, as already remarked, through the overthrow of the Articles of Confederation. But they also came about, and especially in Europe and then the world, through changes in political thought, in particular the modern doctrine of rights. This doctrine is deceptively described as one of equal rights for all. Everything depends on what is meant by equality. Proportional equality, where each gets what is individually deserved, is an equality no less than is mathematical equality, where each gets what is quantitatively the same. Ancient and medieval doctrines of rights applied proportional equality to the distribution of political power and understood the divisions within society between which proportional equality held—notably the lords, the commons, the monarch, and the clergy—as relatively but by no means absolutely fixed. Moreover, because of feudal practice, medieval doctrines recognized the differences of places and peoples and guaranteed to each their many separate practices and customs.[15] Rights in the medieval world were realized in a host of differences between classes and places and persons.

The modern doctrine of rights took offense at medieval difference and sought to abolish it with universal sameness. The cry of equality became, in practice, the cry of uniformity,[16] and hence became at the same time the cry of revolution, for uniformity could only be introduced by overthrowing the existing difference. To quote one historian's judgment:

> Two world wars and the technological and industrial revolution have accelerated a development which began with Napoleon's liquidation of the Holy Roman Empire. Deliberately uprooted, the colourful diversity of life in Europe has gradually withered away. The great drive to make countries, political institutions and men uniform and conformist, the drive so successfully promoted by Richelieu, Mazarin, Louis XIV and the great revolution, in the nineteenth century also made its impact on the German central core of Old Europe. Englishmen and continental Europeans assisted alike in the forward march of this process through which Europe developed its technical, economic and military potential and made for itself new and freely expanding labour markets, spheres of influence and battle-grounds. Much has been lost to Europe as a result. . . . The Holy Roman Empire had contained within it many fatherlands and motherlands, all the greater and lesser principalities and lordships which it sheltered under its roof. Goethe remained a Frankfurter all his life. Schiller was a Swabian in exile. Beethoven's "fatherland" was Bonn.[17]

Perhaps this picture is overdrawn and indulges in romantic idealization, but it contains a basic truth, namely the truth of difference in the parts as opposed to uniformity imposed from the center. Admittedly the difference prevalent and celebrated in all the parts of the Holy Roman Empire was not called difference by the purveyors of the modern doctrine of rights, but rather privilege and despotism. The charge is disingenuous. The modern doctrine of rights has introduced as much privilege and despotism as the older one, if not more. The French Revolution is itself the classic instance, since no man in the old regime, not even the monarch, ever held the power and authority over others' life and property that Robespierre or Napoleon managed to secure. There were too many restraints of law and right and custom, and even of independent coercive power, ever to grant the monarch or lord so absolute a command. Moreover, for the same reason, no monarch or lord of medieval times ever held as much power over the people as modern presidents and prime ministers do. That modern presidents and prime ministers are elected, at least for the most part, while medieval lords and kings were hereditary, makes no difference, for the modern concentrations of power at the center, however one comes by the right to exercise it, exceed by far anything that a medieval monarch could boast of. One has to return, as remarked earlier, to the tyrants of the ancient world to find parallels.

Where equality is understood to be uniformity, as it is in the modern doctrine of rights, the result is not only revolution but also centralization. Ancient and medieval rulers had not been able to control things easily from the center, not because of absence of personnel or technology, but because of absence of uniformity. Each locality, being different in its customs and so also in its rights, had to be treated according to its customs and rights, and a law or command from the center adapted to the peculiarities of one locale would not fit those of another, so that there had to be almost as many commands as there were locales.[18] The new doctrine of equal rights repudiated difference, so that people not only ceased to possess, but even ceased to recognize, the right to be different. The force of command from the center could thus proceed directly to all the parts without being diverted or checked or modified by either the fact or the conviction of local difference. Centralization became real in thought and in deed. When, therefore, through the process of elections and universal suffrage, the reins of centralized power fell, as they have now fallen, into the hands of the wealthy (however dependent the wealthy may be on periodic displays of electoral support), the triumph of oligarchy, oligarchic despotism in extent of coercive power, became complete.

Further Illustration: Representations

Lest these illustrations and their analysis still seem unconvincing, consider the point again from the idea of representation, which as noted is supposed to be the distinctive discovery and mark of democratic states in the modern world. The different ways representation can be understood will serve to reinforce the above contentions about the oligarchy and demagoguery and despotism of the modern state and of the practices of modern liberalism.

A first way of taking representation is where what is to be represented is the common good of the whole community, or the real and objective interests of the people. These interests are those of nature and tradition—tradition as well as nature because a feature of human existence is that we realize our nature in particular places and times and in accord with particular choices adapted to those places and times. To live in accord with conventions and customary practices handed down from ancestors is natural to man, and one of our natural rights is to have these conventions and customs respected and left undisturbed, provided they are not repugnant to reason or justice and are not imposed against the popular will.

Proper representation of the interests of nature and tradition needs persons who, whether by social condition or habit or learning, understand these interests and evince active motivation by them in thought and deed. Such are typically found among the possessors of ancient privilege or high social distinction or traditional authority. That they should be found in the most numerous class or come from the general mass of the folk is not to be expected, although the folk can, as in Plato's *Republic*, be expected by custom and upbringing to embrace with affection the ancient tradition and its practices. They will be found among the few. But not the arrogant few, nor the restless seekers after gain, nor the mischievous lovers of political novelties, though the upper classes may contain many such. They will be the class of gentlemen, those who, along with enjoying, as it may be, the advantages of birth and privilege, possess also the virtues of moderation and prudence. The fitness of gentlemen to represent the common good of the whole is not bestowed or earned by popular elections. It belongs to them, if it belongs to them, by right of natural, intrinsic worth, though confirmation may, for reasons of political prudence, be sought through the suffrage of their peers.

An example of sorts can be found in the Britain of Edmund Burke before the passage of the several reform bills. One special target of these bills was the "rotten boroughs," as opponents called them, or areas of the country with a small, rural population where the representative sent to Parliament was the effective appointee of the local squire or of the men of distinction who alone had the suffrage. Burke protested that there was nothing rotten about these boroughs, however small their populace or narrow their franchise, if by representation be meant, as Burke took it to mean, the representation of the real, common good. The abiding interests of a people or country are not a function of the felt wants of the majority of voters at the time of election. They are a function of the objective needs of human nature as these are historically realized in that nation or people.[19]

A people or a nation is, supposes Burke, not a momentary reality but instead endures through centuries and even millennia. It is a product and a continuing cause of traditions and practices that may be more worth preserving from the point of view of the concrete good of the people than any number of changes that, abstractly considered, are more rational. To overthrow tradition and custom in the name of an alleged universal reason is, more often than not, neither good nor wise. Men are not robots or computers that can be reprogrammed at will. They are living souls who preserve, as they measure, the passages of time, and who thereby come to love the familiar things of their native land merely because they are familiar. Man may be a universal being with a universal nature, but it is part of this nature, and a dispensation of reason too, that he should be formed in the concrete through the accidental and particular circumstances of his birth. To represent this combination of the universal and particular in the political counsels of the nation is neither easy nor simple, and the habits of the ages, as handed down from father to son, likely contain more wisdom, as they surely contain more practical force, than the inventions of a new generation or the nostrums of intellectual fashion. Real appreciation for the concrete good of concrete folk, which is the condition for the proper representation of it, is not to be tested or measured by size of electorate or wideness and equality of the franchise. Such things lie at a tangent to what representation demands. Someone holding office by class or inheritance and who is not elected, or not by all but only by a few, can easily be a better representative of the whole than he who has the united voice of the masses behind him.

In sharp contrast with the first kind of representation is a second and modern one. Here what is to be represented, or what at least there is an aim to represent, is the actual, felt desires of the people or of most of the people. The reason for this difference is a revolutionary change in what is meant by interest. The first way of taking representation presupposes, as just discussed, that there is such a thing as objective interest, whether historically embodied or not, and that knowledge of this interest, of its conditions and its realization, while it will be found in some of those whose interest it is, such as the settled and respectable, whether commoners or gentlemen, need not be found in all of them, such as the restless rich or the envious poor. Actual motivation by this interest may be similarly partial and limited. Representation of objective interest may be realized best if some alone and not all determine who shall be the representatives. The second and modern way of taking representation rejects this understanding. In its extreme form, which also is its more common, it denies there is any objective interest of the sort mentioned that some could know or be motivated by and others not. Interest does not exist as a thing to be determined independently of the actual and felt desires of all the people involved. It is no more than the resultant or combination of these desires, and it is only to be measured by taking the weight of each of them and seeing where the preponderance, if any, is found to lie. No one's desire or knowledge can, in such a case, be adjudged intrinsically superior to that of any other. All count for one and none for more than one (notice here the influence of the state of nature doctrine and its notion of individuals as bundles of equal but conflicting passions). Some may perhaps be better or quicker at discerning what the actual desires are of a given collection of people, and some also may be better at discovering how best these desires or the preponderance of them can be satisfied. But they cannot go further. No representation of these desires can be fair, or is even achievable, unless all of them are fully weighed and unless too the determination of representatives reflects the equal suffrage of those whose the desires are. The majority vote of all is in practice the only means of electing representatives that is just. Where election is not open to all, or where the votes of some weigh more than those of others, there no genuine representation can exist, and a few, in place of all, enjoy the benefits of rule.

The less extreme form of this second way of understanding representation is less extreme in theory only but in practice differs little from the other. There may be, it allows, such a thing as objective interest, for assuredly there are some wants that are common and inescapable for all, such as the wants of physical shelter and sustenance, of emotional affection, of family and friends, of education, and of free expression. Some objective measure also can be taken of these wants and a general determination of the conditions of their satisfaction arrived at. But the particularities and specific modalities of these wants as they exist in this or that group or individual cannot be determined independently of the measuring of actual feelings and preferences. This measuring in turn cannot be done save through the register of majority votes in elections open to all. The practical upshot, in this case as well as in the other and extreme case, reduces, then, to the same.

Elements of representation in this second sense, whether extreme or not, lie ready to hand in the United States Constitution as this was interpreted, both then and now, by the widely read and influential Federalist Papers, in particular by the teaching about faction presented by James Madison (in the paper numbered ten in that collection). A faction, as understood by Madison, is a particular interest or the interest of a part in opposition to that of the whole. Madison has in mind, even if he does not say so directly, actual and felt interests, since he means by faction an interest that is actually motivating and inciting to action some particular group of men. An objective or real interest need not be felt, nor need it be actually motivating anyone whose interest it is. It may be so, or it may not be so. However, Madison hoped, in somewhat Burkean fashion, that the people's real interest would nevertheless tend to be realized, because their felt interests would not govern directly, but only as mediated and mitigated through an elite of elected representatives. Madison's hope about the effects of election was misplaced, as argued above, and anyway it is felt interests that are actually relevant for the workings of the famed checks and balances in the US Constitution. These workings are meant to ensure that what directs US government and which interests politicians and their agents aim to satisfy are, as far as possible, not those of any single faction but the combined resultant of the interests of all the many factions operative at the time. The US Constitution is supposed to operate in such a way that the resultant generally carries the mass towards useful and peaceable ends acceptable to the majority. Possibly this resultant is a true reflection of the real and objective interests of the country (if any there be); possibly the goals of the Constitution are answered if, whether true reflection or not, the resultant renders harmless the clash of factions. No matter: the upshot is the same. Representation is successful, and indeed legitimate, if it is responsive to the actual interests at play in the body politic and somehow reflects the weights of each; and it will be so responsive if the representatives are chosen by the majority vote of all.

We may regard such convictions as one conclusion to be drawn from the doctrine in the American Declaration of Independence that "all men are created equal" (at least when this phrase is read in accord with the state of nature doctrine). For the equality of all men can mean many things. In ancient thinkers it means that all men are the same in nature and have the same end, which is the happiness of virtue and wisdom and which is best achieved if the virtuous and wise, and not just anyone, exercise rule. In modern thinkers, influenced as they are by the state of nature doctrine, it means that all men are equal in desire and do not have the same end, because they do not have the same desires. Further, all desires are equal, and none is intrinsically superior or more deserving of satisfaction. No comparative judgments of worth can be passed on equal desires. It is sufficient if one can devise some way to stop them clashing when joint satisfaction of them is impossible.

Such, at any rate, is the theory. The facts often speak otherwise. For as was explained about elections earlier, these favor, as actually practiced, the privileged (and not seldom corrupt) few. It is unreasonable to suppose that the Founding Fathers, who were well read in both the classical and the modern thinkers and knew the history of political philosophy, were unaware of this fact. Rule by the privileged few, tempered by popular election, was what they aimed for and secured.

There is, to be sure, an argument for defending the undemocratic procedure the Founding Fathers thereby adopted. It turns on the necessity for qualifications among elected representatives and on the phenomenon of political parties. Not anyone is fit to hold office, but only he who has the necessary experience and expertise. Rule is a job and requires, as do most jobs, certain special skills, which skills are the more requisite the more the job of ruling itself exceeds in importance. This argument is, in its origin, an aristocratic one, used at the beginnings of representative democracy to limit the voters as well as the candidates in elections. Voters had themselves to meet qualifications of wealth and property and even birth. The argument is no longer used to limit voters, because if interest is always and only actual desire, and if the actual desires of property owners carry no greater weight nor are more closely connected to the ends of government than those of any other, then all who have an interest, which is to say the whole population, should rightly be counted in determining who is to represent them.

The argument is, however, used to limit candidates. The reason is that a dominant feature of modern representation is what we call political parties. A party is the fixing or concretizing of Madison's notion of a faction. It is a special interest like any faction, but in the case of the major parties, which are alone of consequence in elections, the special interest is of sufficiently broad extent to embrace within its reach a high percentage of the population. This high percentage forms the settled base among the electorate, which the major party relies on and uses to build a majority in the actual voting. A candidate can hardly win an election if he does not first secure some such extensive base, which requires that he first secure the support of a major party. To do so he must profess himself in harmony with the interest that animates the party and makes it influential with the populace; he must also be able sufficiently to articulate that interest in specific policy proposals and legislative action that the party, and chiefly its leaders, will support him and induce as many others inside and outside the party to do the same. Selecting candidates in advance through deals with the party leadership and through the winning of primary elections among those in the populace who typically vote for the party is, therefore, the rational path to follow. It is the path most likely to ensure that the party's candidate will win office and that, if he does win, he will act in accordance with the party interest. To complain that such a candidate may not have virtue or skill for rule is both false and irrelevant. If the candidate has the ability to win first the support of the party and then that of a majority of the popular vote, as a successful candidate necessarily must, he has all the virtue and the skill that either the party or the populace wants. Moreover, no other sort of virtue or skill could be of any relevance, and least of all the aristocratic sort, which assumes the existence of a real and objective interest, independent of the wishes of people and party, as the measure of virtue and skill.

Notice, further, that a party is specially organized to manipulate the people and their interests so as to keep them in line with what the party wants. It manipulates the people through determining how they are divided into electoral groupings, and it manipulates their interests through political propaganda.

The manipulation in the first case is achieved through the drawing of the geographical areas that a given representative will be elected to represent. Areas are drawn that, through creative geometry, are designed to catch that portion of the people a majority of whom can, because of their social class or wealth, be relied on always to favor the party drawing the area. Different parties collude with each other in this process and agree to parcel up the people into electoral groupings mutually favorable to each party's interest. The process has come to be called *gerrymandering*. It is a word not in good odor, but it is hard to see why. If there are no interests but actual interests, and if representation is to be of these interests, there can be little sense in not trying to combine those with similar and compatible interests into the same electoral groupings so that they will be able to choose a representative who will answer to those interests. To leave interests arbitrarily distributed, where no harmony or pattern among them can be discerned or felt, is to ensure that the representation of them will be equally arbitrary, to the annoyance and frustration of all alike.

The manipulation of interests, on the other hand, consists entirely in the arts of the demagogue. Passions can easily be stirred by skillful rhetoric, which, through promises and threats and flatteries, plays on people's fears and hopes, inducing them to vote or act as these passions direct and not as reason or calm reflection might direct. Appeals to reason also may skillfully be mixed in with the excitation of passions, but only if these appeals are kept subordinate to passion. Reason plain will move but the reasonable, who are never in the majority and scorn the vulgarity of demagogues. The arts of propaganda have been much improved in recent times through the time and energy spent in uncovering the springs of popular motivation and in the inventing of powerful new media of communication. The old orators would look on in amazement at the sophisticated skills of the commercial advertising agencies and the devious arts of the *psyops* folk in government offices and military camps.

However, if, as is true in this understanding of representation, all interests are actual interests, then the interests, however temporary, that move people under the influence of propaganda are no less their interests than those that move them without such influence. A demagogue who excites an interest and therewith wins an election is as true a representative of the people as any who might have won through some other interest, whether these interests are enduring, pass quickly away, or only exist when excited for the occasion. A clever demagogue can keep prevailing with the people even when other factors intervene and move the passions in some contrary way. Elections are infrequent, and the demagogue does not need always to be winning the people's support, but only at set intervals. He can even ignore or openly oppose the people between elections, provided he knows how to take advantage even of this practice when he comes again to solicit their votes. The people can be persuaded that sometimes they are foolish and need to be resisted and, for their own benefit, to have another lead them whither, by themselves, they would not go. They can also be persuaded that government is too hard for them and that they should leave judgment and decision in the hands of their representatives and not always be calling them to account. Provided only the representative can excite the passions to his side again when an election is due, he may act and speak as he will at other times. Clever demagogues can so master these techniques as to stay in office many years. But even if a demagogue fails and loses an election, he does so but to make way for another to take his place, who will survive, if he survives, only through practice of the same arts.

The system of elections and the demagoguery of election campaigns have managed to ensure that the people's passing interests are always represented and always satisfied. Their more permanent interests may be often thwarted and for long periods at a time. Yet even here no problem of theory or practice arises. If or when the more permanent interests become so pressing as to overwhelm all other and passing interests, they will themselves be the prevalent interest of the moment and be strong enough to determine the election and the representation. A theoretical problem could only arise if the people had genuine interests that were not a function of their occurrent moods and states and that could be discerned independently and satisfied independently. But modern thought is persuaded that there are no such interests. It is to older and rejected theories that we must return if we would maintain that there are. But who could dare hope to make these theories prevail against modern propaganda?

We must from this analysis, therefore, again conclude that modern government, in the United States and largely elsewhere, is really coercive rule by oligarchic demagogues. The actual rulers are the few and privileged, and they secure and maintain rule by propaganda. There is only democracy here (if democracy it be) in the sense that the people, since it is they who by voting determine which of the competing oligarchs will in fact possess office, are the object of the propaganda—although we must also suppose (as recent events have given us reason not to suppose) that the few and privileged are not changing the vote count to their own interest by outright fraud. Further, and again on the same doubtful supposition, there is only representation here in the sense of representation of whatever the current passions of the people happen to be, and even the representation of these passions is subordinated ultimately to the interests of the oligarchs, especially when no election is imminent.

A system of government based on occurrent passions and interests, and on manipulation of these passions through artificially constructed voting groups and propaganda (if not also fraud), lays itself open to despotism and tyranny. The candidates and the parties they stand for are inevitably tempted to lie and cheat to win elections, for winning is all that matters. Opponents will be ridiculed and demonized by scandalous tales told against them (whether these scandals are true or invented), and rule, when secured, will be used to maintain success in future elections. The people will forever be subject to manipulation and propaganda for the purpose, and since this manipulation and propaganda work on passions, the people will be reduced, for political purposes, to bundles of passions that need to be periodically excited and satisfied. But politicians cannot excite passions without money and leisure for propaganda, and they cannot satisfy passions without taking to themselves as much power and control over common, or even private, affairs as they can. The people cannot be given what they want if the politicians do not have power to give it to them, and they will not have the power unless they take it. The temptation to take progressively more power will be irresistible, and indeed the politicians will have no incentive to resist it. They are successful and remain in office because they have power to satisfy popular passions (the passions that they themselves do much to excite in the first place). Passions uncontrolled by reason, or rather, in this case, stimulated by endless propaganda, have a tendency to grow without limit, both in extent and in amount, so the power to satisfy them must grow in like proportion. The concentration of more and more power in the hands of politicians at the center thus itself grows without limit. The result is not just the state, which in its essence is despotic, but the gargantuan state, and the gargantuan state in its essence is gargantuan despotism.

Things would not and could not develop thus in the United States under the Articles of Confederation, for these left far more in the hands of states and lesser communities without any overarching and despotic central government. Some of the states might, to be sure, have developed in tyrannical directions on their own, but others surely would not. The development toward gargantuan state despotism at the center was only made possible by the United States Constitution. The modern form of representation, which the Constitution made possible and more absolute as time passed, may be viewed as the modern equivalent of Glaucon's greed and Israel's lust for a king. The message of all three, dear to lovers of absolute power everywhere, is as follows: "Satisfy our passions, good or bad, noble or base, in conditions of peace, and we care not what power you need and take for the purpose."

Notes

1. From the King James Version or Authorized Version of the Bible.
2. Translation by Jowett (1871).
3. For some discussion, see in general Fortes and Evans-Pritchard (1940), and for ancient Greece Berent (1994, 1996), Hansen "Was the *polis* a state or a stateless society?" in Nielsen (2002): 9–47, and Beck (2013) especially Part I.
4. For the Articles of Confederation, see Yale University's online Avalon Project, http://avalon.law.yale.edu/18th_century/artconf.asp.
5. For the US Constitution, see Yale University's online Avalon Project, http://avalon.law.yale.edu/18th_century/usconst.asp.
6. Aristotle, *Politics*, 1300a31–b5.
7. The practice of having ballots and of naming candidates on a ballot is not specified in the Constitution, but it is not forbidden and must have become the norm very early on. The option of writing in any name not already printed on the ballot (a write-in candidate), while always available, is of little significance. It does nothing to make the voting a case of all choosing from all as opposed to all choosing from some.
8. *Politics*, 1271a9–18. Note incidentally that the Latin word for soliciting votes is 'amb-itio' (literally a 'going round' asking for electoral support), which gives us our word 'ambition'. In both Latin and at least early use in English the word tended to carry a pejorative sense and to be associated with pride and vainglory.
9. *Politics*, 1303a13–16.
10. *Politics*, 1273a35–b5.
11. *Politics*, 1291b28–30, 1293a26–32.
12. *Politics*, 1305b22–33.
13. The opinion of Hamilton in *Federalist Papers* 9 and Madison in *Federalist Papers* 10.
14. The term may have been coined by Alexander Hamilton, and since Hamilton was no friend of democracy, the fact that the term does not describe anything that can fairly be called democratic should come as no surprise. Many today regard Hamilton and the other authors of the *Federalist Papers* as men of wisdom and prudence whose thinking is much to be admired. The Anti-Federalists regarded them and proponents of the Constitution in general as deceivers and enemies of freedom. One has to read the writings of these Anti-Federalists if one is to have a fair sense of what the Constitutional Convention was all about. As Aristotle's analysis of oligarchy helps to show, the *Federalist Papers* are little other than oligarchic propaganda. See Chapter Eight below.

15. See in particular book 2, chapter 3 of de Tocqueville's *L'Ancien Régime*, and also R. W. and A. J. Carlyle's *A History of Medieval Political Theory in the West*. This work is probably best consulted by going first through the conclusions or summaries of its several volumes. See also Dawson (1954).

16. Article 6, for instance, of the French *Declaration of the Rights of Man and of the Citizen* (1789) reads, "The law is the expression of the general will. All citizens have the right to take part, in person or by their representatives, in its formation. It must be the same for everyone whether it protects or penalizes. All citizens being equal in its eyes are equally admissible to all public dignities, offices, and employments, according to their ability, and with no other distinction than that of their virtues and talents." This article does not, perhaps, strictly entail uniformity, but it suggests it. Certainly it does little to favor difference.

17. Heer (1968: 279).

18. See the references to de Tocqueville and the two Carlyles and Dawson in the earlier notes.

19. See the speech on the Reform of the Representation of the Commons in Parliament for May 7, 1782 (in *Select Works*, 1999). The whole of *Reflections on the Revolution in France* is also of particular relevance to the general thesis.

3

Liberalism in Theory

Liberal Freedom

The previous chapter ended with a discussion of representation and how it divides into two forms according to two ways of understanding human interest, whether as objective and universal (historically embodied or not) or as occurrent and individual. The second way is the liberal way and is tied to the liberal idea of freedom. For it is the contention of liberalism (elaborated by Hobbes and encapsulated by Weber, as noted in Chapter One), that the neutral state is necessary for liberty. It is necessary for liberty first because it is neutral and allows each to pursue what vision of the good life they prefer, and second because it has the monopoly of force necessary to ensure that this pursuit of individual visions by individuals does not end in violence and the war of all against all. A necessary part of this view is the political marginalization of religion, so that religious authorities have no independent political power and certainly none against the state (a point also expressly endorsed and elaborated by Hobbes). Weber, in a way, expresses the point himself: "He who seeks the salvation of the soul, of his own and of others, should not seek it along the avenue of politics, for the quite different tasks of politics can only be solved by violence."[1] Religion is one thing, is the message, and politics is another, and it is a mistake to mix the two, or it is a mistake for religion or the Church, or any body concerned with comprehensive visions of the good, to have any coercive power, whether of its own or through a supplementing of the power of the secular rulers.

This thesis of liberalism may also be expressed in the form of the maxim that political authority should not be involved in the task of distinctively moral education, and in particular should not use force to impose some overall moral code or vision of the good on its citizens. The only proper purpose for which coercive force may be used is the prevention of harm to others.[2] This view has become, for most practical purposes, the dominant view in Western society, even though many more things are nowadays held to be legitimate objects of political coercion than during the classical liberalism of the nineteenth century (where the harm principle was first at home). But the reason is less that the harm principle has been rejected (except perhaps verbally), than that the notion of what counts as prevention of harm has been considerably extended. Whereas before, the prevention of harm was primarily or even exclusively a matter of protecting people's negative rights (the right not to be interfered with in the pursuit of one's goals), now it includes protecting positive rights (rights to be enabled to pursue one's goals through the public provision of certain goods such as wealth, health care, education and so on). For classical liberalism had adopted a primarily laissez-faire attitude, the attitude of *letting* people *do* pretty much what they wished and of intervening only to protect such freedom. But this attitude came to seem objectionable and inadequate because it ignored differences in circumstances. For some people, when left to themselves, could do a great deal and had a very wide field for free action because they had an abundance of other goods, especially in wealth and leisure. But others lacked these goods and could do very little and were tightly confined within a very narrow compass, being forced into a daily and sometimes desperate struggle to survive.

Consequently, in order to ensure that the freedom to act as one chose would actually mean something to everyone (and not merely to the favored few), the active provision of goods by political action, over and above the securing of freedom from interference, was deemed to be necessary.[3]

From this attack on classical liberalism, the ideology of socialism, relatively new at the time, gained a particular advantage. According to socialism, the defect in classical liberalism was not merely an incidental or corrigible oversight but an essential or structural injustice. Under the pretense of laissez-faire, liberalism was enabling the owners of capital and the means of production to take to themselves alone the bulk of the profits from businesses and factories. Such taking appeared to liberalism to be a perfectly legitimate taking by owners of what was their own (the factories and businesses, after all, belonged to them). But in fact it was theft, and a theft of an egregious and offensive kind. For the profits were really produced by the labor of the workers and rightly belonged to them. The owners ought therefore to return these profits to the workers. Instead, however, they paid the workers as little as they could and seized all the remainder for themselves. The theft was thus egregious because it involved large amounts of money and offensive because it was directed against the poor and the weak.

Now, a striking result of this argument was that classical liberalism ceased to be viewed as the expression of a limited system of government that was, on the basis of the harm principle, protecting everyone's negative rights. Instead it came to be seen as a system that, by protecting the rich and strong in their seizure of profits, was using its coercion directly to inflict harm. Liberalism thus seemed to be refuted on the basis of its own principle. For theft is a manifest case of harm, and if the job of political authority is to protect from harm, then political authority ought to be doing the very reverse of what liberalism was doing. Instead of taking the side of the owners, it should be attacking them and forcing them to disgorge their ill-gotten gains. But the best way of achieving this result seemed to be to take away from owners the control of factories and businesses and to ensure by political action the just distribution of profits. Socialism, or the state ownership of the means of production, seemed thus to be justified even by the principles of liberalism itself.[4] But the manifest crimes of socialism when it was actually put into practice, which were worse than anything produced by liberalism (one thinks naturally of Stalin and Mao), have rightly repelled most peoples and nations, and not least those suffering under its thrall. Nevertheless, no practicing statesmen have thought that any sort of return to classical liberalism was the answer.[5] Instead a sort of mixture of the free market and increased government regulation has become the norm through most of the developed world.

The increase in government intervention and control, however, has virtually all been in the area of material welfare, or in what may be called external and bodily good. By contrast, in other areas (notably sexual mores), political authority has been giving up control and is instead allowing and even guaranteeing people the freedom to do more and more of what they want.[6] Part of the rationale given for this policy is, in effect, an appeal back to the original understanding of the harm principle, namely that any public prohibition or regulation in these matters is not sanctioned by that principle but is an undue interference in people's freedom. Yet there is another and more recent belief involved here too: that if political authority does have any job in matters properly subject to free choice, this job is to use its force and its resources, not to limit free choice, but to end or mitigate any misfortune that might follow from the exercise of free choice. So, for instance, with respect to sexual promiscuity, the demand is made for provision of contraceptives, universal availability of abortion, welfare support for unwed mothers, increased spending on medical research to find cures for sexually transmitted diseases, and so on. The job of public authority is not to tell us how to live our lives but rather to enable us to live as we please and without having to suffer any penalties or consequences that cannot be compensated for or put right.[7]

The rationale behind this seductive belief seems to be relatively simple. We all have a right to happiness, and happiness is doing what one wishes; what one wishes is private and individual to each person and is known best by that person. Thus no one is in a position to tell anyone else what his or her happiness consists in. Further, since this right is a universal right and belongs equally to all, no one has more right to happiness than anyone else. Hence not only should no one interfere with anyone else's pursuit of happiness, but also no one should be deprived of what he needs in order to pursue happiness.

The difference implicit here between happiness itself and the means to happiness is rather important. For though happiness itself is understood to be something personal and individual, its means are not. There are certain things that everyone is supposed to need to pursue happiness, as notably health and wealth but also other external goods as a certain degree of respect. These things are also referred to as basic or primary goods,[8] which are understood as goods that anyone needs in order to pursue any other good. It is the securing and fair distributing of these goods that is the proper business of the state and where coercion may legitimately be used. The distribution must be fair, or as equal as possible, because, as already noted, when it comes to happiness, all are equal. But people may or may not be equal in the possession of or need for the means to happiness. Hence, as no one has more right to be happy than another, no one has right to more means than he needs, especially when others do not have what they do need. Consequently a redistribution of means to happiness is required from those who have more or need less to those who have less or need more. But happiness itself, or the end, is not a legitimate object of coercion.

The basis for this view is not just that people in fact differ about what ends to pursue, for this claim by itself is compatible with the idea that there is a single, objective human end that is the same for all (disagreement could be explained on the ground that some are ignorant of this end, or are perverse or lacking in mental capacity). The reasoning is rather that either there is no such end (which is the more widespread view), or if there is, political authority has no business trying to enforce it. For, first, people have free choice and the right to the exercise of it, which right, because of everybody's basic equality, no government may justly take away. Only by being allowed their freedom, indeed, could people grow up and become mature (to be always governed by others in one's actions would leave one in a permanent state of childhood). In addition, public coercion applied to the pursuit of ends might prevent people discovering important truths that they otherwise would have discovered if left free to act and speculate as they chose. Or they might lose the knowledge they have if they are never challenged to explain or defend it.[9] Further, and perhaps more importantly, disagreement about ends exists and seems both widespread and stubborn. To use force to abolish it would require much violence and would likely provoke war (there will always be some who would rather fight and die than submit). Such force, anyway, would not achieve its aim, since it could only coerce outward behavior and never inner consent of the will, but morality and the attainment of happiness require such inner consent.

Contesting Liberal Freedom

It is doubtful, however, whether this or any pattern of reasoning can really be used to set limits to the enforcement of morals or visions of the good. Take first this notion of necessary means to happiness, or of basic goods. Can the moral virtues be excluded from these means? Is it not the case that without these virtues, the things one is pursuing as constitutive or cause of one's happiness will rather be lost, or even bring harm? By virtues I mean qualities of character and intelligence, and it is surely manifest that even if happiness is unique to each individual, still it is by knowledge, self-knowledge above all, that each will know what his own happiness consists in. One can, for instance, easily be deceived into thinking that such and such will make one happy and then discover, when one gets it, that it does not. The satisfaction of momentary pleasures, for instance, is not happiness, as is abundantly proved by the pleasures of drugs, drink, and promiscuous sex. Those who indulge in these things find that they have won temporary plea-sures at the cost of longer and deeper goods (health, family, friends) and at the cost of a lasting happiness. Nor is it just ignorance that can be to blame here. One's character can be to blame too. Weakness of will or lack of self control, the inability to resist pleasures or to stand up to dangers and pains, has ruined happiness for many a man (as in the case of alcoholics and cowards), even when they have known full well in their calmer moments that happiness for them would not be served by pursuit of these pleasures or escape from these pains.

But failure of character need not concern some addiction that causes misery over time. It may concern a single case, as with anger and impatience, which in a moment can lead one to commit some serious crime, even against one's loved ones (such as spouse and child), and blight one's happiness for years. After such lapses and failures, there is nothing political authority can do to set things right again. Yet something could have been done beforehand, perhaps, by education in the virtues, to prevent the lapses in the first place. Perhaps indeed the state not only could but should have done something, for it is hard to see how character traits can be developed otherwise, or in a situation where people are all permitted to follow their passions.[10] For if political authority may rightly use coercion to ensure that people have adequate means to happiness in other respects, how can it not have the right to intervene to ensure that they have adequate means in these respects too? Social and peer pressures generated by other people can be very great, and few have the strength or courage to resist them, least of all among the young. Yet the young are most in need of virtue and are at the age best to learn it (if they grow old in bad habits, applying correction later may be well-nigh impossible). Would not such pressures, then, constitute a harm inflicted by people on each other, and a harm that political authority might rightly intervene to prevent? And do not such virtues constitute a necessary and universal means to happiness, whatever happiness is conceived by individuals to be?

The point here is a very general one: that the basic goods before spoken of are preserved or lost by the presence or absence of the goods of character and not vice versa. A fool and his money are soon parted, we say, but so are a fool and his health or his family or his friends or his respect among others, and one can be a fool through ignorance or through lack of will or through vice. There is another point too. The other means of happiness or the other basic goods seem to have a limit to their usefulness, and having more of them than is needed is not only useless but can even be harmful. Too much money, for instance, has destroyed many, as many or perhaps more than have been destroyed by too little money. The same can be said of freedom and reputation or fame. Further, money and things of this sort can also become absorbing and seduce one away from other goods and even lead one to lose these goods—friendship in particular. One needs to know where to stop in one's pursuit of things like money and how to prevent them from becoming absorbing, which can only be done by character. But by contrast, the more one has of the proper virtues of character, the more one is helped and benefited, rather than less. The need for training in character would seem to be as necessary or more necessary than the provision of these other basic goods.[11] So if political authority may act to ensure the presence and fair distribution of the other basic goods, and if these basic goods are in fact less basic and indeed less good than the virtues, then political authority should act to ensure the presence of the virtues too.

But there are reasons to suppose that the virtues are for everyone constituents of the end or of happiness and not just means to it. First of all, happiness would seem to involve the loving presence of others, especially of family and friends (the friendless are held to be most unfortunate). But to acquire and keep love and friendship, one needs oneself to be loving and friendly or to have those qualities of character and mind that make one ready to give oneself to and for others. These qualities are not included among or generated by the other basic goods. These other basic goods are indeed of a more self-interested or self-focused nature, being primarily a matter of one's own immediate benefit.[12] Other-focused goods, however, or the qualities of a loving and self-giving character, are precisely the virtues. It is virtues that make for the best friends and that make one most fit to be a friend and keep friends. The unkind, the mean, the self-centered, the cowardly, the rash, the bitter, or the jealous and suspicious would be desired, and could be kept, by no one as friends.

Further, the other basic goods are not in our control but can be lost despite our best efforts and despite the best efforts of public authority (even though it is to overcome the risks and uncertainties of life that we call upon the state to intervene and provide guarantees in these areas). So to locate happiness in such physical and external goods is to make oneself a hostage to fortune and so subject to all the anxiety, frustration, and bitterness involved when things go wrong. In such a condition, we are more like spoilt children than grown men. The virtues, by contrast, are in our control and are not subject to fortune in the same way. They will not be corrupted by prosperity or destroyed by hardship, since even at the height of fortune or in some gloomy dungeon, nothing can prevent one exercising courage, patience, and self-control if one does not oneself wish it.

Indeed in this regard, it is surely a fact of experience that the virtuous lead more contented lives than the vicious and the weak-willed. They fall less into misfortune (they fall only by chance and not also by their own folly); they can handle it better when they do; they are not racked by anxieties for things whose presence depends on chance; they are more satisfied with what they have; they are at peace with themselves and with others; they have better and more lasting friends; they have sanguine hopes for the future, and no or few regrets about the past.[13]

Trumping Liberal Freedom

Yet despite the force of these considerations (which could indeed be multiplied), it might nevertheless seem that at least one of the earlier arguments furnishes a decisive reason for keeping the competence of the political authority to a minimum, especially in matters of morality, and that is human freedom. In fact, this reason will retain its force even if the end or happiness is a something definite that can be known and is the same for everyone.[14] For it is of the essence of human beings to attain happiness through their own free choices, and so it cannot be the job of political authority to intervene and force people into happiness against their will. Indeed this job would be impossible, since no one can be forced to do something voluntarily.

The reply here is twofold. First, force is not put forward as a sufficient means to virtue but only as a necessary one. It is meant to ensure the conditions (notably freedom from vicious examples and restraint of the passions) in which virtue can grow in those who, through these conditions, come to appreciate the goodness and beauty of virtue sufficiently to want to get it for themselves. The regulation of behavior is a way, and typically the only way, in which virtue is acquired, for those who yield willingly can come to love good actions for their own sake, simply from the fact of being required to do them. Indeed in no other way typically do people become enamored, for instance, of certain artistic skills, such as playing a musical instrument. For acquiring such skill calls for long and often tedious practice that the young, at any rate, would never do without the compulsion of parents and teachers. Yet as these skills become more developed and the child begins to feel the delight of mastery, love for the activity begins to take over and to stimulate to action spontaneously, something that would never have occurred without the initial compulsion. Nevertheless it must be admitted that neither skill nor virtue will grow in anyone who is not willing. Hence all that force can do for such as these is to keep them in check. But this keeping in check is nevertheless necessary, both for their own sake, since it will help prevent them from committing crimes, and for others' too, since the unfettered behavior of evil men spreads its poison through the whole society and not only undermines social life but corrupts character, especially of the young. There is no need to be disturbed here by Mill's objections that force will prevent the making of experiments that will generate new knowledge, or will even prevent us retaining the knowledge we already have since we will never be challenged by disagreement to keep the reasons for it sufficiently alive. For, on the former point, what we do not know should not prevent us from acting on what we can and do know (and we can know that the learning of virtue requires force as a necessary condition). In addition, the inculcation of virtue could never be an impediment to the discovery of truth; it is rather the failure to inculcate virtue that would be so, since it would leave people subject to ignorance and passion. On the latter point, truths can be and are still questioned even when known to be true, for there are two ways of questioning something: either so as to reject it or so as to understand it. The first way would be objectionable (for, *ex hypothesi*, the truth in question is known, at least as to the fact), but not the second. Teachers regularly question truths in the second way, so as to teach them better. Theoreticians do the same, so as to understand them better. Indeed, the art of arguing well on both sides of a question is an integral part of understanding truth (handed on already in Aristotle's *Topics*), and something a trained philosopher should be doing even independently of any actual interlocutors.[15]

The second part of the reply is that, as has been in a way already implied, freedom is itself twofold, internal and external. External freedom is freedom from coercion. Such freedom can be either good or bad, depending on how it is used. A criminal, for instance, uses his external freedom badly and needs to have it taken away. Internal freedom is freedom from one's own passions or having such control over oneself that one is not driven into some action or decision by impulse or emotion (even though one knows this action or decision to be wrong), but that instead one acts according to rational judgment. External freedom really depends on internal freedom, because someone who is driven by passion is like a wild and untamed animal needing to be caged. It is those who have control of themselves who are fit to be externally free. Such self-control is the autonomy required by happiness, but it is not given or automatic; on the contrary, it is achieved, and law is the best means to achieve it, for well-laid law encourages and enforces all those acts that the internally free, or the virtuous, do naturally and by choice. Such law is never in fact a restraint on the virtuous (since they would do what the law commands even without law) but only on the vicious.[16]

There is, however, an ambiguity here also in the meaning of law; or rather, law itself can be understood in two ways. The first way is the common one nowadays where law is understood as imposing, by its prohibitions, restraints on action or on the unfettered pursuit of one's own ends. This may be called a Hobbesian notion that understands law as a sort of side-constraint on action. Law in this sense is opposed to freedom, or rather external freedom, and is a diminution of it, even if a necessary diminution. For the underlying idea is that there is no universal human end, but we naturally pursue whatever ends we wish, and that the only reason we need to be prevented by law from pursuing these ends in this rather than that way is that there are other people around who will be harmed by our action if we do not refrain. Here in fact is where we return to the harm principle, for this notion of law would seem to be what lies at the bottom of that principle. Law is an application of the harm principle: people's freedom to do as they please is only to be limited to the extent that the prevention of harm to others requires it. For were it not for other people with whom we have to live, or were it not the case that we cannot safely hope to make all of them follow our choices all the time,[17] there would be no need for legal restraints on action, because there would be no one else around who could resist us or be adversely affected by anything we did. Law is thus essentially about limiting the means of pursuing the end; it is not about limiting the ends themselves.

The second way to understand law is the more ancient one, the way associated with the traditional notion of natural law.[18] Law in this sense also imposes restraint on action, yet this restraint is not understood as a diminution or inhibiting of freedom in one's pursuit of the good, but rather as making both freedom and the pursuit of the good possible. For the underlying idea is that there is a universal human good or end and this good is not an automatic given, or is not the immediate object of desires or feelings. On the contrary, the good is something that needs to be discovered and reasoned out, and law is precisely the result of such working out. It is a making explicit or an articulating of what the good is. Law is not a laying down of side-constraints on means of pursuing the good; it is rather a defining of the end or the good itself. Indeed there are no limits on means; or rather, any means that the law forbids, it forbids precisely because they are not means to the end, however much they may appear to be, but to something evil instead.

If one takes law in the first way and combines it with the view that freedom is the external freedom of doing whatever one chooses, then law and freedom appear to be necessarily opposed. But if one takes law in the second way and combines it with the view that freedom is the internal freedom of having sufficient self-discipline and knowledge to use well one's external freedom in pursuit of the true human end, then law and freedom turn out not to be opposed at all but identical. Ignorance of the good and subjection to passion would prevent us making a choice for what we want, since we would neither know the good nor have sufficient control to pursue it if we did. Law is meant to give us the necessary knowledge and the necessary control. Such law, as backed up by the coercive power of political authority, is not in opposition to freedom but is the necessary precondition of freedom. Even to suppose an opposition here would be to misunderstand both law and freedom.[19] But law in this sense not only generates and preserves internal freedom; it preserves external freedom too. For the greatest threat to external freedom is tyranny, and a people or nation that is foolish, undisciplined, or otherwise vicious is an easy prey to clever tyrants who well know how to manipulate passions and those enslaved to them.[20]

To fail, then, to use the coercive force of law to impose and inculcate moral virtue is in effect to leave the way open for the use of force to impose slavery, the force first of one's own passions and then of a ruthless tyrant. There is really no other option.[21] Fears that the use of force to impose moral virtue will lead to war are, in most cases, exaggerated. Some of the worst wars (those waged during the twentieth century) arguably arose not from the attempt to impose moral virtue and restraint, but from the failure to do so (such as the failure to restrain the passions for worldly glory, empire, and wealth on the part of both rulers and ruled). These wars were also, it is worth remarking, not religious wars but secular or even irreligious ones. Further, the religious wars often referred to as evidence of the evils of imposing morality and religion, namely those following the Protestant Reformation, were themselves arguably the result not of the imposition of religious discipline, but rather of its rejection (for the rejection of the prevailing religious discipline, as opposed, say, to its reform, marked Protestantism almost from the beginning). But anyway, if war can sometimes be good and necessary and there really are causes worth dying for, then religious ones would seem to be chief among them – the cause of God (his real cause, not some pretense) cannot fail to be greater and more glorious than a cause merely of man. Finally, should there be societies that will not tolerate much by way of coerced discipline and that cannot be moved toward virtue, then we will just have to conclude that these societies are rather low down on the scale of moral worth and that not much can now be done to make them decent. The existence and recalcitrance of such societies should, nevertheless, not prevent us from acknowledging, and treating differently, those societies that are capable of being moved by discipline to higher levels of virtue.

The understanding of the nature and functions of political authority is going to differ according to the two different views of law just explained. According to the first view, the dominant question about political authority is going to be the limitation of its competence over morals and over views of the good, and how its coercive power is to be used to ensure this limitation while permitting individual freedom in such matters. The attempt thus to draw some hedges around the moral role of political authority was, indeed, the original motivation of the appeal to the harm principle. But note how different the political question looks when law is taken in the second way, as defining and articulating the human end. Here the question about political authority will not concern how to limit moral discipline, but how to expand moral discipline by making the public teaching of it better, or rather how to have an authority—whether political or religious or both—that perfectly knows and declares the truth about the end. The aim will be to describe and secure, if possible, the wisest government reason is capable of. Politics in this latter understanding is not primarily about coercion but about guidance,[22] not primarily about restraining the will but about enlightening the mind. Coercion will be a secondary consideration, and only required to the extent the guidance is opposed or rejected.

Of these two understandings of political authority, the former coerces means and not ends, while the latter coerces ends and not means. The former is also necessarily coercive, while the latter is not. For men, both in liberalism's understanding and in fact, naturally pursue their ends, whatever these are, as much as they can, and this inclination, being always there by nature, always needs coercive restraint by the liberal state so that the means used stay within the limits imposed by liberal theory. The latter understanding of political authority, by contrast, aims primarily to teach what the true end is, toward which all men are naturally inclined, and coerces only as required against those who in some way resist nature. The latter's coercion therefore reinforces nature, while the former's opposes it. In addition, the former does in fact coerce ends and not just means, for in practice it does impose an end: the end of not allowing ends to determine politics, or the end of tolerating all ends. Opposition to this end (and this opposition is natural to man, because the drive for the comprehensive good is natural to man, as will be argued in the next chapter) has to be coercively suppressed. The latter understanding of political authority, then, is simply freer: both understandings coerce as regards ends, but the former also coerces as regards means, while the latter does not; and the latter coerces secondarily and in support of nature, while the former coerces primarily and against nature.

Herein is found the essence of illiberalism and of illiberal freedom in contradistinction to that of liberalism. But this essence needs further elaboration, both in itself and in its realization in communal life. For, in particular, one should not suppose that its realization will be simple or straightforward, or take the form of one coercive power (where coercion is necessary) and not rather of several and distinct forms. Fitness for teaching morals and the objective good of human life need not be found, or found equally, in all forms of authority. These and similar questions must be dealt with in the chapters that follow.

Notes

1. *Politics as a Vocation* (1965: 126).
2. This thesis was classically stated by John Stuart Mill in Chapter One of *On Liberty*. It was restated by Hart (1979) and has, with modifications, been defended by Feinberg (1987–88).
3. See, on this point, Kymlicka and Norman (1994: 352–381, especially 354–355).
4. This argument for socialism, though plausible, is nevertheless insufficient. For, first, it takes no thought of whether the means chosen do not involve worse evils than they are designed to remove (as in fact quickly proved to be the case), nor of whether there are not other and better means to the same result; and, second, it denies the right to private property despite the fact that this right has a foundation superior to and independent of classical liberalism and its deficiencies. These faults in the argument for socialism were prophetically made by Leo XIII in his encyclical *Rerum Novarum* of 1891.
5. As regards theorists, it is different matter. Apart from the inevitable Hayek, von Mises, and Nozick, see also Flew (1981 and 1989).
6. A classic instance would be abortion or assisted suicide, where governments have used their authority to deny subordinate public authorities the right to prohibit or regulate abortion or assisted suicide within their own communities.
7. There are theorists of the liberal welfare state who expressly acknowledge and require a moral component in the state's activity. But this moral component is limited to the virtue of social justice, and the demands of social justice are defined in terms primarily of material welfare. Hence the morality

involved is essentially the morality of ensuring such welfare for all (Rawls 1993: 194–95); it does not embrace what one would find in a more extensive and more traditional morality. Or if a need for the public inculcation of more virtues is recognized, it is only for virtues necessary to preserving and operating a liberal welfare state, as in Galston (1991), and contrast Beckman (2001), George (1995), Raz (1986).

8.   Rawls (1971: 92–93).

9.   These points are contained in Mill's *On Liberty*.

10. "The right to do whatever one wishes is incapable of providing defense against the base element in each man" (Aristotle, *Politics*, 1318b39–19a1).

11. The importance of character for happiness seems to have been generally ignored by apologists for liberal democracy. Even Galston (1991) only speaks of liberal virtues in the sense of virtues that liberal societies need to survive and not in the sense of virtues that people need to be happy.

12. The way Rawls generates them, namely from what a self-interested individual would rationally choose in the original position (1971: 92–93, 119).

13. Note Aristotle's litany in *Ethics* 9.4 and also his arguments in 10.6–8.

14. This argument has been powerfully presented, and in an original form, by Den Uyl and Rasmussen (1991).

15. The Scholastic theologians, such as Aquinas and Scotus, probably raised more and better objections to Christian doctrine than many non-Christians or atheists; but they did so, of course, to understand and expound the meaning and grounds of the doctrine. Note, therefore, that the deliberative democracy of Talisse (2005: chs. 6, 7; 2007: chs. 3, 4; 2009: ch. 5; 2012: ch. 6) does not overthrow the point in question here. Definitively known truths are not things whose truth one can or should, whether epistemically or morally, retain an "open mind" about. Further discussion of them will only be about their meaning or reasons, not their truth. So their truth can be firmly held and firmly acted on too.

16. Here is to be found what seems to be the flaw in Den Uyl and Rasmussen's argument (1991) against using political authority to enforce moral virtue. Autonomy is indeed necessary to virtue and happiness, but as a constituent and not as a means. In those who use their autonomy badly, for instance, or who have never been trained to use it well, the exercise of autonomy is an impediment to happiness (as with the criminal). The means to getting them to use autonomy well is precisely enforced moral education (as is manifest especially in children). Once they have been educated and autonomy has become in them a formed habit of choosing the good and avoiding the evil, moral education is no longer necessary or, if continued, will not need to be enforced but will be willingly embraced. Either way, autonomy cannot be used to generate an argument against the political enforcement of moral virtue. It is only because Den Uyl and Rasmussen slide from the (correct) view that autonomy is necessary as a constituent of virtue to the (incorrect) view that autonomy is necessary as a means to virtue, that they think autonomy can generate such an argument (1991: 70–95).

17. This argument is the one Rawls gives about the original position (1971: 119).

18. St. Thomas Aquinas gives a classic statement of this notion in *Summa Theologica*, Ia–IIae, qq. 90–97, but see also the fine statement of it by Blackstone in *Commentaries*, Introduction, section 2, *init.*

19. Part of the point of Pope John Paul II's encyclical *Veritatis Splendor* and of his oft-repeated claim that it is an error to separate freedom from truth.
20. Compare Milton, *Paradise Lost*, bk. 12, lines 86–90: "Reason in man obscurd, or not obeyed, immediately inordinate desires and upstart passions catch the government from reason, and to servitude reduce man till then free" and lines 97–100: "Sometimes nations will decline so low from vertu, which is reason, that no fault but justice, with some fatal curse annexd deprives them of their outward libertie, their inward lost." Rawls acknowledges the need for virtue in the people to prevent tyranny and the like, but he seems unaware of the full implications of this fact (1993: 205).
21. The political theory adopted, among others, by Talisse (2005: chs. 6, 7; 2007: chs. 3, 4; 2009: ch. 5; 2012: ch. 6), and based on epistemic virtues and a theory of epistemic perfectionism, while commendable as far as it goes, does not provide a third option. It does not escape the need for forced inculcation of properly moral virtues (deliberation and knowledge are hindered as much by anger, lust, pride, sloth and so on as they are by ignorance or failure to reason; that is, they are hindered as much by faults of will as faults of mind).
22. Compare Rawls (1993: 136): "political power is always coercive power."

4

First Principles of Illiberalism

A Fresh Beginning

If the state, then, is an invention of liberalism's myth, and if political phenomena are distorted by being looked at through the myth of the state, as both theorists and practitioners now do, the first need in political philosophy, not to mention political practice, is to remove the phenomena from the distortion and see them and analyze them as they really are.

Where, then, to begin? At the beginning, naturally, and the beginning, since politics is about the organizing of people into certain kinds of communities, is people or human beings and what it is about them that makes community something they want and invariably, if differently, pursue. Modern political philosophers sometimes in part follow this procedure when they begin their analysis of political phenomena by returning to what is called the state of nature or, more recently, the original position. This state or position is imagined to be where we would all naturally find ourselves before any political organization had come into existence. But this return to some pre-political state or position is never taken far enough. It stops at people who are already conceived of as being adult, as being capable of speech, as having a grasp of complex notions like justice and rule and fair distribution, and as willing to form and to keep mutual agreements. Admittedly the proponents of this idea need not be taken as supposing such a state was ever a historical reality; they need only be taken as positing, in imaginary form, the position from which an analysis of politics and a construction of a just political community should take its start. But why is this position, however imaginary, the one to begin with? In fact, as the presentation of the state of nature doctrine illustrated when Hobbes was discussed above in Chapter One, to start with such a state of nature is to start at the point from which the modern idea of the political state is and was first constructed. To start here, then, is to beg the question and to assume the liberal myth about politics in advance.

But the liberal myth is precisely a myth and is what most needs to be rejected. Starting at the beginning, therefore, cannot mean starting with liberalism's state of nature or original position.

The obvious place to start instead is with the brute facts of biology. Human beings come to be through birth from parents.[1] For many years they are totally dependent on parents and other adults for everything from food, clothing, and shelter to education and character formation. There is no choice exercised by the child over such things, either at birth or for many years afterward. The child's life and conditions are just given. It begins with them, it grows and matures through them, and it more often than not ends up living its whole life in them and producing children of its own, who begin in exactly the same way and who end up doing exactly the same things. Changes can indeed occur, either by chance events such as natural disasters or wars of invasion or conquest, or by the deliberate choice of the elders, who may consciously set up some different system of life and community. Such elders have gone down in the history of such communities as the first founders, and around them there tends to grow up a special reverence, founded, no doubt, on real facts but elaborated on by later mythical additions.

The first beginning, then, is not the birth and upbringing of children, but instead the parents who give them birth and bring them up. Where did the first parents come from? In our modern understanding, this question is answered, to the extent it can be answered, by reference to evolution. The human species came to be by a slow process that passed through many earlier and more primitive species. In these other species there was a succession of parents and offspring from one generation to the next, each passing on to the later what it received from the earlier, rather in the way we see that birds and other animals still do. The bearing and raising of offspring would develop as the several species developed, until something like the human species emerged on the scene and, from purely animal acculturation, began to develop the moral and intellectual cultivation now distinctive of that species. This cultivation would no doubt have received particular impulse from individuals or groups of individuals who, by natural ability or chance, exercised a greater influence over those they lived with than anyone else and were able to give their common life distinctive forms. Finding these forms to be of benefit to their communal life, people would look on the authors of them as great benefactors. They would even tend to look on them as more than human, because indeed their achievements did make them more than the other human beings around them. People would look on them as gods, and the foundations and beginnings of human goods would be given a divine origin.

Perhaps indeed some of these founders or supposed benefactors would have been more like tyrants, in fact (as some parents are, even today, with their children); and the concern with the divine might have sprung from fear as well as from admiration. Perhaps indeed the concern with the divine was present from the beginning, for some sense of superior powers in the world would have been borne in on everyone by the mere fact that humans were not the cause of, and could not account for, the existence of the world around them or even of themselves. All these things were just there and just given. Where did they come from? Who or what gave them? The only plausible answer is that they came from some god or gods. Who were the gods? They were mysterious beings that were the authors, in some way, of all other beings. These mysterious beings were regarded as the explanation for what otherwise was just inexplicably there. Since these beings, if they exist, are nevertheless hidden, their presence had to be deduced from what was visible, and their nature had to be guessed at as being some-how like ours (for we had no other experience to go on) but so much greater and more magnificent. They were endowed with properties fitting their superiority and their hiddenness: they were immortal, they were invincible, and they were all-knowing, being aware of the future as well as of present and past. They were everything men were not, though they were like men in having intelligence and will and power, albeit intelligence, will, and power that vastly transcended, even if it also mirrored, what humans themselves had.

Human community begins thus in parents and the gods. Human community is, first and foremost, family and religion. But why go beyond the family? And why insist on worshipping and honoring the gods instead of just recognizing their mysterious existence? Indeed, why gods, instead of grand, impersonal forces that operate without intelligence and will? Why religion instead of evolution?

As for evolution, it is too sophisticated a theory to be conceived without considerable cultural and scientific advance among men and could not have been there at the beginning. Besides, it does not dispense with the gods or some being prior to it, for the processes that make up evolution do not operate on nothing; they operate on things that already exist and already have inner tendencies and potentials. Otherwise the processes would never produce anything and so would not produce evolution either. Therefore something must have preceded evolution that, *ex hypothesi*, could not itself have evolved. Religion is more rational as an ultimate answer about the world than evolution could ever be.

As for the question about going beyond the family, the answer can only be desire, the desire for something more and better and more fully answering to human needs and potentials. It is obvious to a mere view that the things we moderns now have and enjoy are impossible of realization in simple families or in small groups of extended families. They are only possible in large and developed political groupings. Even so, it is no less obvious that the things we moderns now have do not fully satisfy. We have urges and longings that transcend our own best efforts to attain them. The gods return here, as they do also with evolution. Our reach, as it is said, exceeds our grasp. The gods or God are our hope, if there is one, of grasping what we reach for. The drive to large and developed political groupings among men, like the drive to learn and understand all that is around us, points ineluctably to what lies beyond. The drive for the political and the scientific is the drive for some comprehensive attainment of the good that, in the last resort, could only be provided by the gods. Human comprehensive visions are not enough to satisfy; they never go far enough. We want what we cannot encapsulate in any theory or vision of our own.

Still, these facts give us a truer beginning of political analysis and political philosophy than any state of nature doctrine could supply. We want a political life, or even at the limit a politically transcendent life, that fully answers to our deepest longings. Perhaps, indeed, the political life will not get us where we want to be, but it seems to be a necessary step on the way. The tradition of political theory, as we have inherited it from the past, always understood politics in terms of the drive for a complete life, for the fullest attainable happiness. Politics is thus not only inseparable from happiness; it is also inseparable from religion, for religion is our name for the beyond and the beings (or being) that constitute it and control it. Of course, it may be, as analysis proceeds, that something like the state or liberalism will emerge as an option within political phenomena. Yet it will hardly emerge as the only option, and, if what has been argued in previous chapters is anything to go by, it will not emerge as the best option, either.

But if we must begin political analysis with the drive for happiness, the contours of political philosophy have long been outlined for us by the tradition of political philosophy from Plato onward, if not also from before Plato, in the stories of the Bible. We are not necessarily limited to these outlines or to the achievements of the tradition, but they are the context within which we should start and from which we should proceed.[2] For this same reason, we should proceed from the ineluctable presence of religion in political life. Religion, or the gods, cannot fail to arise in politics, if politics is the expression of the human drive for fullness of happiness and comprehension of the whole. The state of nature doctrine and the liberalism it has spawned tried from the start to marginalize religion and to remove it from the center of politics, leaving it only a place in what was reserved as the private sphere of individuals and individual associations. The fact that liberalism has not planted itself in traditional religious countries such as Islamic ones, or in comprehensive atheist countries such as communist ones, only serves to highlight the artificiality or unnaturalness of the liberal solution. To wrench comprehensiveness from the political context affronts the very foundation that politics has in man's drive for fullness. Liberalism does violence to the humanity in man and can only succeed by continual marginalization, if not outright suppression, of his longing for more. Communism confirms this claim as much as religion does, for communism is in its fundamental form a rival to religion; it is a comprehensive vision of the whole that excludes God, just as religions are a comprehensive vision of the whole that includes God. Comprehensiveness of vision is the badge of both.

Liberalism, of course, defends itself on the ground that where comprehensiveness of vision is allowed to remain integral to politics, the result is war and general misery. One can avoid this fearful result and still allow man all that he wants from comprehensiveness if one removes the comprehensiveness and so limits politics, in the way explained before, to securing the conditions in which each can pursue their own vision in peace. That these claims are false was also argued before. Liberalism has not ended war but instead has introduced a new and fearful war of its own: total war. It has also not made room for the pursuit by each of their preferred comprehensive vision. For not only does it itself, as already argued, harbor a drive to comprehensive tyranny, but by marginalizing comprehensive visions and removing them from the political, it has taken their comprehensiveness from them. The visions, by their very nature, want to embrace everything, above all and especially the political, since the political is the furthest development of the communal life of man; and the comprehensive vision, if really comprehensive, is a vision that embraces all of man's being, from individual to family to full-fledged community. To deny it any of these is to deny it itself.

Indeed, if truth be told, liberalism is itself too, even in its so-called limited forms, a comprehensive vision that suffuses the life and thinking and morality of everyone subject to it. Liberalism produces a liberalist society and liberalist citizens. What it marginalizes, they marginalize. What it makes central, they make central. But since it marginalizes religion and moral restraint, and since it makes central the free pursuit by individuals of what they judge or feel at any time to be their good, and since judgment and feeling without religion and morality focus almost always on the satisfaction of the passions, the resulting liberalist society tends to become a fevered embrace of degraded lusts and refined extravagance, often enough in the same places and among the same people. Attend a swanky soirée in a billionaire's penthouse in Manhattan or London or Paris, and amidst old masters on the wall and golden fittings in the bathroom, one will as likely find designer drugs on the drinks bar as expensive liqueurs, refined debauchery in the lounge as refined conversation, a blasé atheism at the dinner table as a blasé liberality. Perhaps it was ever thus among the rich and fabulous, since the like was surely found in the past at the courts of kings. But the doings of kings were as often kept hidden from the toiling, religious masses, who would have been scandalized had they known. Now the doings of billionaires are admired in glossy magazines and held up for the toiling masses to imitate rather than deplore. Surely we can do better.

Comprehensive Politics

If human community begins from the family and for the sake of more complete realization of full human good, and if concern for religion, or wonder about the origin of things, especially about the origin of man himself, manifests itself as part of this realization, then certain fundamental features of the nature of human community may be deduced. First and foremost is precisely the longing for the comprehensive good, and not just for any such good but for the *true* such good. The longing is not for illusion but for reality; it is for genuine good, not merely apparent good. Second, and as a result, the longing stimulates the development of possible answers, and these answers become concrete motivations. But because the question is so broad and the evidence about the answer so hard properly to discover and penetrate, the concrete answers themselves become various. Material goods, such as greater possessions, larger and more powerful communities, and conquest and control of other and lesser communities, will figure largely in this variety. But so will theories about the gods or the ultimate beings (or being) that lie at the origin of things. The more obvious answers will take hold first, such as that the gods are present in other and more mysterious and uncontrollable things, like storms and earthquakes and sun and moon and stars. Since these things are many, and since many of these many seem to have their origin in birth from other things of the same kind, the idea that the gods have a similar origin will typically present itself. This idea will lead back to the thought that the first origin was some primeval father or mother from whom all other things, such as sun and moon and stars, came to be, through progressive generations. Since, further, men find among themselves that parents are replaced, sometimes even violently, by their children, the same idea will be suggested about the first things (a classic ancient account is found in Hesiod's *Theogony* and other primeval tales).

Most of all, indeed, the fact of death will impose itself forcefully on human consciousness. What happens after death, if anything, will be a pressing and even disturbing question; the manifestation of strange and inexplicable phenomena, which seem to run counter to the normal course of things; dreams and waking visions and striking coincidences, even paranormal events (such as happen still today); all these and similar things will tend to induce men to people the world with mysterious presences that come and go. Some of these presences, because of dreams or waking visions (prompted by loss, perhaps, of a loved one), will be identified with the dead, who will thus be thought still to exist in a way, though without bodies of flesh and bone. Some sort of devotion to these dead spirits, to solicit or appease them, will naturally arise, and with it devotion also to things that never seem to die, such as sun and moon and stars, or that seem always to keep happening, such as storms and earthquakes and peace and calm. These apparently impersonal forces will take on a personal character to provide a ready explanation for why a storm happened then and not later, and destroyed these people and things and not those.

These originary explanations, hesitant, uninformed, based on what is obvious and to hand, will not permanently satisfy the inquiring mind. Some of the more reflective will seek out other and different explanations, explanations that oppose and perhaps mock the ones already in place, saying that events like storms happen by chance or by the necessary workings of material forces and not by supposed bodiless spirits. The sun and moon will be said to be big pieces of burning rock and not gods. Those who think otherwise will find these suggestions disturbing and fear that the gods will be angry at such denial of their existence and power. The inventors of these irreligious ideas will be attacked or expelled or even sacrificed to appease the supposed offended deity. But thinking will not stop, and men will go on asking the same questions and trying out new and different answers. The advance of community itself into more extensive and more sophisticated forms will stimulate the process, as men discover that success in many things, like farming and sailing, requires method and principles. The practical arts will develop, and people will experiment with different materials, applying fire and water to test results. Mining and forging and tempering hard earth, or the metals, will come into existence.

Further, methods and principles will be looked for everywhere, and those who, because of advancing community, have leisure from necessities through being served by others, will look for principles and methods in the things of leisure, particularly in counting and numbers, and in the regular motions of the heavens. Records of the past will be examined and ways to preserve memory fostered, in particular by forms and patterns of words that in their rhythmic features lend themselves to easy recollection. Poetry will develop, and those skilled at composing or remembering poems will be prized and honored. At some point, ways of recollection that do not rely on living memories will be invented, such as by marking shapes on long-lasting material objects: walls of caves, pieces of wood, cured animal skins, baked clay, or beaten metal. Pictures that are direct copies of visible objects will likely come first, but the need for more abstract shapes, such as to record numbers or the sounds of human speech, will be felt and find varying solutions. But throughout all will remain the mysterious riddles of the universe and whence it came and how it always remains, and where and what are the hidden things, the dreams and visions of the night, strange foretellings of the future, sudden intimations of events far away. The riddles of man himself will figure largely among these mysteries, the mysteries of love and peace, hatred and war, success and failure, advance and decay, birth and death.

The comprehensive unlimitedness of this activity and progress, and its religious dimension, will mark human community from the beginning, and it will form itself into concrete versions. These versions will become the specialized preserve of experts, poets and priests and scribes, who will hand them on to future generations. But the versions will vary from place to place, and none will ever be so complete or convincing as entirely to satisfy the inquiring mind. The desire to have not simply a comprehensive vision, but a comprehensive vision that is true, will drive speculation always onward. Still, it will be this drive, manifested in all the areas of life, that will fundamentally mark human community and its development.

Authority in Human Community

One particular feature of this drive is the way it will tend to create in human community two different kinds of authority: the authority that is concerned with the present and living human things, and the authority that is concerned with the trans-human, or divine things. Rulers and kings will not only have officers to lead the army, to judge disputes, to deliberate about future needs, and to maintain records and deeds, but also priests to honor and solicit and placate the gods. Communal life will have a temporal or material dimension on the one hand and a spiritual or religious dimension on the other. These two dimensions will not be sharply divided, since all human activities, from war to farming, are subject to the mysterious unknown forces whose care is the preserve of the priests. Success in war and prosperity will depend as much on the gods as on man. But still, it is one thing to know how to marshal troops for battle or how to prepare the soil for planting, and it is another to placate the gods of war and grain so that unexpected and uncontrollable events do not intervene, or intervene to help and not to hinder.

The pagan world presents such a picture to us, where the temporal and spiritual powers, while distinct, tended to combine in the same hands, so that the rulers were as much head of the priests as of the judges and generals and managers. But the two parts differ, if only because the latter are under the control of human art and skill, while the former are not, but instead in the hands of the mysterious and the divine. What is ours to make or mar contrasts with what is not ours but is made or marred by powers we do not own, save, perhaps, by prayer and sacrifice.

The pagan world united what the world of Judaism, Christianity, and Islam has divided. The political or temporal authorities in this second world are not the same as the spiritual or religious authorities. The latter instead come to be a separate class and to have their own rights and their own powers to justify or condemn, to free or confine. That the two authorities or powers nevertheless belong together as integral parts of human community follows from what was argued above about the drive for comprehensiveness. Human community ultimately exists to satisfy this drive, but the drive of necessity embraces the temporal things we can manage and control by art, and the spiritual things that perhaps we can, to some extent, penetrate by science but that we cannot fully know or command. Human community, therefore, includes both, and not simply as parts within it but as authorities and powers over it. Communist countries had and have their spiritual authority, namely the ideology of communism, whose form and content are carefully watched and controlled as much by scholars deputed to the task as by rulers. The same holds increasingly true of modern Israel, where the guardians of Jewish religious orthodoxy seem as integral to the management of affairs as the politicians, and indeed where some of these guardians become politicians because they are guardians. Analogous things were true of medieval Christendom, where the two powers of temporal and spiritual were distinct, culminating in emperor and pope, yet both exercising control over communal life, the spiritual being able, where the spheres overlapped, to command and control the temporal.

A human community that knows of temporal command but not of spiritual is, in the light of the above, deformed and stunted. Only in the so-called liberal state is such a stunting expressly aimed at, and only in such a state is the spiritual power systematically deprived of independent public authority and relegated to the private sphere without power to command the temporal in any way. The reasons for this development were explained in earlier chapters, and the consequences of it too.

There is one consequence, however, that has not yet been fully explored, and that consequence is the effect of the liberal state on man's drive for comprehensive truth, which, as argued, is the ultimate nature and point of human community. The liberal state professes not to deny or limit this drive but rather to deny it any authority or power over the temporal and political. The profession is disingenuous, and in two main ways, first in that it marginalizes what by its nature should be at the center, and second that it denies any real possibility of an authoritative divine revelation.

The first point has already been touched on, where it was argued that the marginalization has the practical effect of making the spiritual seem irrelevant or merely a matter of taste and not a matter of truth (however hard the truth may be to find). So it has the practical effect of saying that the human drive for truth need not direct itself to spiritual questions but only to temporal ones, and it has this effect not by having established determinately that there are no gods and no afterlife (for it expressly denies any competence in these things), but rather by the simple fact of marginalization. Its practice sows a likewise public practice of atheism, even if a theistic interest is allowed as a personal option. It sows, that is to say, an answer to the human drive for truth that excludes the spiritual from the drive and from the truth. The spiritual nevertheless continues to manifest itself, if only in a religious rage for atheism or a dangerous fascination with the occult. At all events, the religious, benign or sinister, is supposed to be for personal choice, not for public formation and education.

The second point, about divine revelation, follows from the first. For if the spiritual is to be marginalized and not to be at the center of public life and authority as itself part of that life and authority (though a distinct part), if indeed it is a matter of personal choice, then the idea that there has been given to man an authentic and public revelation about God is undermined. For were there such a public revelation, it could not rationally be marginalized or reduced to personal choice. It would have to be as much in the public center as, or even more than, anything else.

Let us then entertain, for purposes of argument, the hypothesis that there is a public revelation from God or the ultimate source of all things. The hypothesis is eminently plausible, since the three great religions in the world today, Judaism, Christianity, and Islam, all claim to be such revelations, either for all men in the case of the latter two, or specifically for Jews in the case of the first. Hinduism also claims to be a public revelation (while Buddhism, by contrast, seems on the whole not to, but to record rather what can be naturally known of the divine through intense meditation and experience). Further, the evidence for the existence of some supreme being that has power over all things is, if not uncontroversial, extensive and rationally persuasive. It covers not only, or even especially, the classic theistic proofs (beloved of philosophers for endorsement or denial), but even more so miracles and exorcisms and other historical facts on the ground.

Since at this point, however, philosophers are likely at once to retort with Hume's celebrated argument against miracles,[3] it is necessary to point out here that this argument is doubly defective. First, Hume defines a miracle as a transgression of a natural law. This definition is wrong, because no natural law states as part of itself that it operates in the presence of a supernatural power; it states only that it operates in the presence of natural powers; but a miracle is by definition the work of supernatural power. A miracle does not transgress natural law, therefore, but is rather the exercise of a higher power. It is not unlike the way we "transgress" the law of gravity when we pick a stone off the ground. By itself a stone will not rise. In the presence of a human being, who has power over a stone greater than gravity has, it can rise because it rises with the human's hand. Consequently, and second, because miracles do not transgress natural law, Hume's claim that a witness to a miracle is more likely to be lying than that a natural law has been transgressed, so that the evidence against a miracle is always stronger than the evidence for it, at once falls away. If there is a supernatural power, the evidence of a witness to a miracle performed by such higher power is no less reliable than the evidence of a witness to a purely natural event. All depends on the standard conditions required for determining if a witness is to be judged reliable: namely whether he was really present at the event, whether he was in a good position to witness it, whether or not he has any strong motive to lie, whether he has proved himself a reliable witness on other occasions, whether his testimony stands up against cross-examination, and the like. Since the witnesses for at least some miracles seem to meet these conditions (as even Hume allows in the passage referred to), their existence can hardly with reason be denied.

However, there is no need to insist on these claims against critics. The main point here is simply to establish the intrinsic plausibility of the hypothesis that there is a supernatural being that can and does intervene in the world, and that therefore can and quite possibly has vouchsafed to men a public revelation of his existence and will. For on the supposition of this hypothesis, and on the supposition of what was argued earlier about the drive of man for a comprehensive understanding of things, a drive that is integral to his drive for community and the goods that community enables, the conclusion follows that a public revelation from God, if there is one, should decisively fashion human community and in a public, open way. Those charged with the care of the revelation and its faithful preservation and promulgation would be entitled to exercise a public authority in the public sphere, and to do so not in place of the authorities whose care is with properly temporal affairs, but instead alongside them and, if the temporal power in any way threatens the revelation, against them too. The temporal authority would also have some duty to assist and support the spiritual authority to the extent that the management of temporal affairs impinges on the management of the spiritual ones.

The result would not be a theocratic community, for a theocratic community is properly one where the two powers are united in the hands of the spiritual authority because it is the spiritual authority. But one could call it a *theonomic* community, in the sense that the spiritual power would have at least equal public authority along with the temporal, and in cases of conflict, superior power. The reason is plain. The spiritual is not only superior in its nature to the temporal (for the divine is superior to the human), but it also is superior in man's drive for comprehensive truth. Only the spiritual power, if it preserves and preaches a genuine public revelation, is able to satisfy that drive, for only it could teach the truth about the highest and ultimate things. The range of the temporal does not extend beyond truths that are temporal, and these are limited and never enough to satisfy the human drive for comprehensiveness. A temporal power that stood in the way of a public revelation, if only by denying it public authority, would not be serving community, as it naturally should, but opposing and thwarting it.

Classic examples of theonomic power are found in medieval Christendom, in the medieval Byzantine Empire, in Islamic nations past and present, in Old Testament Judaism, and, increasingly, in modern Israel. There is no need here to arbitrate between these instances or to assess their respective merits, although some general points will be discussed shortly. But one important conclusion does immediately follow. A political arrangement that, as a matter of principle, denies public authority to any public revelation, however well authenticated, is not a boon to human community but a bane. It thwarts the drive that has formed human community from the beginning and that still and always will continue to form it. Liberalism is such a political arrangement. It claims, of course, to be neutral and not to be thwarting any human longing or drive but to be ensuring the conditions for this drive's full and multiply varied realization. But liberalism's claim to neutrality is as much a myth here as it is everywhere else. To deny public authority to a public revelation is to deny that it is, after all, a public revelation. It is not to permit it to exist in fair conditions of peace. For if a public revelation presented by God to all men is not allowed to exercise public authority, it is effectively prevented from being that public revelation, and so is reduced rather to being a private one. It will of course still function, but it will be prevented from functioning as it ought, for it will be prevented from exercising spiritual authority in public life and from correcting temporal authority where temporal authority impinges on spiritual things.

This argument, recall, is being presented hypothetically, as an explication of what must be true on the supposition of a public revelation from the Supreme Being. The argument, however hypothetical, is enough to point up an ineradicable flaw in all forms of liberalism, or all forms of political authority that deny, as liberalism does in its very idea, public authority to a publicly revealed religion. Liberalism can only make this denial by denying the existence of such religion, for if such a religion exists, the denial of public authority to it is a denial that it is what it claims to be. As noted in a different context before, liberalism is a doctrine that, willy-nilly, claims to itself the authority to preach the truth about religion. In this case, indeed, it claims to itself the authority to preach that there is no religion endowed with public authority.

One might retort that even if there were such a religion, neither liberalism nor any temporal power would ever be in a position to allow it public authority. Judgment about spiritual things belongs to the spiritual power, not the temporal one, so that, *ex professo*, the temporal power could never have the authority to judge whether any religion had public authority and, if so, which one it was. This retort only goes so far. For while the temporal authority could not judge the content of a revealed religion, it could judge whether some proposed religion made a rational claim to be publicly revealed. The former judgment may be beyond man's natural powers, but the latter is not. From natural first principles one can work out the sort of conditions that a religion would have to meet if it were to make a rationally valid claim to be publicly revealed.

As a general truth one can say that the political can judge natural truths and so can judge religion to the extent that the evidences for religion, or for this religion over that, are also natural truths, or truths that fall within the competence of natural reason. If there are no such natural truths giving evidence for one religion over another or for any religion, the political power will have no ability, even if it otherwise has the duty, to foster this religion rather than that, for it will have no ability to discern the truth. But truth is the goal of community, and its protection, or the protection of the search for it, belongs to the political power. So in such a case, the political power would be unable to act and would have to be neutral, save insofar as a given religion proved itself to be inimical to the search even for natural truths. But, by the same token, if there is no natural evidence for religion, no one at all will have any evidence to accept or follow this religion rather than that, for no one will have any evidence as to which is true or truer than which others. Accordingly, not only will the political power be unable to protect the true religion, if there is one, but also the community itself will be unable to embrace it. The best that could be done would be to leave the question open for whatever search could be conducted, and to impose no limits other than those that natural justice might independently impose on human communal activities in any event.

The question, therefore, naturally arises as to what the natural evidence for a particular religion might be. There are here two sorts of evidence: natural evidence naturally available, and natural evidence supernaturally available. The former would concern those evidences for religion that have traditionally fallen within the sphere of philosophy, such as the classic proofs for the existence of a god and the like. But these proofs do not point so much to a particular religion as to religion as such, and they leave particularities open to difference. For no doubt some ways of honoring the god might prevail in one place and others in another, all of which, if not morally offensive, would be presumptively legitimate. If there were a way of determining between particular religions over and above moral acceptability, the evidence would have to be supernaturally given natural evidence. The evidence would have to be natural in order to be judgeable by men, but it would have to be supernaturally given if it were to point clearly and decisively to one particular religion rather than another.

There are in principle two things here that natural reason can judge: first, whether a religion professing public authority makes a coherent and rationally defensible claim to that authority; second, whether there is evidence proving that the profession is not just coherent and defensible but also true. On the first point, natural reason can judge that a publicly authoritative religion would have to have God as its author, either directly or indirectly through messengers sent by God. The great religions in the world claiming to be revealed—Christianity, Judaism, and Islam—do claim God as author, citing for their founders Moses and Mohammed as divine messengers in the latter two cases and Christ as God incarnate in the first; Hinduism too claims an origin in revelations given by God to the ancient Rishis of India. But natural reason can also judge that such religions, to be genuine, would have to claim not only to be exercising an authority given somehow by God, but also to be doing so with infallibility. For we must assume that God is at least as rational as we are, and it would be absurd for God to bestow divine authority on a religion and not bestow on it at the same time infallibility in matters of teaching and divine cult. A divine authority capable of mistake could never be trusted, because the truth of what it said and the validity of the cult it practiced could never be relied on. A true revelation falsely taught and wrongly practiced is worse than no revelation at all.

Note, however, that such infallibility in matters of religious truth, while required by the idea of a divine revelation, has no place outside such revelation. In particular, it has no place in matters that are properly subject to human investigation and research. The knowledge or science that men are naturally capable of is open to all for examination and check, provided one has sufficient intelligence and has gone through the requisite training. Since revealed religious truth, by contrast, is only known by revelation and cannot be independently examined or checked, there can be no place, for there is no ground, to challenge the revelation or the authority that infallibly proclaims it. The truth of what it says is only known by the fact that it says it, and says it by divine authority. An infallible teaching authority is indispensable in the case of divine revelation; it is absurd anywhere else.

One conclusion that immediately follows from these considerations is that no written document could constitute or found a religion possessed of public authority by divine decree. A written document, such as the Bible or the Qur'an or the Hindu Vedas, needs authentication and interpretation. The Bible, for instance, is neither self-authenticating nor self-interpreting. For one thing, we need to know which books actually belong to it, and to use the books currently taken to belong to it to prove they belong to it plainly begs the question. Books are also capable of being misinterpreted, and the more so the more difficult they are; even the best readers can err. So the Bible (and also the Qur'an and the Vedas) must get authentication and interpretation from some other source. That source must be public if the authentication and interpretation are to be public. The source must be living and visible if the religion is to retain its authority and to go on being made intelligible to all the generations that successively come and go. It must be possessed of an authoritative teaching that is authoritatively and infallibly proclaimed, and it must be open to the view and examination of all if it is to proclaim, by its authority, a teaching accessible and necessary to all.

The second point concerns the existence of evidence proving that a profession of divine authority is not just coherent but also true. Such evidence would have to be supernatural (so as to prove divinity) yet also judgeable by natural reason (or else the evidence would not be evidence for us), namely displays of supernatural power manifest to human sense and reason. The obvious instances here are miracles, prophecies of the future, exorcisms of demons, and the sanctity or the luminous goodness of individual believers and practitioners. That such things, if they happen, can rightly be judged miraculous and supernatural by natural powers was argued earlier (in the discussion of Hume's argument). All that is further needed is sufficient evidence that such things have happened and go on happening, and the availability of this sufficient evidence in the records of actual witnesses. Where there is authentication by eyewitnesses, there is no rational ground for rejecting the evidence: if it is irrational to believe without sufficient evidence, it is no less irrational not to believe with sufficient evidence. An interesting example here, reported by Bede,[4] is the way St. Augustine of Canterbury and others converted the king of Kent and thereby progressively his whole kingdom to Catholic Christianity. The preaching of St. Augustine and his companions was accompanied by so many and so striking miracles that any other response by the king and his subjects would have been irrational.

An obvious response to these contentions is that miracles and exorcisms and prophecies and saints and the like are found in more than one religion or church, so how can they be used to make a decision for one such religion over another? The question is too simply posed. That certain religions contain holiness and miracles and prophecies shows that they must in some way be divine. It does not show that they have, by divine appointment, public authority. But what is key in the present context is precisely such divinely appointed public authority. For it is one thing that the divinity of something be manifest; it is another thing that that divine thing have public authority to speak and rule in the name of the divine. One must therefore turn directly to the religion itself and see whether or to what extent it makes the claims and does the things that are rationally required of such authority (such as, notably, infallibility). If and only if a religion is coherent in what it claims and does in this regard will the public manifestation of its divinity (by miracles and the like) be also a public manifestation of its authority to speak in the name of the divine. If the divinity of some other thing is publicly manifest, its authority to speak in the divine name will not be manifest, for either it does not claim such authority, or it does not make a rational claim to such authority, or something else of the sort.

The Catholic Church is, of course, a prime candidate here, because it does claim the relevant authority, does make the claim coherently (for it claims infallibility at the same time), founds this claim on grounds internal to and consistent with the revelation it also teaches (as the special status accorded by Christ to the apostle Peter), and has on its behalf multiple testimonies to miracles, exorcisms, and other divine acts taking place over many centuries. There is, however, no need, for present purposes, to assert or to assess the truth of these statements. For whether or not the Catholic Church, or any church or religion, has the public authority it claims to have, this claim, in order to be rationally defensible, would have to take the form just outlined. For if a religion is to have public authority as divine and to be acknowledged as such, it must meet the above conditions of infallibility and authentication by miracles and the like. Otherwise its claims can be dismissed as incoherent from the start. For instance, in the case of the king of Kent, while one might question whether the miracles happened, one cannot question that *if* they happened, the king responded in the only rationally defensible way. The conditional proposition holds that *if* there are miracles, *then* divine power is at work and the messengers through whom the miracles are performed have divine approval, whether or not one denies the antecedent. One should, of course, have good reason for denying the antecedent in order to be rational about it, but since the antecedent asserts empirical facts, the rationality of denial or acceptance will depend on the way we assess any alleged empirical fact: by examining the trustworthiness and reliability of the witnesses. Once this examination has been done, and the antecedent accordingly asserted (or denied), the rest follows.

We can at least conclude, then, even on the basis of the hypothesis alone, independently of empirical investigation, that liberalism, as already remarked, is flawed in its very idea. For liberalism denies in principle and as a matter of doctrine that any religion can have public authority in political community. But to deny this possibility in principle and as doctrine is to deny the truth of the hypothesis, for it is to deny, in advance of all possible evidence to the contrary, public authority to any religion whatever, even to one that could prove itself to natural reason to be divinely endowed with such authority.

Note finally that one cannot defend liberalism here in the way that is typically done, by appeal to the so-called burdens of judgment. These burdens of judgment, which are the many "hazards involved in the correct (and conscientious) exercise of our powers of reason and judgment in the ordinary course of political life," may be briefly listed thus: (a) empirical and scientific evidence is often complex and conflicting; (b) we may reasonably disagree about the relative weight of different considerations; (c) concepts are vague and subject to hard cases; (d) the way we assess evidence and weigh values can be shaped by our total life experience; (e) different normative considerations on different sides can make overall assessment difficult; and (f) the number of values any social institution can incorporate is limited.[5] But none of these "burdens" applies in the case of clear and manifest miracles and other supernatural acts (of the sort, for instance, allegedly witnessed by the king of Kent). Here the evidence is plain to view, and doubt by eyewitnesses is irrational. To doubt it would be like doubting that the sun was shining or rain was falling when standing outside in the open air. Likewise, doubt by those who receive the reports of eyewitnesses, provided that these reports are well authenticated, would also be irrational. It would be like doubting that Napoleon lost the battle of Waterloo or that Caesar crossed the Rubicon. To defend, therefore, by appeal to the burdens of judgment, liberalism's denial in principle of public authority to any religion, even to one authenticated by manifest miracles, is subterfuge.

Notes

1. The ethics of care theory and the communitarian and civic republican theories also take their bearing by the situated or communal character of human existence; see Held (2006) for the first theory, and the review and references in Talisse (2005: 1–32) for the second two. The position adopted here is in some ways similar, but its line of argument is rather differently directed.
2. For some discussion of this tradition of political philosophy in its application to forms of government, see Chapter Seven below.
3. *An Enquiry Concerning Human Understanding*, section 10.
4. Bede, the Venerable, *Ecclesiastical History* chapters 25–33.
5. Rawls (1993: 54–58). The summary follows the Online Stanford Encyclopedia of Philosophy s.v. Public Reason. See also Talisse (2012: 25–28).

5

The Personalism
of Illiberalism

The Person

Political thought, since it is about community, and since community
is about the drive for comprehensive truth, should take that drive as
its principle and goal. The principle and goal, then, is the drive, rather
than a comprehensive vision of the good as such. For perhaps no vision
man can conceive will ever be the comprehensive truth; perhaps such
truth has to be a gift from the highest being, as the great religions
anyway teach, for they teach not attainment now but pursuit now and
attainment hereafter. Nevertheless the drive for comprehensive truth
will determine the nature and primary structure of political life, subject
no doubt to the limitations of time and place and persons.

The decisive term here is not so much that of "comprehensive" as
that of "truth." A comprehensive falsehood is not what is wanted, and
if no comprehensive vision can be constructed by us that would lack
falsehood, let us have truth without comprehensiveness rather than
comprehensiveness without truth. Note first, then, that truth is not
opposed to freedom, nor is the pursuit of it or even the honest claim
to it a threat to freedom. In fact freedom is enslaved by falsehood and
set free by truth. This assertion seems paradoxical, for how can freedom be freed or enslaved? Is not freedom freedom regardless? The
answer is that freedom is not simple or single, and it can exist in some
ways but at the same time not in others. The point can be illustrated
by thinking of situations where one is free to choose but one lacks
knowledge of the good, or of what one really wants, or what will really
satisfy. Choice here exists but is hindered by ignorance, or worse, by
falsehood. What we want is good, the most complete good attainable,
but if we do not know what it is, we cannot choose the way to it, and if
we mistake it for something else, we will choose a false way. Freedom

in this case is bound by ignorance or error. It is not free, because it cannot do what it wants, namely pursue the good. Truth, then, sets freedom free, because it gives freedom what it needs to choose what it wants and not what it does not want. The principle and structure of political life must therefore be determined by a pursuit of truth that will set freedom free to choose the good.

Nevertheless there is controversy about truth and about whether indeed there is a truth that, in the case of the human good, is the same for all. So something more must first be said about freedom and the truth about the good and whether there are many such goods or one. For if there are many, there will be as many freeings of freedom as there are differences of human goods and the truth about them. Consequently a single political arrangement focused on one such good will free some but enslave others, according to whether the good aimed at is their own good or another's.

The question, however, about the general connection between freedom and truth, whatever the truth may be, is prior. The question about the truth itself is better dealt with after the general connection has been more fully explored. For it may seem, and does seem to some, that a focus on truth within freedom is inimical, if not to freedom, then to the uniqueness and the personhood of the individual. One of the things we want, especially today, is to give a place in our communal life to that special uniqueness and dignity that we say and claim belongs to each of us.[1] What counts is not just that I am a human being but that I am I and that I have rights and choices and a life that is uniquely mine and uniquely mine to determine. We want, therefore, a communal existence that permits—indeed, that enables—me to be me and you to be you. Hence such communal existence must be, first, pluralistic, because I and you are unique persons who cannot be captured in or reduced to some single category (something "true" for you that is not "true" for me), and second, democratic, because if others can determine my communal existence without (or even against) my consent (for they "know the truth" but I do not), I am denied my uniqueness and become someone else's cipher.

We can all readily acknowledge and feel the force of these considerations; they have for us moderns an immediate resonance. But what is not so easy is to pin it all down, to analyze it, to bring it to conscious expression. Indeed the problems of analysis begin already with that simple expression, "I." Nothing, one might think, should be more obvious to us than our very self. In one sense, nothing else is.

The existence of myself, the immediate presence of my own reality among all the other realities around me, is the most undeniable fact of experience. Yet it is an existence that I *use* more than I experience. I use it to negotiate my way around, to secure my needs, to satisfy my desires. The focus of my attention is from me to things. Only in rarer moments does my attention turn back on me, and those moments tend to be moments of frustration or annoyance, when the things do not yield to my wants, when they stand stubbornly contrary. Rarer still are the moments when I try to seize myself directly, unmediated through the presence of things, and try to discover who or what I am, when I stop using myself and, as it were, try to find myself face to face. "Know thyself," said the Delphic oracle, and imposed on us a task that is as obvious as it is hard. For what really am I?

The word "I," Elizabeth Anscombe perceptively remarked,[2] is not a name or a referring expression. "John" and "Bill" are names, but "I" is not. How then do John and Bill refer to themselves when they want to? If the nurse asks John how he feels today and John says "I feel better," is he not saying the same as "John feels better"? Indeed, would not the nurse herself say the same when reporting back to the doctor? So if "John" is a name, and if when John says, "I feel better," this remark is equivalent to "John feels better," how is "I" not a name? Of course, if "I" is a name, it is a rather special name, because it names everyone, just as "you" and "he" or "she" name everyone. It is, as we say, an indexical. It indicates someone or something in the immediate environment (physical or contextual) that one can pick out by a sort of pointing. But to indicate is still to refer, so, to this extent, indexicals must have some characteristic of names. Perhaps, though, we should regard this fact as merely linguistic. For "I" has deeper resonances than a name could have. It is, for instance, a sign of a child's undeveloped consciousness that, in speaking to its mother, it refers to itself not as I but by its name. A child in this condition has not yet fully appropriated itself to itself, as it were, but is still externalizing itself as another of the things out there to be named as they are named. Saying "I" consciously and with maturity is to see that one is saying more by "I" than one would say if, referring to oneself, one said not "I am hungry" but "John is hungry." What is this more?

There is a peculiar transparency to "I." To say "John is hungry" requires no more than a successful reference beyond oneself to John— whether John is one's child or one's goldfish. But "I" is not a reference *beyond* oneself. It is a reference *to* oneself. The referrer and the referred are one and the same. More, however, is that the same word expresses the one referring and the object referred to at the same time. When I say, "John is hungry," the two are different: I am the referrer, and John is the object referred to. When I say, "I am hungry," the two are one. I am both referrer and referred, both subject and object, and I achieve both at the same time and with the same word. Collapsing the two functions into one is what a small child has not yet mastered, and instead it externalizes itself so that it can refer to itself in the same way as it refers to other things. Indeed, this collapsing is an extraordinary thing to master. Linguistically "I am hungry" is the same as "John is hungry," but really the two are worlds apart. "John" signifies another outside me; "I" does not. Yet I can only say "I" because I do somehow make myself sufficiently other as to signify myself. I somehow make myself two, a referrer and a referred, without, however, ceasing to be one. For if I really became two, I could no longer say "I"; I would have to say "he." Hence the need to speak of the transparency of "I." The "I" that is referred to is transparent to the "I" that refers, so that the referring "I" refers right through the referred-to "I," so to speak, and comes back to hit itself. Thus the referring "I" ends up referring to the referring "I," and the referred-to "I" ends up being referred to by the referred-to "I." It is as if an archer, shooting at the target, were to end up shooting at himself.

Nevertheless, if the self-referring of the "I" is a sort of self-transparent vanishing (if one may so speak), the point is not that the "I" has no structure to uncover and analyze. Typically the "I" is understood in terms of intentionality; that is, of consciousness as a cognitive act directed to, or intending, an object of cognition. Knowledge is intentional in this sense, and self-awareness is intentional too, insofar as it is knowledge. But the "I" comes to view less in terms of self-knowing than in terms of a self-possessing that is also a *self-governing*. Part of the reason is that even in knowing, the "I" is *active* and involved in a special *energizing* of itself. The phenomenon of "I act" is, here as elsewhere, decisive.[3] Like any case of "I," the "I" of "I act" is a self-referring transparency, only now this self-referring is viewed under the idea of self-governance. For self-referring here is not only a taking hold of oneself in self-awareness; it is also a taking hold of oneself for action. The former taking hold, the taking hold that is a self-possessing in self-awareness, has more of a passive character: it is a sort of registering in oneself for oneself of all that one already is and has become.

The phenomenon of "I" in question here has a multiple analysis. To begin with there are the mirroring and reflexive functions of consciousness. Mirroring is the self retaining for itself, in immediate self-awareness, all that the self does and undergoes, and reflexivity is the self turning back on itself to realize for itself that it is that very self. The taking hold of oneself for action, while it involves the same two functions of mirroring and reflexivity, has now the added function of what one may call an engaging of oneself for action. This engaging for action may be termed self-governance, and together with self-possession, it constitutes what may itself be called *self-determination*. Self-determination is peculiarly constitutive of the person. A person is precisely a self-determining agent. Even in acts of knowledge, he is self-determining, for though the content of what he knows is determined by the object known, that he knows it, or that he is now engaged in knowing it and not something else, is determined by himself and his own acts of choice about what to study.

The self thus comes fully to view or, more properly, fully into existence in acts of self-determination. In the exercise of its capacity self-consciously to initiate action, the self not only brings something about in the real world—such as, say, a table or a book or a judicial sentence—it also brings itself about. It makes itself to be an actor: an actor of this rather than that, and an actor of this quality rather than of that. In fact the self is engaged, in each of its acts of self-determination, in constituting or creating itself. This creating is, however, not a pure creating *ex nihilo*, for the person exists in the first place as a real, substantial thing—a real, individual human being. This reality is the metaphysical reality, so to say, of the person, which the person does not create but which he preexistingly is. The various acts this person thereafter performs come to the preexisting individual as modifications conditioning that individual, or as accidents conditioning the substance (to speak metaphysically). These accidents and substance together, however, constitute for the person who is them the lived reality of what he is. They make him to be this unique individual. They are, if you like, his personalistic essence, and the fact that they can also, metaphysically speaking, be differentiated into substance and accident is secondary.

The human person, therefore, is at the same time a natural and a human creation. For the natural powers with which every human creature is endowed become, when freely exercised, the continuing cause and abiding subject of the several acts that, over time, constitute the "I." Each "I" is thus not only a self-creation but also a unique creation, and the reason is in both cases the same: self-determination. Nothing makes the "I" what it becomes but the "I" itself, and this "I" is unique not only because each "I" makes itself differently, but also because each "I" is a different and independent cause. The unique self-causality of the "I" is accordingly inviolable. But what is meant here is not that people cannot try to violate each other, or, indeed, that in trying to do so they cannot cause considerable damage. What is meant is that, ultimately, none of this trying and none of this damaging can penetrate to the center of the "I's" causality and take that causality away or make it dependent on another for its acting. True, this causality can be subjected to another's causality by force or trickery, but such subjection could not happen without some consent, however minimal, on the part of the one subjected. Hence it could not happen without the "I" retaining the power, when it chose, of throwing off the subjection. If there were no consent given at all, as can happen, say, with hypnosis or extreme brainwashing, the "I's" causality would be rendered wholly inoperative. The "I" would be suspended, not subjected.

Love of Self, Truth, and Participation

The constitutive self-determination that thus prevents the "I" being unwillingly *subjected* to another is what gives the "I" the special privilege of being able willingly to *participate* in another. The uniting of many into one that despots and tyrants have vainly pursued by force is effortlessly achieved through love by the lowliest of men. For love is the typical as well as the most complete exercise of self-determination. This love is first love of self, the love whereby, in acting freely, we choose this self and not that self to be what we shall become. In every free act, we are loving, because we are choosing to create, the self of that act. This reality is why our free acts are so precious and so important, and also why we should take great care to ensure that the self we are choosing is a self worth loving and a self worth being. For while we are free to choose what we want, we are not free to choose that what we want shall be good rather than bad. The good or bad belongs to the acts of themselves, and it is from the goodness or badness of these acts that we who choose them become ourselves good or bad.

The objectivity of the good is a matter of much dispute among philosophers and the population at large, but the fact is sufficiently proved by the phenomenological experience of truth. What needs to be stressed here is the *experience* of truth rather than truth itself. When we choose something, we choose it as a value, and we so choose it because we judge it to be a value; and to judge something to be a value is to judge it as true, to be the value we suppose it to be. Of course we can be mistaken in our judgments, but the possibility of mistake just confirms the importance of the experience of truth. For there can be no question of mistake if there is no question of being right, and there can be no question of being right if there is no question of truth. Here is the difference between acting from choice and acting from instinct or passion. In both cases the act is, to be sure, focused on a value, but in the latter case, the value operates immediately on the instinct and, passing judgment by, directly determines the action. The instinct or passion, called into operation by the value, just takes over, as it were, and causes the act willy-nilly. The act, then, just happens in me rather than being something I do. In the case of action through choice, by contrast, the act is not caused by the value unless or until the value has been taken into my self-determination and been judged to be a true value and a value that I *ought* to pursue here and now (for assuredly one cannot judge that one ought to do something that one also judges not to be truly good or not to be truly worth doing). Judgment, not instinct, intervenes between the value and the act, and what judgment judges is truth. Thus and only thus can the act be mine and something that I choose and that I do. This moment of truth is integral to self-determination and an essential part of the experience of "I act." Without it there can be no "I" doing any action.

We might call the moment of truth the *personalistic* truth of the act, as opposed to its *ontological* truth. By the latter is meant the factual goodness or badness of the act, which falls under the province of moral theory, where the truth about which sorts of acts are really good and which really bad is investigated and established. By the former is meant the judgment of good and bad that any self makes in determining itself to act. The two need not coincide. But they ought to coincide; that is, we ought to strive to make sure that our judgments are not mistaken. If we do make this effort but still, despite ourselves, make a mistake, our act, while ontologically bad or deficient, is personalistically good. Moreover, this mistaken act is the one we ought to choose unless and until we are able to realize and correct the mistake. Honest error is better than dishonest rectitude. Honest rectitude is, however, better still, and we ought to strive for it. Thus, because we know we can err, because we know that the good is sometimes hard to discern, and because we know that the good is what we should nevertheless pursue, to act as if this point were not true—to act, that is, as if we need not care about the good and about getting it right—is to have denied or compromised the personalistic good. The same would be the case if we were not to care about the moment of truth at all and simply chose to follow our passing instincts or pleasures. For in every such case, we would nevertheless have made a judgment, in particular the judgment not to care, and a judgment, moreover, that we knew to be false. So, in this case, regardless of the ontological truth or rectitude of the act we performed, our choice to do it would be directly against the personalistic truth of it, or against honesty.

These remarks have been made by way of commentary on the idea of loving ourselves, that the way to love ourselves is to love the truth in our acts, the personalistic truth first and, though this, the ontological truth too. Thus to love ourselves is the foundation for and the beginning of loving others. It is the foundation because it makes the truth about others the foundation of our actions toward them; it is the beginning because to love the self-determination that is "I" is to practice loving the self-determination that is you. The truth about you, of course, is that you too are a self-determining "I," and I cannot act on this truth unless I treat you as another "I." The way this truth is best captured is to talk about the "I-Thou" relationship in contrast to the "I-It" relationship.[4] An "It" confronts me as something that I may treat as I will and for my own benefit. There are no doubt limits on how I should treat this or that "It," but these limits do not so much arise from the "It" itself as from the relations to myself or to other "I's" that it happens to stand in. By contrast a "Thou" confronts me as something that may not be used and that may not be treated as I will for my own benefit. I must treat you as an independent source of activity, making independent choices through your own judgment of truth and your own power of self-determination. This point does not mean I have to agree with you or think your choices wise or good. But it does mean that, despite my disagreements, I have to go on treating you as your own agent, as having your own power to originate acts and not as derivative from me. I have to go on treating you as "Thou" and not as "It."

The "I" and the "Thou" are individual self-determining subjects or supposits (to use the traditional Latin term), and individuals are, strictly speaking, the only such subjects. A group or a community of individuals is not another subject. It is a relation among subjects. Nevertheless it is a relation of a special kind, for it is constituted by the joint action of several "I's" for the common good. The "I" by itself is not yet a "We," and the "I-Thou" is not yet a "We." For while the "I" should affirm the dignity of every "Thou," this affirming may be done without the "I" and the "Thou" joining together in choosing and acting for a common good.

The "We" only arises when the "I" and the "Thou," or several "I's" and "Thous," each exercise their self-determination in choosing the same good as others are choosing, and in choosing it because the others are choosing it. The upshot need not be that each does the same act. Often it means they do different acts. But it does mean they do acts that together constitute the realizing of a good that is common to them all, and that they all share in, and that they all exercise their self-determination for. Obvious examples would be team sports, like football or soccer, where each member of the team occupies a different position and is in charge of a different task, but where all do their tasks for the common good of the team's victory. Here there is one common good, victory; there are many specific tasks, such as defense, attack, running, kicking, or passing; each individual performs his task through the exercise of his own self-determination; each does this task for the good of the whole team; each makes this good the object of his own act and does so because the others are making it the object of their own acts too.

There are certain conditions that must be met if a number of "I's" is to form a "We," and once a "We" is formed, certain implications necessarily follow. The first and fundamental condition is that each "I" be able to act, and does in fact act, as a self-determining person. Any difficulties put in the way of any "I" to make action harder, or even to prevent any "I" from acting, will compromise and eventually destroy the "We" because they compromise and halt the acting of the "I," or of one of the "I's," in which the "We" subsists. It is not even the case that the remaining "I's," whose self-determination is not compromised or halted, still constitute a "We." For, first, if the other "I's" whose self-determination is compromised are needed in the "We" so that this "We" can realize its proper good, then the "We" is compromised to the same extent that the "I's" are. Second, if these other "I's" are not needed, or while desirable are not strictly indispensable, but yet they are subjected to the "We" anyway, then the "We" in question has, in its own act, denied the truth about the "I's" it thus subjects. For it is no longer treating them as "I's" but instead as kinds of "It." Perhaps ignorance could sometimes furnish an excuse here, so that the "We," or those "I's" that constitute it, is not personalistically blameworthy (as may be true of some primitive peoples in their treatment of other tribes). But it could hardly furnish an excuse in modern liberal democracies, whose chief claim to civilization is their recognition of the equal dignity of all men. For if such dignity is to mean anything, it must mean allowing or enabling all men to realize their self-determination in their own free activity.

Another and in some ways more powerful way of putting across this basic insight about community and participation is in terms of the idea of *neighbor*.[5] The idea of *neighbor* is based on the simple fact of our common humanness; that is to say, it is based on what is common to all men everywhere, including myself, and not on what is common to these or those men who compose this or that separate community. As such, the idea of *neighbor* is the fundamental basis of, and deeper than, all membership of particular communities. It forms, in a sense, the idea of the human community as such. Any of the more particular communities that deny this base of common humanity lose their properly human character and, in a way, cease to be communities at all. For in denying or relegating humanness, the humanness of the excluded others, they deny the dimension of participation that makes human community. Participation is, first and foremost, a human thing and cannot be realized in its fullness if humanness is anywhere denied. The term "neighbor" thus brings out the full significance of participation. The ability to share in the humanness of every man is where participation reaches its personal depth and its universal dimension. It is also the core of participation and the condition for the personalistic value of acting along with others. It establishes and confirms the universality of human existence, or the fact that, despite all the particular differences that separate us from one another (historical, cultural, personal, and so forth), we all share in the one humanness, and all achieve fulfillment through the same authentic dynamism of freedom and self-determination.

The idea of *neighbor* brings with it the commandment of love, the commandment to love one's neighbor as oneself. This commandment expresses a special attitude of regard that we should have toward every person, simply by the fact of his or her personhood. Every person should be treated as a person and not as a means for furthering one's own interests. Love of one's neighbor is in fact the necessary basis for any community that is to be human, and for any relation to a member of a particular community. Without it there arises the phenomenon called *alienation*.[6] Alienation signifies that man is deprived of the personalistic value of his action. Such privation can, indeed, happen because of the system of things; but its root is deeper and more personal in man himself. For it is man who creates and operates systems and who is responsible for the alienation present in a system. The fundamental source of alienation is disregard of the command to love one's neighbors, one's fellow human beings, in all their fullness as persons.

In order to overcome alienation, love of one's neighbor must be at the foundation of all the communities and systems that man develops and establishes at any level. Alienation is only in the system because it is first in man, the acting person who embraces or fails to embrace, in his action, the true human good and genuine participation with others.

The Family and Religious Truth

Since truth and the striving for truth are integral to what it is to be free and a person, the community of persons, which arises for the fuller development of persons, must itself be marked by the same striving for truth. This striving will give to community, and especially to the political community, its fundamental form and character, so that communities that do not have truth and the striving for it as their aim will, to this extent, be imperfect and indeed unnatural, as going against the natural form of community. The striving, however, as was already remarked, is not properly described as a comprehensive vision; it is better described as precisely a striving for such a vision or as close to it as community is able to go. There will thus be a certain open-endedness to the striving. It will not close off rival comprehensive visions but instead subject them all to the measure of truth. It will, to be sure, close off or resist visions that oppose truth or the search for truth, but it will do so in the name of the fundamental form and character of community, which is truth. No genuine and honest searching for truth will be contrary to political community as such, but a demotion or relegation of this searching from political community will be contrary to it. Liberalism, therefore, which wishes to relegate the search for truth to what lies beyond the properly political, is intrinsically unnatural and intrinsically unjust, because it opposes the common good of community. There may indeed be structures to political community that are not as such about truth and the search for it but rather about preserving and organizing community in peaceful and prosperous ways. Still, these structures will have truth as their fundamental measure, since peace and prosperity will themselves be measured by the search for truth and will be pursued as and how the search for truth best requires.

The implications of this fact are many. First, of course, is that justice and injustice in political communities will take their measure from truth and the search for it. There may indeed be more than one way of justly organizing communities, but if so, each of these ways will be just because of the orientation to truth and not otherwise. There may also be limitations imposed by conditions extrinsic to the orientation to truth, limitations that cannot easily or at all be removed. For instance, physical preservation and survival may be so urgent that little else can be thought of until these are secured. Or the complexion of the peoples who make up the community may be so diverse that the political community is compelled to be more like liberalism in its actions and to focus on the conditions for the search for truth rather than on directly enabling and assisting that search. To what extent such limitations exist and have to be accepted, rather than lessened or removed, will depend on circumstances and prudential decision by agents on the spot, and not by a straight application of first principles. But in order to be able to make such decisions, agents must know the principles and aim to follow them as far as possible. Consequently a first task is to lay out the principles and only from there consider the variations in ways of implementing them.

Since the chief desiderata for persons, both individually and in community, are truth and its pursuit, a first principle is that community, if it is to have these desiderata as its end, should have as its end the forming of the community and its members for that very end. This forming will not be first about material needs (or if so, only first in time) but instead about moral character and intellectual habits, namely whatever character and habits best orientate people to truth and its pursuit. That this character and these habits will themselves take the form of the virtues, moral and intellectual, long sanctioned by philosophical and religious tradition, may, for the present, be assumed as intuitively obvious. At all events the forming of community in question here will embrace, first, the acceptance and preservation of truths already discovered and, second, the qualities of mind and will and heart to do such accepting and preserving as well as to advance further. The measure of material goods will be given accordingly, and neither wealth nor empire will be the aim of a just community, but only as far as circumstances and truth require (which, as varying in time and place, may sometimes make empire just and sometimes unjust).

The community, however, cannot be directed to this forming for truth and its pursuit if the leaders of it, and at all levels of leadership, are not themselves already directed and formed in the same way, or are as well formed as possible. Accordingly choice of rulers, where choice must be made, will be determined by virtue and wisdom and by where they are found in the different parts of the community. So as virtue and wisdom vary in their presence, either simply or in this or that part of the community, so the possible forms of just and legitimate rule will vary. A first implication to notice, then, or rather to recall, is that elections and election campaigns, expensive or not (whose deleterious effects were discussed earlier), will hardly be the method to follow in choosing leaders. Only as election ensures virtue will it have a place, and not as it represents rival and merely occurrent interests instead of the interest in truth. Virtue, by contrast, whether in rulers or ruled, will include all those qualities of character that enable life in community, such as justice and moderation and courage especially, but also and more so those qualities of mind that directly enable the search for truth. The latter are typically referred to as epistemic virtues but may be summed under the idea of philosophy taken in its primary sense of love of wisdom, and so as embracing all aspects of wisdom and love of it.

A second point, however, needs especially to be reintroduced here, namely the point about religion from the previous chapter. For while the love of wisdom knows no intrinsic limits, the natural capacity of men to discover truth need not be taken as reaching to all that is in principle knowable. The truths about the highest beings may, apart from certain general facts, be beyond natural human capacity. They cannot, however, be beyond human desire, if human desire is, as it has been argued to be, directed to the comprehensive truth. Such comprehensive truth, if it is beyond human capacity to attain naturally, can only be made known by the gods themselves, and if the gods bestow of their knowledge through priests, then the religious dimension will transcend and be superior to the political. The political will have to make a special place for religion within community and give it special privileges and protection so that this superior knowledge may be properly propagated and preserved. By the nature of the case, then, the political will have duties in respect of the religious, to provide it a place and preserve and protect it from political interference or overthrow. The religious will thus have a certain political power, not direct or immediate, but instead indirect and as occasion demands; and the political will have a religious duty, not to teach or rule religion, but to promote and foster it so that it can flourish and do its job without impediment.

The evils introduced by the modern idea of the state are particularly evident here. The state is necessarily hostile to religious beliefs (they derogate from its power) and would, if it had to tolerate them as a public force, twist them to its own purposes. State education, because of what the state is, is necessarily nonreligious if not antireligious. But non-state education, to be real, cannot just be lessons taught in private classrooms. It must find support and reinforcement throughout people's lives, which it will not do as long as the state is possessed of extensive control over people's material and personal existence. Internal checks, such as one finds in the US Constitution, are not enough. Such checks can and do exist alongside monopolistic and despotic power. There must be external checks coming from within society, or society must have a real separation from and independence of the state. Or better still, there should be no state, no monopoly of coercion in community.

An independent religious authority is the most powerful of these checks, but its power extends further. People are individually weak and dependent on others for almost everything in life. The dependence of individuals on the state destroys freedom and truth. It tends, moreover, to make people idolaters toward the state, for its distant and impersonal welfare structures and functionaries are, because of their distance and impersonality, too easily idealized and divinized. Their all too human faults are too far away to be noticed, but their pervasive acts of seeming beneficence, from pensions to welfare checks, endow them with semidivine status. It is far better if people depend instead on those immediately known to them, their families and personal friends, whom, because of personal closeness, they cannot divinize but whom they can love. The family is not just parents and children but also grandparents and grandchildren, uncles and aunts and cousins, as well as acquaintances and associates in the larger but still local community. The family has historically been the most powerful source of independence from central political control. It has received its strength mainly from religion, since religion has given the family its first roots and surrounded it, and the rights and duties of parents, with the awe and sanction of the gods. Further, the family provides, when not corrupted, the means and substance of common life requisite for firm and lasting friendships, for mutual loyalty and trust, for sustained joint action, for the inventions of thought and art. It provides too the haven where there will always be a welcome, and the last resting place where the dead may be honored, remembered, and supplicated. Other associations can generate similar bonds, from those forged at school to those forged in common physical or intellectual endeavors. The friendships that such unions create form fixed centers of action independent of the state and uncontrollable by it.

Not surprisingly, therefore, the more complete the central authority, especially when of a despotic character, which the earlier argument showed the modern state was, the more hostile it has proved itself to be to such things, and in particular to the family, where they all begin and to which they all somehow relate. The central authority cannot be all-powerful if there are powers among men that do not depend on it. The modern liberal state, for instance, has acted in many ways to undermine the family and the independence of the family. The state control of schools takes from parents the right to decide how their children are to be educated. It also requires high rates of taxation that deprive parents of the freedom to decide how to spend their own resources. Similar high rates of taxation are required for the provision of public welfare, whose bureaucratic inefficiencies and invasions of family privacy must be endured by all except the very rich. The free availability, even the active promotion, of abortion and artificial means of contraception are also not without deleterious effects on the stability and health of family life. To say that all these things are key elements of individual freedom, which only killjoys or the indifferent could oppose, betrays neither thought nor honesty. Free sex is not part of freedom, unless yielding to the passions is freedom. Nor is freedom having one's money or other resources taken by others to determine how they are spent. Freedom is when one can make one's own decisions for oneself and one's family, and when one does so by following reason, not passion. Such is the message of the idea of the person, and of the self-determination, noted above, that distinguishes the person.

The destruction of the family, and of the religion that supports it, is also an effective way to destroy the wider bands of comradeship, since the latter so often and so naturally finds its roots and supports in the former. The destruction is complete when there is added to it the ideology of individualism, born of liberalism's state of nature doctrine, where each person is considered a separate unit, endowed, as a separate unit, with his own individual rights, and beholden to none in his choices, provided he not interfere with the choices of others. A doctrine more calculated to divide people than this doctrine of rights and of mutual noninterference is hard to imagine. A doctrine more calculated to reduce people to slavery is hard to imagine too. If the good, as liberalism teaches, is what appeals to each and what each has the right to follow, then not only will most people follow their passions most of the time, but also an all-powerful coercive state will need to be always on hand to stop those passions driving people into violent conflict. The result is that people are made into slaves and political authority into a despot. Such a condition is not freedom, nor is it happiness or peace, at least not a happiness or peace worthy of self-determining persons.

The solution is to be found, as it has always been found, in traditional religion. By traditional religion is meant religion that teaches the existence of a transcendent god who cares for, as he will also finally judge, the creatures whom he has made. But a distinction must be drawn between religion's moral teachings and its speculative ones. This distinction is necessary, both in its own right and in view of the principle of toleration to be discussed in the next section.

By speculative teachings is meant teachings about the nature of God and his creative activity. The Christian teaching that God is a trinity is such a teaching, as is also the Jewish teaching that God spoke the world into existence in six days, the Muslim teaching that Mohammad is the last prophet of God, or the pagan teaching that things were created by the sexual congress of the first gods. These speculative teachings are often incompatible with each other (unless interpreted allegorically), but the moral teachings they are associated with are not. Nor do these moral teachings so depend on the speculative that if the latter are rejected, so must be the former. They are, moreover, largely the same, while the speculative ones much differ. The speculative are also optional, even sometimes within the same religious community. The moral are not optional and can safely be required.

The moral teachings are twofold. The first, already mentioned, concerns the existence of a suprahuman power that is guardian of right, avenger of wrong, and final judge of the deeds of men. The second concerns the principles of right and wrong or how men ought to behave, in which alone (and not in the pursuit of the passions of liberalism's state of nature) is happiness to be found. Despite surface differences, these principles are basically the same. The well-known Ten Commandments, inherited from the Jews, are a neat summary of them. For although the first three commandments about God and the sabbath are not, as such, the same for all, they are nevertheless so in what they say about the need to pay divine honor, through determinate acts on determinate occasions, to the supreme being or beings. All these commandments, while universal as regards their immediate content, admit of much particularity of interpretation and application as one descends to the details of concrete actions. In such interpretation and application, differences between peoples and religions increasingly appear. But the same is true of all principles and laws, even those in force in liberal states. Men's actions, despite a general sameness, vary infinitely in particular details, and require, for correct judgment, the prudence born of age and experience. Yet even here the conviction is universal that there is a correct judgment to be made and that particular actions, like general ones, are in themselves right or wrong and not merely in relation to opinion or passion or interest. Implicit in these commandments are the habits to be developed through them and to be used for the better keeping of them, commonly called virtues. These virtues, like the commandments and principles, are also essentially the same and universally acknowledged. Their opposites, the corresponding vices, are no less universally recognized and no less universally condemned.

Religions fundamentally agree in these doctrines. Even those who profess no religion agree in them. While it is true that people sometimes act against the moral laws and virtues, and while it is also true that none is free of the temptation so to act, few are brazen enough to believe, or to say they believe, that the laws are wrong and the virtues detestable. Those who are thus brazen make themselves hated and feared by everyone else, even by each other. Who would not hate and fear someone who cares not for the life or property of others? Such an one is ready to kill or rob whomever he meets and has made himself the enemy of mankind.

The moral doctrines form a consensus shared by everyone, religious and nonreligious, which one might fairly call an overlapping consensus. It embraces everyone despite their differences in other matters, the religious ones in particular. In order to understand and explicate this consensus, there is no need of the lengthy disquisitions or controversial thought experiments beloved of professional academics. The principles of right (as summarized in particular in the Ten Commandments) are this overlapping consensus, which has, in this form, existed explicitly within Christian, Jewish, and Islamic civilizations from the beginnings of each, and has existed implicitly and in effect in every other civilization and religion (however limited the range of others to whom it has at times been applied).[7] There is no need to hunt about for it in hidden places. It is right there in the actual knowledge and practice of everyone's ordinary and daily life. That this consensus overlaps all religions and is separable from the speculative doctrines proper to each does not mean that it is separable from all religious beliefs and behaviors. Since the moral doctrines divide into a set of principles of right and wrong on the one hand and a belief in a transcendent guardian of these principles on the other, and since the latter involves religious convictions, religion is integral to the moral doctrines. Still, the precise relation that holds between these two elements needs explication.

Note, first, that the principles have a certain immediate self-evidence that makes them logically independent of the conviction about a divine judge. They retain their truth and universality even in the absence of this further conviction. So the nonreligious can hold to them no less than the religious. The moral principles do not logically need to be derived from, or to receive confirmation in, any prior truths, whether religious or not. They can and do stand in and by themselves.[8]

Note, second, that these principles can be used to judge religions and actions undertaken in the name of religions. Those, for instance, who claim religious sanction for murder or theft or deceit can be judged criminal, and the religion that gives them such sanction can be judged corrupt. Or the principles can be used to show that those who think their religion counsels action against the principles have misunderstood or corrupted their religion. One can argue on these grounds that al-Qaeda's support of terrorism is a corruption of Islam, and Muslims have so argued. Another case is Bartolomé de Las Casas, who condemned, in the name of their shared religion, the way Spaniards conquered and ruled the Americas.[9]

Note, third, that despite the separability of the moral principles from religion, religion is their best and most effective support. People, for whatever reason, are naturally religious and are affected in their actions and their convictions more or less by religion. Out-and-out atheism is rare among mankind and seldom an early or a natural development when it is. But nonreligious men and atheists, or those who are so by persuasion and not by vice or passion, can have no grounds for complaint against the dominance of religious convictions in public life and education. Provided they accept and follow the associated moral principles that form the overlapping moral consensus (which they cannot fail to do, except at the expense of what even they must concede to be reprehensible irrationality), and provided there is no state to force them to be educated in this way rather than that, they will suffer no inconvenience nor be forced to live in any way they do not wish.

Note, finally, that even were the religious doctrines false, their utility could hardly be denied. While there are many motives for virtuous behavior, not least that virtue is good and the source of happiness, nothing seems to be, for most men, a more powerful deterrent from vice than the conviction that, even if they escape human judgment, there is a divine judge whom they cannot escape. Such a conviction lacks too, in this form, all disutility since, if true, it informs men of where lies their ultimate happiness and, if false, inflicts on them no harm or loss. No one suffers or is penalized by living, if only through fear, a life of virtue. True, it would be better to live a life of virtue through love of virtue. But the religious conviction, properly understood, cannot but be a most powerful support for this purpose too. It teaches, and in a simple way accessible to all, that virtue could not be an object of love to the gods nor vice an object to them of hatred were virtue not, of its nature, surpassing fair and vice not, of its nature, surpassing foul.[10]

Toleration

The distinction just made between the moral and the speculative teaching of religion, and thus too the separability in principle of the first teaching from the second, already points to one clear way in which the question about the toleration of those who may disagree and hold rival opinions can be answered. For as already indicated, disagreement in matters of moral teaching can rightly and forcibly be resisted or marginalized, and for reasons that no one, not even the nonreligious, can rationally disagree with. Disagreement in speculative teaching, by contrast, can more readily be tolerated. Still there is need to speak further here if only because of what has often been said before, namely the human striving for the comprehensive truth and the consequent orientation of community to serve that striving. If a divine revelation about the comprehensive truth has been given, and given in ways that natural reason is able to judge and recognize (in the matter stated in the previous chapter), then the teaching of this revelation naturally comes within the ambit of community life. Otherwise community would lose its orientation to comprehensive truth.

An important question therefore arises. For if the religious authority is to have, by divine right, some power over the political, and if the political authority is to have, by the same divine right, some duty to the religious authority, and if the religion in question is opposed by other and rival religions, then the political will have some duty to suppress these other and rival religions. The natural freedom of persons, therefore, and their duty to follow truth as best they see it, will be infringed, for if they see other than the prevailing religion sees, their freedom to pursue such perceived truth will be denied them. Consequently the political power will have to get involved in religious suppression and persecution, which seems not only bad in itself but properly beyond its competence. For how is the political to judge which religion is true, if it is not also to have some authority in determining religious truth, and so if it is not itself to be in some sense also a priestly or religious power and no longer a purely political one?

There are two parts to this question: first about how the political can have competence to recognize religious truth, and second as to what sort of tolerance is to be allowed to those who do not accept the prevailing religion, but instead accept some other one or none at all. For the treatment of everyone within a political community, since such a community arises from the natural structure of human freedom in the search for truth, will have to be such that the freedom of everyone is preserved and enhanced and not hindered.

The first question was already dealt with in the previous chapter (about miracles and infallibility and the like), and nothing more needs to be added here. The second question is about how and to what extent those who reject the religion embraced by a community and fostered by public authority should be allowed to live within the same community. This second question embraces matters both of truth and of freedom. For one particular religion could only rightly be embraced if it were publicly known to be true, and it could only be embraced if it also, at the same time, fostered and enhanced the freedom of persons, including those persons who, for whatever reason, do not accept the publicly known truth.

We speak of the tolerance not only of people, but also of material things like bodies and bridges. The tolerance of a bridge is how much weight it can carry without collapsing, and the tolerance of the body is how much of a certain substance it can absorb, or the like, without illness or death. Tolerance in this sense is not wholly different from the tolerating of other people that is meant by political toleration, for we tolerate those things in political life that we are able or willing to bear with. Toleration means how much difference of opinion or behavior a community (or individuals) is able or willing to bear before the community collapses or the individuals forcefully resist. Toleration, in its most general sense, is a capacity to bear things, and the capacity to bear something is the capacity not to be adversely affected by that thing (such as a bridge that bears a weight or a society that bears differences). Hence tolerance might be defined as a capacity not to be affected by another, and political toleration as a community's capacity not to be affected by that which is other, whether in opinion or behavior.

Toleration is a capacity both of nature and of choice. A community is both a definite thing with definite features and something determined by the choice of those who compose it. A community's natural capacity of toleration is what it can in fact tolerate without being corrupted or destroyed. A community's voluntary capacity of toleration is what it chooses to tolerate, whether or not what it chooses to tolerate is something that it has the natural capacity to tolerate. Toleration as a public policy is a community's voluntary capacity of toleration (a community's natural capacity of toleration is determined by the community's nature and not by the choice of its rulers). Choice is of the good, but when mistaken or perverse, it is of the bad. Choice and action in the case of toleration are also of someone and by someone and about something, for they are someone's tolerating of someone about something said or done. Further, they are for some reason or end and at some time and place and in some way or manner and for some duration.

Of these differences, the most important are the "by whom," the "of whom," the "about what," and the "why," for these constitute the substance of the choice and action. The others constitute the circumstances. The "why" is more determinative than the "by whom" or the "of whom" or the "about what," for it is in view of the "why" that one decides who is to be tolerated and by whom and in respect of what. The "why" itself is the good, or some part of it, or the opposite. Good tolerations will be those that tolerate for the sake of the good, and bad tolerations will be those that tolerate for the sake of the bad. Conversely, good intolerances will be those that are intolerant for the sake of the good and bad ones those that are so for the sake of the bad. The people who do the tolerating, the "by whom," are the rulers or the ruled, and the people who are tolerated are also rulers or ruled but contrariwise (rulers are ruled insofar as they are subject to the rules they make). The "about what" will be either words or actions or both (and thought and character too, insofar as thought and character issue in words and actions). The kinds of toleration based on these differences are many, but it would be tedious to list them. It is sufficient to notice the principles of the division.

The "why" is the chief determining factor in the kinds of toleration and distinguishes toleration into good and bad. So the first thing to consider is the "why" of toleration, or the end toleration must serve. This end must naturally be the end that the community that is to exercise toleration serves, and, as has been now extensively argued, the proper end of community is the common good of the truth and its pursuit. Rulers who pursue their private good (their own power or fame or wealth) at the expense of the common good (the welfare of the people as a whole) are corrupting community and reducing it to tyranny (the classic definition of tyranny, going back to Aristotle and beyond, is precisely that the rulers pursue their private good and not the common good).

The most important factor after the "why" is the "what." The "what" is words and deeds. Thoughts will only be included insofar as these cause and are manifest in words and deeds (things not manifest, or that cause nothing manifest, escape human control). All those deeds and words will be tolerated that fit in with the common good. All those that oppose it will constitute the range of candidates for not being tolerated. Which of these candidates should not in fact be tolerated and in what way will vary. In a simply just society, none of them will be tolerated, but the use of force will not be required, because no citizen will want to do or say them (education in justice will teach them otherwise). All citizens will judge them to be bad and to be avoided. Only in less than simply just societies, where not everyone is just, will there be need for any appeal, subject to the vagaries of time and place, to the use of force.

Religious Toleration

If such may be laid down about the nature and kinds of toleration, the question of religious toleration may now be directly confronted. The assumption must of course first be made, as it has been made throughout so far, that religion is a matter of truth or falsehood. If this assumption is not made, religions and the differences between them do not rise above differences in tastes, and it would be absurd to talk about the toleration of tastes qua tastes or to make them, by themselves, an object of public policy. The discussions of religious toleration typical in liberalism do not begin to be serious, because the assumption is made, at least for public and political purposes, that religion is not a matter of objective truth or falsehood.[11] The liberalist position on religious toleration is incoherent. No serious debate about the question can be had on the assumption it adopts.

If the assumption has to be made, then, that religion is a matter of truth or falsehood, and if, further, religion turns out to be false, it should, if possible, be gotten rid of—unless it is trivial or has some incidental advantage, such as easier control of the passions and more effective suppression of crime. In this case one might suppose that religion should not just be publicly tolerated but publicly promoted, and that all popular religions with the same incidental advantage should be thus promoted. A policy of this sort was adopted in the ancient world. In the medieval world, it was also adopted, but with a difference. Religion was held at this latter time not only to be practically beneficial but also theoretically true, whereas in the ancient world it had often been held to be practically beneficial but theoretically false. The ancient world only faced a serious question of religious toleration when a religion arose (namely Christianity) that was popular, had the incidental advantages just mentioned, and claimed to be simply true and the others to be wholly or largely false. The rulers did not know what to do with a popular religion that made truth, a truth rationally defensible before learned men, its distinctive badge. Other popular religions, being intellectually bankrupt, could not do the same. The rulers took the easy way out: let nothing disturb the status quo, and let the new religion be suppressed. They failed. The new religion conquered not just the masses, but the rulers and the intellectuals too. It won without force of arms, and the other religions lost despite force of arms.

The success of the new religion created a new world in which religion was on all hands acknowledged to be a matter of truth and not just of utility. Settling for utility at the expense of truth, as the ancient world had done, was never a happy compromise. It went directly against the point of community, as has been argued at length above, and so also against the deepest human yearnings. The human mind wants truth as much as the human heart wants goodness. Only in a world like that of medieval Christendom, ancient Israel, or medieval and some modern Islamic countries could a serious question of religious toleration arise. What to do about false religions, even and especially useful ones?

A false religion can have no rights of principle against a true one. A society that accepts the true religion, and does so on rationally compelling grounds in the way argued before (namely, the intrinsic rationality of the religion and its claims, the evidences of miracles, and so forth), must have a right to resist or marginalize other and opposed religions. It would have no obligation to tolerate them as equals. Such policy would be imposed on it by the common good, which is the measure of correct toleration. Obedience to the true religion must be part of the common good, if not indeed the most important part.

A standard response to this conclusion, of course, is that even if religion is a known and public truth (and not, say, a matter for merely private judgment), the use of force to impose assent is not justified. The truth should be allowed to operate and persuade by its own conviction. One can rationally assent only to what one recognizes by one's own mind to be true. A forced verbal assent would never be more than external and insincere.[12] The answer to the objection is that there are many sorts of truths, and the mental grasp of them does not happen in the same way, nor is it subject to the same impediments.

The proper organ of truth is the mind, and if the truth is evident, the mind naturally embraces it. Instruction and reasoning and evidence are the means for making truth evident. But some truths, even if they can be made evident to the mind, may be opposed by one's desires. Moral truths are especially liable to this opposition. Desires can impede the intellect and blind it to evident truth, even truth accessible to natural human reason. They can also be an impediment to truth not accessible to natural human reason but known only by divine revelation. Truth by revelation has to be accepted, if it is accepted, not because its truth is seen from within (such as when, say, we see the truth of some mathematical proof), but because it is guaranteed by divine authority.

Acceptance of truth on authority is something we do all the time, as in medicine, where we trust the authority of doctors, or in schools, where we trust the authority of teachers. In these cases the truth that we do not know ourselves but accept from others is a truth we could come to know ourselves if we went through the right training. In the case of divinely revealed truth, we can, *ex hypothesi*, never know it directly for ourselves (at least not in this life), but only on authority. The name we give to acceptance of truth on authority is "faith." Faith is of truth; it is knowledge; it is knowledge derived from authority; it is rational. These features are present in the case of putting faith in what a doctor tells us about our health. What we know in this way is truth (it is truth about our health); it is knowledge (it is a coming to have what the doctor has, though not as the doctor has it); it is based on authority (it is based on the authority of the doctor); it is rational (it is rational to accept the authority of one's doctor, *ceteris paribus*). Such knowledge is indirect. It goes to the truth through another. But it is knowledge. The difference is between knowing, say, that water is H_2O because a chemist has told us and knowing that water is H_2O because we have ourselves performed the experiments that prove it. The first is knowledge by faith, and the second is knowledge direct.

Knowledge by faith, while it exists in the mind, is attained by an act of will. We must choose to trust our doctor or the chemist, and only because we do so do we have knowledge about our health or about the chemical composition of water. The choice must be rational, in that it must be based on adequate evidence. The evidence will not be about the fact known (we would not then need to trust anyone to know it); it will be about the trustworthiness of the authority. We are rational in trusting our doctor, because we have evidence that, say, he went through the right training, that he is licensed by a known medical authority, that he is acknowledged as an expert by other doctors who went through the right training and are licensed by the same authority, that what he told us about our health before turned out correct (we, or people we know, were cured of this or that ailment by following his instructions), that he is not a liar or corrupted by bribery, that he has an upstanding character, and the like.

Such faith is rational, but it is also an act of choice. The evidence, because it is about the trustworthiness of the authority and not about the things the authority says, does not convince the mind of the truth of these things, but only of their trustworthiness. To believe their truth, the mind must be moved to do so by an act of trust. But an act of trust is an act of will. We can, if we like, refuse to believe the doctor or the chemist, however convincing the evidence of their trustworthiness may be. We cannot, by contrast, refuse to believe that the angles of a triangle equal two right angles once we have seen the proof, though we can contradict it in words if we like, for speech is an act of will. Where acts of belief dependent on acts of will are involved, coercion can be legitimate—not to force the act of will (an act of will cannot be forced), but instead to facilitate it by the suppression of opposed irrational desires and opposed irrational contradiction. The force is used to facilitate the act of trust, not to prove its rationality (which is done instead by the evidence). That there is such force with respect to belief, and that it is legitimate, is ignored by liberalist doctrines of tolerance (even though, if truth be told, they have to rely on something like it to justify their own coercive acts of rule and self-protection).

As argued before, the only adequate proof, accessible to natural reason, about the authenticity of a revelation will be miracles, fulfillments of prophecy, and the like that, while accessible to observation and natural reason as to the fact, have no natural explanation, but only a supernatural one, and so are known, even to natural reason, to be manifestations of a supernatural power. That this power is supernatural will be known and easily known to natural reason, because the miracles that prove it will be thus known. The fact of a miracle is, as noted before, no harder to establish in principle than the fact that Caesar crossed the Rubicon or Napoleon lost the battle of Waterloo. There is here no problem of the burdens of judgment, so called, that do and can arise over proposed comprehensive visions of the good. The judgment is not about the religious vision as such but about the evidence that it is divine. Once the divinity of the vision has been proved to natural reason through miracles and the like, the question of the truth of the vision has been settled too, and all that is required is to learn from the revelation, or from the priests to whom it has been given, what it actually says. There may be difficulties here, but they will raise no problems of truth, for the truth has already been established; they will raise only problems of meaning and definition and can suitably be left to experts.

The community as such will be entitled to take the revelation as the public measure of religious truth and to do so on the basis of well-established evidence that is not problematic and does not labor under any burdens of judgment (in the way illustrated before with the king of Kent and St. Augustine of Canterbury). There can, in principle, be no reason for anyone to reject this truth, and even less any reason for the community not to embrace it and fashion itself and its life and education around it, rejecting all other and rival religions or comprehensive visions, at least as to their having public authority within the community. Those who reject the religion may be rightly suspected, because they will also have rejected the naturally manifest evidence for its truth but, in light of the principle of self-determination that constitutes the "I" of persons, they need be no more than marginalized (at least as to religious matters) within the community. In properly civil matters and before the law they may rightly be otherwise equal, provided they do not attempt to overthrow by violence or subvert by deceit the publicly accepted and proved religion. They will enjoy toleration, therefore, but they can hardly have public status to act as if their vision were as equally acceptable as the manifest and proved one. For *ex hypothesi* it is precisely not so acceptable and may not in truth or justice be treated as such. It should be marginalized in the name of truth and justice itself, and therefore of course in the name of freedom itself, including the freedom of those who are so marginalized. Only if those who espouse the marginalized vision proceed to hostile attacks, open or secret, on the community may they be forcibly and rightly restrained or, *in extremis*, expelled.

Notes

1.   See, for example, the document *Dignitatis Humanae* of the Second Vatican Council.
2.   Anscombe in Guttenplan (1975: 53, 62).
3.   This point is especially the focus of Wojtyła's work, in particular his 1979. A fuller exposition of this work and of its significance can be found in Simpson (2001). The thought of Wojtyła is relied on heavily in the following pages.

4. A distinction made famous by Martin Buber (1923).
5. As expounded in particular by Wojtyła (1979) ch. 7 sect. 9
6. Again following Wojtyła (1979), ch. 7, sect. 10.
7. The commandments about not lying or stealing or killing or committing adultery are universally recognized within groups (even a gang of thieves needs a basic trust and honesty among its members if its thieving is to be successful). What is not so universal, but should be, is extending them to those outside the group.
8. Moral truths may depend, ontologically, on a supreme being, but they have a certain epistemological independence. Indeed, if there is a process of inference between the moral truths and a supreme being, it is from the former to the latter rather than the reverse.
9. Hanke (1959).
10. One could also mention the works of charity, the involvement in community action, and the practical love of neighbor that religion also properly inculcates and inspires. These are implied in what has already been said about religion and the family and virtue, and an explicit discussion of them would figure in a fuller discussion of the values of religion and religious education.
11. This assumption underlies Locke's famous discussion in his *Letter Concerning Toleration* and vitiates his whole argument.
12. This argument is the only one Locke gives in his letter on toleration, and he ignores its obvious response.

6

Political Principles
of Illiberalism

Citizenship

Political life is the life of those who make up the community (for communities do not exist save as their members exist), so we must ask who those are who make up communities. Those properly belong to community who in some way contribute to its work, which is, in the first instance, the pursuit of the comprehensive truth, but includes also, since men are reasoning animals with both animal and spiritual needs, the defense of the community against enemies within and without, the reconciling of disputes (especially, but not only, for the unlearned), and the deliberating about policy and structure and judgment, or about all things that concern rule for the common good of all. Those who actively share in these and similar functions will be members of a community in such a way as to be also integral parts of it; that is, the parts that make it up and constitute it. Other members may be necessary for the community, as being that without which the community cannot exist, but not properly parts of it. The parts of health, for instance, are the actual dispositions or chemical balances in the body that are health, while those without which health cannot exist, such as food and medicine, are not parts of health but instruments or materials for health. It will be the same in a community, and those will be parts of it who directly share in its proper activity. Others who provide materials or tools for a community will not be parts of it, though they will be necessary.

Of the functions proper to community, deliberation, judgment, and defense would be the chief practical tasks, and philosophy, science, religion, and the like would be the chief theoretical tasks that its practical tasks are directed to. Not sharing in any of these things would make one not be a proper part of a community, even though one was included in it. But further, since matters governing the practice and pursuit of

113

philosophy, science, religion, and the like would be determined by those who deliberate and judge, the chief parts of community would be deliberation and judgment, since these parts would, in practice, control all the others. Accordingly those who share in deliberation and judgment are members of the controlling part of the community, and those who do not are not, even if they share in other things. We may, for this reason, restrict the term "citizen proper" to those who thus share in deliberation and judgment, for it is they in whose hands the life of the community rests and who exercise control over it.

This restriction in the meaning of "citizen proper" is not entirely arbitrary, though it is stipulative. The point of it is to achieve a certain sharpening of focus and not, as such, to exclude or discriminate. For citizenship, as taken in this strict sense, is a concept of political rule and not a moral or membership concept. That one is not a citizen proper anywhere does not deprive one of being fully human and a person. It just excludes one from the exercise of certain functions, and exercising these functions is not necessary for personhood or even for moral or religious perfection. Those who have chosen a life removed from the exercise of rule—as some philosophers have done in the past, as well as many religious like monks and hermits—may achieve higher levels of human perfection (because they achieve higher levels of access to the comprehensive truth). Everyone, including hermits, begins in community, but not everyone need stay there. Nor need all those who stay there be citizens proper in order to attain the good of community life. Priests, for instance, are often excused or excluded, by virtue of their office, from all citizen and military functions, so as to devote themselves to what is higher and divine.

Nevertheless, when it is a question of citizens proper, one must recall that the system of representation (or representative democracy, as it is called) that exists today effectively deprives everyone of citizenship (in the sense stated) save the actual representatives themselves. The reason is the special character of electing and election campaigns described earlier in Chapter Two above. Voting in elections is less an exercise in ruling than an exercise in following: "vote for him, or him, or her, but no one else." If voting is going to be a serious exercise of choice, candidates will not be chosen in advance, there will be no campaigning, there will be regular and full account-giving by the elected to the voters, and the voters will be able to ensure that delinquents are recalled and properly punished. Only thus will voting count as a sharing in rule that is adequate, at least in some measure, to the conditions of citizenship proper. If it be said that such voting, to be manageable, will require the political community to be small, let the point be conceded. Large communities are not necessarily good things. Certainly, as argued before, the state, which is huge, is not a good thing, but rather the bad thing of monopolized coercion or despotism. Besides, largeness of political authority, if desired or necessary, can be secured not by states but by loose and federated empires, where lesser bodies of control are systematically related to higher ones, and the higher ones can take a larger view; these higher ones can also be appealed to against the mistakes or faults of lesser ones, though ordinarily appeal should not be needed. This question of empire, however, and its superiority to the state will be returned to later.[1]

Subsidiarity and Solidarity

There would appear to be two general principles in need of being observed if citizenship is to be real and broad, and especially if communities are to be federated with others in some way. What these two principles are and the need for them can be deduced in two ways. The first is from the idea of the person as a self-determining "I" and as capable of participating in a "We." The former fact, that of self-determination, points to what is called the principle of subsidiarity and the latter to what is called the principle of solidarity. Subsidiarity is the principle that decisions should be made at the most local level possible, so that all or as many as possible of those involved can exercise their self-determining "I" in these decisions. The latter fact, that of participation, points to what is called solidarity, or the principle of cooperating with others in matters of joint concern, so that joint decisions and joint actions are the expression of many self-determining "I's" in one self-determining "We." Solidarity in these joint decisions and actions need not necessarily take the form of agreement, since protest and opposition may, on occasion, be the way one can best express one's solidarity. To opt out and abandon joint activity because one disagrees, or does not wish to face the problems of opposition, is to opt out of and abandon solidarity. It is to say that one no longer cares and no longer wishes to share with others in acts of joint decision. The two principles together of subsidiarity and solidarity will tend to produce subordination between more local and less local levels of joint action. Everyone will have a say and exercise decision at the most local levels, but fewer will be able to do so at less local ones (indeed there may be those who do not have the necessary moral and intellectual ability to function much beyond the most local decisions). Some means of delegation or representation will intervene, whereby a few from each local community come together to share, as representative of their community, in decision about more central concerns. Communities will express solidarity with each other through their leaders and representatives, and express subsidiarity by the fact that only the central will be decided centrally, while the local is decided locally.

The second way to deduce these principles is from the contrasting merits and defects of two dominant systems in modern political thought, classical liberalism or libertarianism on the one hand and recent liberalism or socialism on the other (see the first section of Chapter Three above). Classical liberalism, or libertarianism, has generally been judged wanting because of its failure to arrange for or encourage the care and protection of all. Instead of uniting citizens in bonds of friendship and of generosity and gratitude to each other, it has tended to split them up into hostile or at least rival factions. The reason, to repeat, is roughly as follows. It has been a maxim of libertarian theory and practice that the only proper purpose for which coercive force may be used is the prevention of harm to others. Such prevention of harm has been primarily, or even exclusively, a matter of protecting people's negative rights (the right not to be interfered with in the pursuit of one's goals) and not any supposed positive rights (rights to be enabled to pursue one's goals through the public provision of certain goods such as wealth, health care, education, and so on). But this limitation ignores differences in circumstances. As noted earlier (in Chapter Three), some people can do a great deal and have a very wide field for free action because they have an abundance of other goods, especially in wealth and leisure, while others lack these goods and can do and enjoy very little. The result is prosperity for the favored few and misery and resentment for the rest.[2]

Socialism, by contrast, has made the principle of bringing people together the essence of political life and has striven so to organize things that, as its name implies, all the people come to form a single social unit. This principle of bonding people together is an expression of the principle of solidarity. But socialism failed, and disastrously, in its false understanding of how to promote such solidarity. It sought to do so through the absorption of everything and everyone into the state, so that the state became the ultimate determiner of all aspects of people's lives and decided who was to get and do what. But establishing a friendship of everyone with everyone at so abstracted and extended a level is clearly impossible and in fact was never achieved. Friendship has to begin locally and among few and can only be spread out through the whole mass by means of a multitude of mediating associations. Socialism failed in not allowing and encouraging these mediating associations. Everything became top-heavy and autocratic. Libertarianism, by contrast, has prided itself on allowing people to lead their own lives in their own way, independently of regulation by the state. The principle, then, that socialism failed to observe was the principle of subsidiarity, the principle that common life is a complex of authorities subsidiary one to another, and all with their proper spheres of competence and independent rule.

By failing to take notice of solidarity on the one hand and subsidiarity on the other, both libertarianism and socialism failed, in the end, to preserve either principle. Their one-sidedness meant that even what they did make some effort to pursue was undermined. Socialism's centralization dissolved the possibility of genuine solidarity at the only levels at which it can really be exercised and felt, that of individual friendships, close families, and small communities; and libertarianism's letting loose of the individual and his passions undermined the solidarity that even subsidiary groupings need to cohere and survive. The better approach would be to combine both principles together. The observance and inculcation of them, however, cannot be a matter of external or merely mechanical means. For it is a joint fault of socialism and libertarianism to try to reduce rule to certain techniques, systems, and institutions and to ignore the importance of the persons operating them and of their character.[3] Subsidiarity and solidarity require and are both the effects of character or moral virtue, since much prudence, charity, and courage in particular are needed in order to see what must be done and to set out actively to do it. But morality is the work of education, and education is not something mechanical. It requires, rather, the contact of mind with mind and heart with heart, and such contact begins first and endures longest within the family. It is the family that is everyone's principal educator. Hence political authority should do much to foster and support the family. But by the family must not be understood the nuclear family. Such may be the kernel of the family but not its fruition. The family reaches completeness in its extended form; that is, through grandparents, aunts, uncles, cousins, and also close friends. It is all these together who carry the first and vital burden of moral education to the young.

The extended family is already on the way to becoming itself a larger and more political body, the village or the township. This further level of human community has also its proper sphere of competence and its function in preserving and fostering the work begun in and by the family. From here the growth of community into larger and more complex associations can proceed into a fully political community. But these further levels of community and organization do not destroy or supplant the earlier ones. On the contrary, they exist to preserve and perfect them by carrying on at more complex levels the work already begun in the home. For the process being described here is one of genuine development, and the mark of genuine development is that it preserves and enhances what went before by bringing it to the perfection it was already then aiming at. The mark of corruption and decay is precisely the reverse, when what comes later destroys and diminishes what went before, as in the case of disease and death.

That socialism is a corruption of humanity and of human community becomes especially visible here, since socialism destroys all other and prior associations as far as it can, especially the family, in order that it might remain alone. The corruption of libertarianism is also made visible by the same fact. For if the later communities are genuine developments of earlier ones and exist to perfect and enhance them, then it is clear that one of the jobs of these later communities is to intervene, if necessity requires it, to preserve the earlier ones and to remove disease and decay. They cannot just stand aside and let things be, as though it were none of their concern. Nevertheless, it remains true that this intervention must not take the form of replacing the other communities and doing their job for them (as socialism wishes). Such a procedure would deny the principle of subsidiarity. The intervention should rather be limited to cases of necessity or emergency, when all remedies available through other communities have failed, and it should be continued just as far and as long as the necessity lasts.[4] Only a local authority can properly perceive and put into suitable practice what is needed locally, here and now. A remote central authority, if it imposed the same rules and policies everywhere, would, in its ignorance of local differences, destroy rather than enhance the good. For even if the good is something universal and the same for all, its instantiation or realization is always particularized.[5] Indeed it is in this fact, or the fact of the individual and self-determining person, that the principles of solidarity and subsidiarity find their ultimate and joint justification. The good is universally one for all and is realized along with others, and so there is need for a principle of solidarity in people's actions with each other; but this good is realized locally and according to endlessly variable particular differences, and so there is need for a principle of subsidiarity in the dividing up of rule and decision.

Property and Education

Things necessary to community but tools or materials and not parts proper are principally those to do with material provisions, such as food, clothing, shelter, and the things for making and providing them. Let these be summed under the general heading of "property." Ensuring a sufficiency of property for the life of the community will be one of the matters that fall under judgment and deliberation, but the actual getting and managing of this sufficiency need not be, and those engaged in this latter task need not be among those engaged in the former, although they could be.

As to material property, or to property ordinarily understood, we can say that food, clothing, and shelter are the most obvious such needs, and because of these there is also need of land to provide the food and the materials for clothing and the places for shelter. But before all these, there is the need for parents. No human body comes to be or continues to be without parents. The family, as composed first of parents and children, is the first expression of natural sociality and natural peace. It is the first origin of the need for property, and it entails that property too is first a social thing, not an individual thing. It also entails that property is not first a thing of the larger community but exists prior to and independently of any such community. Since the care and use of property are how property comes actually to serve its purpose for the family and the community, the things integral to such care and use are also part of property. Slavery is therefore also integral to property, though slavery has to be carefully understood. This term primarily refers not to a social condition but instead to a function or a job, and it means those functions or jobs that are fundamentally uses of the body for necessary helps. Beasts of burdens are slaves in this sense. But if there are some human beings whose best work is the like use of the body and who, for whatever reason, cannot or will not rise beyond such work, then they too fall under the heading of slaves. Such persons might indeed be legally free, in the sense of not being owned by anyone, as beasts of burden and inanimate equipment typically are. They may, therefore, even be receiving wages or other kinds of remuneration, possibly of a substantial nature. But they would be functionally slaves.

In modern society at least some of the jobs that people engage in are functionally slavish, from direct manual labor even to various clerical activities. Those who perform such work will need to have some intellectual skill, for even manual work requires some intellectual skill, such as to carry out commands and complex instructions. Those who work out such instructions, if they are to do it for its due purpose (which is property for use and not for unlimited increase), will need a grasp of the use of property and so of the comprehensive aim of community that property is meant, in its own way and at its own level, to subserve. To this extent their function and their grasp will transcend the limits of slavery, for slavery exists to serve the end and does not, of itself, require knowledge or articulation of the end. Still, the slavish functions exist and need to be performed, and those whose lives are devoted to them (without any needed grasp of the comprehensive aim that transcends these functions) are effectively slaves, whatever other status they may or may not have. One should not, therefore, when thinking of slavery, judge what it is by the feature of legal ownership (such as one sees in the antebellum South of the USA). One should judge it by its function. Consequently one must concede that slavery not only existed in the North of the United States before and after the Civil War (even though factory workers and suchlike were not legally owned by anyone), but also exists to this day all over the world. However, no derogatory or negative implications need result from this fact. Those who perform slavish functions in a community devoted to the pursuit of the comprehensive human end are caught up, at least ultimately, in this pursuit and share its benefits. In time, indeed, they may be able to leave behind their slavish status, in whole or in part. Further, nothing excludes them from partaking in religion; indeed they would naturally be included in religion as sharing its liturgy and rituals and practice. Politics and engagement in political life are not the best thing. Exclusion therefrom is not necessarily bad.[6]

If property as so understood is part first of the family, then the preservation and protection of property are likewise part first of the family and exist prior to and independently of the larger community (and especially of any state that may emerge). Weapons of self-defense, therefore, and nowadays primarily guns, belong naturally to the family. By nature weapons exist for hunting and defense. By nature the first defense is against wild beasts and human attackers. By the situation of present times, the first defense is against the state. If land naturally belongs to property, weapons for defense also naturally belong to it. Weapons, therefore, naturally belong in the hands of the people, and it is intrinsically unjust for any higher authority to confiscate or forbid them. Thus, by the same token, separate police forces do not naturally belong to property. Separate or professional police forces, as we call them, are creatures of the state, brought into being, sustained, directed, and exploited by the state so as to be the visible form of its self-serving doctrine that it alone can and should coerce. Standing armies are creatures of the state in the same way. Both are an attack on natural property, the natural property of families to possess their own means of defense and to determine the correct use of them. Even as families naturally combine into larger associations, they never lose their natural property or their natural right to natural property. Police forces and standing armies are a denial of nature and right. All policing and military functions belong directly to the people and always remain directly the property of the people. Some limited delegation may be necessary and desirable; but alienation is intrinsically unjust and conceptually impossible. Lest these ideas seem utopian, consider only the case of Switzerland, which, despite slippage in recent years, has held closest to the natural vision of natural defense by natural society.

Material property has two natural uses: consumption and exchange. Exchange is the natural way to secure a sufficiency of what is needed for consumption, since by nature not all property or the produce of property exists equally in all places and at all times. The exchange of property naturally belongs to natural society; therefore, the means of exchange do as well. The chief such means is money; therefore, money belongs to natural society. It does not belong to the state, which, as argued, is unnatural and repudiates natural society. All modern money does belong to the state, because all modern money is paper sanctioned by the state. Without the state's sanction, all modern money would be worthless. In fact all modern money is worthless in its intrinsic nature, because it only has the worth that the issuing state says it has. The state, because it claims a monopoly of coercion, has to claim a monopoly of money, if only because money, as the means of exchange for property, is the means of exchange for the means of coercion (especially weapons). To control all the money is ultimately, therefore, to control all the property. State money is an assault on natural property and the natural right to natural property. It should be abolished, and the money needed for exchange, its creation as well as its control, should be entirely in the hands of natural society.

The body is for the soul, and the property of the body therefore is also for the soul. The soul's chief manifestations and functions in man are thought and will and feeling and deliberate action. Man's natural sociality and peaceableness naturally express themselves in naturally social and peaceful thoughts, choices, feelings, and actions. But as the body, when immediately born, is dependent on mature bodies to grow and flourish, so also is the soul. The soul's food and clothing are education. These are, as it were, the natural property of the soul, and they belong as naturally to natural society as any other property does. They do not belong to the state. But the state seizes them all, and necessarily so.

The state's monopoly of coercion exists only in idea, because the means to make it exist in practice are lacking and will always be lacking (even if the lack asymptotically declines). The state's existence, thus, depends far more on teaching than on force. If it does not control teaching, it cannot preserve its own existence. The state's control of teaching is first unnatural because contrary to the natural property in teaching that belongs to natural society, and second perverse, because all it teaches, and all it wants to teach, is its own preservation. It has no interest in the natural development of the mind, or the will, or the feelings, or choice; for if these develop naturally, they will develop against the state. They will develop in, through, and to the natural sociality and peaceableness that man is. Therefore the state uses its coercion in education too and arrogates all of education, directly or indirectly, to itself.

Accordingly, just as man has a natural right to material weapons—that is, guns—against the state, so he also has a natural right to spiritual weapons—that is, education—against the state. No education, therefore, of any sort, from cradle to grave, should be in the hands or in any way under the control of the state. It should all belong to natural society. But in order to be done well, it will have to belong, ultimately, to some organ or institution that has a special concern with education. Such an organ or institution, in order to be true to its function, will itself have to possess, and by nature, a fundamental orientation to truth. Therefore, again, such an organ or institution cannot be the state or any part of the state, or in any subordinate relation to the state. For the state has no fundamental orientation to truth. It has a fundamental orientation to its own extension and self-promotion, and it will use lies as much as truth for this purpose. Science, for instance, although as a natural human endeavor it has an orientation to truth, yet as subordinate to the state, it is not seldom perverted, not just to promoting means of coercion and surveillance, but also to promoting lies in the service of the state. Moral education, therefore, of the sort needed, properly belongs to the family and its immediately connected communities of village and town. The principle of subsidiarity requires the local authority to take the lead in these matters. A central authority, remote from and ignorant of local differences, would corrupt education rather than enhance it, and all the more so if the central authority is the state, which, as just noted, has no orientation to truth in the first place.

There are other factors too that are relevant here besides the communities that stand, as it were, in a direct line between family and the higher political authority. For there are many sorts of associations that exist alongside these and indeed interpenetrate them, among which should again be especially mentioned that of religion. Religion has always been one of the most penetrating and effective of all educators. For it and it alone enters into the heart of each man and speaks to him in the depths of his being. The influence of a merely human government is always external and externally imposed and can, without the aid of religion, barely penetrate further. Such was manifested especially in the old Soviet Union, where the ideology of communism did not live in the hearts of men, not even of the leaders, but was like a decaying outer garment. Communism was not the animating principle of communist nations; it endured in them only through force. Hence the communist system collapsed as soon as the force was removed. Religion, however, can and does appeal to the inner springs and consciences of men. Its education is more lasting and profound. Indeed it proved its vitality precisely in those communist nations where it had been most suppressed, for it has come visibly to life again afterward, almost as if the communism that suppressed it had never been. Human government cannot take over or duplicate the role of religion, but it can allow for and promote it.

By religion is meant, in the first instance, the natural desire for truth about the ultimate meaning and end of human existence. This desire, as already noted earlier, is nevertheless peculiar in a special way. It is a natural desire for what, as far as we naturally know, is not naturally attainable. If there is a God or gods, they are not subject to us, but we are to them. The truth about God or the gods is naturally known only to God or the gods, and to man only to the extent that God or the gods are naturally known through things naturally known to man. But there is no reason to think that what is naturally known to man about God is all, or the most important, of what can and needs to be known to man about God. The natural desire for religion is also, and necessarily, a natural desire for revelation, a revelation that will depend on the will of

God and not on the will of man. To the extent that there is a revelation, since it will be made to man as he naturally is, and since man is social as he naturally is, revelation too will be social. It will throw itself into some social form or some more or less organized institution within society.

Historically there are three or four organized revealed religions in the world: Hinduism, Judaism, Christianity, and Islam. Abstracting for the moment from the truth or adequacy of these religions, we can say that all of them are and must be independent of the political power and of all functions and coercion of the political power. If there is any power of coercion here, it must be all from religion against the political power and not from the political power against religion. The right of religion, especially revealed religion, to be superior to and independent of the political power is a natural right inherent in man's natural right to spiritual property, above all his natural right to property in truth. It is thus an indispensable element of his freedom. (So to the extent that religion in Iran has and exercises this right, to that extent Iran is freer than any country in the secular West.)

One might say, and opponents of religion in the secular West do say, that religion, especially organized religion, would be a threat to liberty if it had over the political power the authority that it had in medieval Christendom, say, or has now in Iran. The charge is false and self-serving. The modern state is a far greater threat to freedom than religion ever has been or ever could be. Man's freedom consists in his right to pursue his good through his natural property. The chief such good is truth. The state does not care for truth as such. It spreads error indifferently and systematically whenever such error will serve its purpose. The state does not deny its essence when it spreads error. Religion, by contrast, always does, for it claims authority in virtue of the truth it teaches about God. A challenge to religion in the name of truth is a threat that religion cannot ultimately resist. And the human mind, being itself naturally oriented to truth, would eventually issue such an irresistible challenge. Any religion, therefore, that has survived for any considerable length of time among any considerable body of people must have truth at its core. The state, by contrast, can always resist truth and has no intrinsic need to welcome it. The survival of the state depends not on truth but on power.

From the point of view of freedom, religion, even organized religion, is always superior to the political power, and indeed all religions, where they exist in any number, operate as so superior. A religion, whether natural or revealed, that is not superior to the political power and is not capable of laying down limits to it in the name of truth, is confessing that it has no divine authority, because it is confessing that it has no authority superior to man. So it is confessing that it is not a religion, or not a doctrine and worship directed to what is higher than man. Even the old pagan religions never made so self-negating a claim.

These considerations about religion lead to the result that freedom cannot be preserved in or by the political power but can be preserved if this power is subordinated instead, at least in all matters that concern man's interest and property in truth, to some religion, revealed or natural or both. Without such subordination, in fact if not also in idea, there can be no freedom, because there can be no property in truth. This conclusion holds all the more so of the modern state, where all property has become the plaything of the state and stands at the disposal of the state. The superiority of religion to the state, or rather the abolition of the state and a return to natural forms of social life, is alone the path of freedom.

For recall the argument about freedom presented in Chapter Three, that there are two kinds of freedom, internal and external, and that the latter, which is freedom from coercion, is good or bad depending on how it is used (such as that a criminal uses his external freedom badly and needs to be coercively restrained). Internal freedom, by contrast, is freedom from one's own passions, or having such control over oneself that one is not driven into some action or decision by impulse but acts according to rational judgment. This internal freedom is integral to what it is to be a person, since a person, as argued in Chapter Five, is essentially self-determining. To be fully a person is to be fully internally free. External freedom, while desirable, is secondary. It is religion, therefore, and revealed religion in particular (if it exists and can be had), that preserves freedom, not the state. The state can provide or take away external freedom, to be sure, but it does nothing for internal freedom (which it ignores or even opposes). Since external freedom is ultimately dependent on internal freedom, the tendency of the state is inevitably toward destroying both.

Public Reason

In illustration of these facts about freedom and education and religion, consider the idea of public reason. This idea is in particular favor among liberal theorists of political life, and by it is meant the set of reasons that may legitimately be appealed to in public debate, especially where what is being debated is some policy or constitutional arrangement that will involve coercion in its implementation. The claim is that if citizens or members of a state are properly to assent to such coercive measures, the measures have to be justified by appeal to reasons that such citizens can rightly be expected to endorse. So appeal to comprehensive views of the good, and in particular religion, fall outside public reason, because citizens cannot rightly be expected to endorse the comprehensive view or religion in question. They may instead have other comprehensive views where the appeal fails, because these comprehensive views do not include or endorse the reasons on which the appeal is based. If citizens are to comply with public reason in their advocacy of policies and rules to be imposed on the whole community, they must refrain from appealing to anything that cannot be justified to the whole community, and so they must refrain from appealing to religions and comprehensive views that are controversial and not shared by all those on whom the rules or policies are to be imposed. Not to do so is to fail to treat others with the respect due to free persons who have comprehensive views other than one's own. Public reason thus introduces a duty of civility whereby citizens are required to explain to each other that the positions they advocate can be supported by reasons that all citizens can in principle be expected to endorse.

Connected with the idea of public reason is the idea that there are deep and intractable disagreements among citizens, and that these disagreements are not a result of irrationality, or self-interest, or prejudice, or perversity but instead arise naturally from the exercise of human reasoning under favorable conditions of freedom. This fact of reasonable pluralism, as it is called, is itself connected with the so-called burdens of judgment (discussed earlier at the end of Chapter Four), which are supposed to explain why reasonable and rational people will be permanently divided over matters of philosophy, religion, and other aspects of the good life.

As a result, reasonable persons will appeal only to those public or political ideas that are part of a liberal democratic political culture and can be assumed to be acceptable to everyone, insofar as each is reasonable and rational.[7] These public or political ideas may well indeed be endorsed from within the several comprehensive views or religions that citizens adopt, but they can, as it were, be extracted from any such view and stand on their own as forming the content of a political conception of fair cooperation that all can accept as reasonable, regardless of the comprehensive views they also hold. Public reason is the overlap between comprehensive views and is the residue of agreement, as it were, that is left when the controversial aspects of these views are set to one side. Citizens agree to confine themselves to this agreement when matters that affect them all are proposed for public policy and enforcement. For thus no one will be required to endure as public policy what satisfies someone else's comprehensive view but not his own. All comprehensive views will thus be respected in debate and decision, not as comprehensive, but as limited to what other and incompatible comprehensive views can also endorse. This asceticism in reason will enable incompatible comprehensive views to coexist in peace in the same community, because no comprehensive view will be forcibly subordinated to any other. Instead each will be respected in its difference and required only to agree to what all comprehensive views can agree to under fair terms of cooperation. No view will get all it wants, therefore, but none will be forced to accept things peculiar to some other comprehensive view and not also to itself.

There are a number of qualifications and differences in the way public reason is understood, and a number of objections have been raised to the whole idea.[8] However, for present purposes it is not necessary to discuss or summarize them, for public reason in all its forms falls foul of two main problems. First, and principally, it confuses the pragmatics of rhetoric with a principle of justice. Second, it begs the question, and its associated notion of the burdens of judgment not only is falsely stated but also makes public reason self-refuting.

First, then, public debate on matters of common concern must perforce be conducted on the basis of reasons and premises generally acceptable, or able to be made acceptable, to the audience. Otherwise the debate will be pointless. Rhetoric is the art of persuading an audience on the basis of what is persuasive to it. What the audience does not believe, or cannot be persuaded it believes (for we may believe things when we are told them that we have not yet consciously noticed that we believe), will not be usable as a basis for persuading it of something else. However, there are no limits in principle here, only limits in practice. Any common belief that is widely shared, but goes beyond what public reason would allow, can fairly be used in public debate, for it will be persuasive. And if the thing being argued for is good for the community, no disrespect or lack of civility is involved if reasons beyond public reason are used. Rather there would be disrespect and lack of civility, and certainly a failure in the art of rhetoric, if such reasons are not used, for something capable of persuading the community of an attainable good would have been rejected, and so the attainable good would, to this extent, have been rejected too.

Second, to exclude matters to do with the comprehensive good, or with the striving for it (as the burdens of judgment require), is to deny the very idea of community, which, as argued before, is marked precisely by such striving. The comprehensive good needs thus always to be at the center of public debate, since it and its pursuit will give the measure for the pursuit of all other goods. That there is disagreement about this good is not an impediment, for perhaps one can give several arguments, each of which appeals to different goods and yet has the same conclusion. Or, since the whole of a given comprehensive good is unlikely to be in play at once, one can appeal to a part of it, or use arguments that show this part should be accepted even if other parts are not, or argue for the comprehensive good, not of course by assuming it, but by giving persuasive reasons in its favor.

In addition, the problem of the burdens of judgment is falsely stated. The idea in fact is an old one and can be and was used in the past as an argument for religious revelation, and a religious revelation the manifestation of whose truth escapes all such burdens.[9] The comprehensive good does indeed seem in some way to transcend human capacity to recognize surely or to penetrate adequately. The profounder truths of religion, for instance, such as about the existence and nature of God, are only with difficulty proved by natural reason alone, even if everyone, including the uneducated, has some sense or inkling that there is a supreme being behind the manifest things we perceive and know. Accordingly, the right response is not to give up trying to make the comprehensive good known to all (which, as remarked, would deny community), but instead to look for ways of doing so that transcend merely human capacity. The obvious such way, or rather only such way, is divine revelation. Indeed if there is a god (as most men at least dimly divine) and a god who cares that humanity should know or be guided to the comprehensive good, one would expect such a god to provide special assistance to men for the purpose. One would expect, therefore, that there would be divine revelations in human history, varying perhaps from time to time and place to place, but sufficient for those in that time and place to seek after God and find him. One would expect, further, since humanity is one, that there would at some point be a special and authentic revelation vouchsafed to all humanity to embrace and follow. One should therefore look to see if there is any such revelation. One should also look to see if there is compelling evidence for its being a revelation. For a revelation meant to remove human ignorance and the burdens of judgment would be useless if the fact that it was a revelation was itself subject to the same burdens. It would just regenerate the problem it was meant to solve. As argued earlier, evidence for a revelation that overcomes ignorance and the burdens of judgment would have to be manifest even to the ignorant, and of such kind are things supernatural, like miracles, prophecies, expulsion of demons, luminous holiness, success in persuasion beyond human power and by means beyond human power, and appeals to all sorts and conditions of men and not to one ethnic group more than another.

Such supernatural happenings are often denied, of course, but seldom, as they should be, on the basis of an impartial examination of the evidence. Too often prejudice and even perversity get in the way. Yet the proponents of public reason allow that the prejudiced and perverse are not reasonable, and that to limit what one says or what premises one adopts in public debate to those that the prejudiced and perverse would adopt is no requirement of public reason. When the king of Kent was persuaded by the miracles of St. Augustine and his companions of the truth of Catholic Christianity and helped bring his whole kingdom over to the Christian faith, he was acting on the basis of evidence that was not subject to any burdens of judgment but was instead manifest to all, in a way that all who were rational and not prejudiced or perverse would accept. The advocates, therefore, of public reason who exclude the actions of the king of Kent from the scope of public reason, and who wish mass conversion of a kingdom to be no part of political authority, are thus denying the public reason they claim to be upholding. If reason is to reign in public debate, and public reason too—that is, a reason accessible and endorsable by all who are rational, even if they are uneducated (for the uneducated can recognize the rationally persuasive force of a miracle as much as the educated can)—then what the advocates of public reason exclude from public debate and action is altogether unreasonable and against the requirements of public reason.

Notes

1. See Chapter Nine below.
2. See again Kymlicka and Norman (1994: 352–381, especially 354–355).
3. See Kalb (2008) and his stress on the technocratic and bureaucratic ambitions of liberalism.

4. See Pope Leo XIII, *Rerum Novarum*, sects. 11–12, 29.
5. This point is forcefully and correctly made by Den Uyl and Rasmussen (1991: 34–35, 39).
6. For further discussion of slavery and its defensibility in principle, see Simpson (2006), especially pp. 114–115.
7. Rawls (1993: 217).
8. See the comprehensive discussion in the online Stanford Encylopedia of Philosophy s.v. Public Reason, and also Talisse (2012: chs. 1, 7, 8).
9. St. Thomas Aquinas, *Summa Theologiae* Ia q.1 a.1.

7

Justice and Political Forms — Aristotle versus Rawls

Posing the Problem

Principles need to be realized, and the principles of politics need to be realized in concrete political forms. But if, or rather since, politics is about the human drive for happiness or the comprehensive good (as argued above), then the fundamental features of these political forms can be already found, more or less, in the long premodern tradition of political philosophy from Plato onward, and especially in the distinctions worked out by the unrivaled analytical acumen of Aristotle. One may in principle, therefore, take over from that tradition these fundamental forms and apply or adapt them, *mutatis mutandis*, to present conditions.

Nevertheless, because the tradition in question is so different in orientation as well as in results from contemporary theory and practice, there is some point in approaching it, so as to bring out the difference, by way of comparison and contrast with what is typically done nowadays instead. For when raising the question of forms of rule, or of correct forms and right government, we today will begin, if we follow current procedures (whose origins, as earlier noted, lie in Hobbes and the so-called state of nature), with social justice and rights, with the legitimacy of political rule and freedom from oppression. Such is what Rawls does in his *Theory of Justice* (perhaps the most influential of recent writings on politics in the English-speaking world). Rawls begins with justice, which he calls the first virtue of social institutions.[1] How is an institution just? It is just by how it fashions itself in view of the equal good of equal individuals. What are individuals? They are different combinations of desires and interests, which combinations individuals may and perhaps should put into some hierarchy or order but which have no hierarchy or order by nature. The institution is the state, and the state is an impersonal structure of rules and of mechanisms designed to enable individuals to satisfy their desires in peace, or without coming into conflict with each other in pursuit of their different interests.[2]

If by contrast we follow Aristotle, for example, we will begin with communities and the good and show how the political community is the highest community pursuing the best good (*Politics* 1.1.1252a1–7).[3] Aristotle talks not of individuals but of men and not of structures but of communities (or only of structures in view of communities).[4] Aristotle talks of the city and man, but we talk of institutions and individuals. For Aristotle, what matters are not individuals but men, or only individuals insofar as they can become men. The city exists for man because, as an education in virtue, it exists for the perfection of man. The modern institution or state, by contrast, exists for the individual, because it exists for the satisfaction of the individual.

It is hard for us nowadays to begin with the city and man as Aristotle does, because we have lost a clear grasp of these concepts. For us the city is a sprawling metropolis like London or New York, and "man" is a word of offense that political correctness bids us no longer use in its generic sense. When we meet Aristotle's *polis* or *politeia* (city and regime) and his *anthropoi* or *andres* (humans and men), we must transmute them, and translators generally transmute them, into our categories of state and individual. What, by contrast, remains common to Aristotle and us is the idea of justice, which is where Rawls begins. Which justice? We distinguish, like Aristotle, the justice of punishment and exchange from the justice of distribution. The latter we consider to be the justice of the institution, the justice of assigning shares in political life. Let us begin, then, with Aristotle on the justice of distribution in political life.[5] In this way it will be easier for us to see beyond the limitations imposed on our political thought by the dominance in that thought of the modern idea of the state. We will understand better what governmental forms and structures most fit the natural condition of man as that condition has been examined and analyzed so far.

From Justice to Government

Aristotle raises this Rawlsian question of justice in political life in *Politics* 3.12.1282b14–83a22. He frames it as a question about who should rule. He answers it in terms of the common advantage, or of what benefits the whole community. His discussion is as down to earth in examples and as brief in statement as Rawls' discussion is complex and drawn out. Everyone agrees, says Aristotle (speaking for our day as much as for his own), that justice is something equal, and that it is equal for the equal. But (and here's the rub) who are the equal?

Aristotle's discussion turns on finding out who the equal are. For most moderns, as for Rawls, that question does not arise, or it arises only to be at once answered as "everyone." Rawls begins with people in the original position, and what Aristotle would find striking about that position is not the veil of ignorance but the equality of everyone behind it. All are equal, and all are supposed to think and choose as equals. What they choose is the structure of the institutions under which they are all to live and which is encapsulated in Rawls' two principles of justice.[6] Aristotle too is interested in structures, but he is first interested in the kind of constitution or the government.[7] The government is the people who rule, and the structures are what enable and preserve their rule (*Politics* 3.6.1278b8–15, 10.1281a34–39). Who, then, are the rulers, or who should rule? Rawls assumes that the idea of offices open to all, under a fair system of elections, answers the questions that need answering about the determination of rulers. What moderns and Rawls care about is how rule is exercised, whether or not it is exercised according to the two principles of justice or the like. Aristotle also cares about the "how" of rule, but the "how" is determined by the "who," for the "who" determine the structure that concretely embodies the "how." Aristotle puts the persons first, because the character of the structures is derivative (Rawls puts the structures first, because the character to be developed in the people is derivative[8]).

For Aristotle the question of who are equal and who unequal is very much a live one, and it dominates his discussion of distributive justice and of government. Ancient oligarchs thought themselves equal and the common people unequal, and ancient democrats thought, contrariwise, that all were equal (or all who were not slaves or barbarians; *Politics* 3.9.1280a11–25). But equality is not only *of* someone; it is also *in* something. People are not equal *simpliciter* but equal in height or color or ability or the like. Some might think, says Aristotle (*Politics* 3.12.1282a23–83a22), that if people are in other respects equal, then those who are superior in any good at all will be unequal and should have greater shares in rule. But this answer leads to the result that those who are superior in things like height and color should rule, which is plainly false. Merely because you are white and not black, says Aristotle in effect, or tall and not short, you should not thereby have political control. To illustrate he takes the example of pipes for playing music with. People equal in playing the pipes should not get more or better pipes merely because they are better born, for the better born are not thereby going to play the pipes better. Again, if there is someone superior in pipe playing but inferior in birth and beauty, then even if birth and beauty are better goods than skill in pipe playing, the one superior in that skill should still get the better pipes. For birth and beauty, however good they may be, contribute nothing to the work of pipe playing. The distribution of pipes, or of all goods generally, must follow features relevant to the work of the good in question, and those who excel in these features should receive more of that good, regardless of how much they are excelled by others in other goods.

The good to be distributed in politics is shares in the life of the political community, and principally shares in ruling. These shares should be distributed according to equality and inequality in things relevant to the work of the city. What is the work of the city? The good life of the citizens. What features are relevant to the work of good life? Birth, freedom, and wealth, says Aristotle, listing first the things that most people think about first. Life is impossible without resources to satisfy material needs, and decisions about how the city is to act cannot be made without the freedom to make them (birth is thus part of freedom, because native birth is the standard way, both then and now, for determining who is a citizen and so who is free to take part in the city's decisions). More important than these features, however, are the virtues, notably justice and military virtue, the first of which is the virtue for making right decisions (including the right decision about who should rule), and the second of which is the virtue for preserving life and freedom. Virtue, understood as embracing courage and temperance and prudence as well as justice, turns out to be the chief determinant for shares in rule. Those who are superior in virtue should receive greater shares in rule. Indeed, for the same reason, those superior in virtue should have, and in the best government would have, wealth and birth too, so that in them all the relevant features are combined (*Politics* 4(7).9.1329a17–39). The claim of such people to exclusive rule would be unimpeachable. No other group claiming any other feature could be relevant. The result of Aristotle's reasoning is that justice in political life is inequality. For justice is only equality for equals; it is inequality for unequals. But those superior in virtue are unequals. Therefore they should have unequal shares in rule.

Everything that Aristotle says about governments follows of necessity from this result, as in particular the fundamental division of governments into correct and deviant (*Politics* 3.7.1279a22–31). If virtue is the chief claim to rule and other claims are subordinate to it, then those governments where the virtuous rule will be just or correct, and those governments where the non-virtuous rule will be unjust and deviant. But since a city is a multitude of people, the rulers must be some part of this multitude, either all of them or some of them or one of them. So there must be three kinds of government in each division, correct and deviant, according as the rulers are one or few or many. The correct governments, then, are kingship when the virtuous one rules, aristocracy when the virtuous few do, and polity when the virtuous many do. The deviations are democracy when the non-virtuous many rule, oligarchy when the non-virtuous few do, and tyranny when the non-virtuous one does.

The Classification of Governments

Aristotle's division is not merely numerical. Numbers drive it, but the division is of people with a certain feature: virtue or its lack. The division is of numbers as *qualified* (*Politics* 3.8.1279b20–80a6). One has not understood Aristotle's sixfold division of governments if one thinks merely of the number of rulers. One must think of what these numbers are when concretized in persons. If justice in shares to rule goes with virtue, and if one man is justly to be ruler, then his virtue must so far exceed that of others that no one can compare with him in virtue (as in the case of the one superior pipe player who justly gets all or the best pipes). Likewise in the case of the few, their virtue must be similarly supreme, and also in the case of the many, whose virtue too must be supreme. Aristotle's division forces us to ask what supreme virtue is like when it is in one or few or many. Is the virtue the same in each case, or do the numbers make a difference?

Aristotle's division now becomes empirical or sociological and appeals to actual facts about men in smaller and greater numbers. Concretely, he says, the virtue that exists in one or a few can be perfect virtue, the virtue that makes its possessors so superior to all others that they are like gods among men. The virtue, by contrast, that exists in many is not perfect virtue. It is rather military virtue, the sort of virtue that can exist in a large body of citizen-soldiers, the virtues of courage and discipline and self-control (*Politics* 3.7.1279a39–b4, cf. 2.11.1270a4–6). The virtue of the virtuous many is not the virtue of the divine king or the aristocrats. It is a lesser virtue. The structure of a polity, which is the rule of virtuous citizen-soldiers, is different from the structure of kingship and aristocracy. In fact kingship and aristocracy have no structure. They do not need one. The divine kings and aristocrats rule entirely by their own will, which, because supremely virtuous, is always just. Their rule is without law, because it does not need law; the rulers, as embodied justice, are themselves law (*Politics* 3.13.1284a3–14, b27–34). No law that could be written down could ever be superior in justice to their decisions and so could never have a just title to rule. A city run by kings and aristocrats needs not structure or written law but education, to ensure that the young are brought up properly and acquire the supreme virtue that will fit them in their turn to be kings and aristocrats. Aristotle's discussion of the best government in the *Politics* is about education and contains no discussion of structure or law. The best government is not an institution, and justice, which is nevertheless its virtue, is not the virtue of an institution. It is the virtue of men who are beyond all institutions. The best government is a community of divine friends devoted to a life of courage, justice, and temperance in war, and to a life of justice, temperance, and philosophy in peace (*Politics* 4(7).15.1334a11–34). It should remind us more of the medieval Knights Templar than of modern states or governments.

Structure and laws independent of men only arise for Aristotle when we descend from the heights of godlike virtue to the military virtue of polity and the non-virtue or positive vice of the deviant governments. In all these governments, there are no men good enough to be trusted to rule without law, because there are no men good enough to be themselves law. The measure of law is still virtue, though as qualified and even compromised by the incalcitrance of sociological facts. The problem the lawgiver faces at this point is likened by Aristotle to the problem faced by a gymnastic trainer (*Politics* 6(4).1.1288b10–35). If the bodies such a trainer has before him are the best bodies and their possessors fully committed to achieving the best, he can give them the best training and need make no adjustments or concessions to lack of capacity or lack of will. A lawgiver in an analogous position would be the ruler and educator of the best government who is training the noble young to be kings and aristocrats. But gymnastic trainers, to say nothing of lawgivers, are seldom fortunate enough to have before them the best subjects. They have before them bodies ranging from good to mediocre to bad, and wills ranging from enthusiastic to indifferent to hostile. The scientific trainer, insists Aristotle, will do the best he can by these bodies too. He will consider what suits these bodies and how to get them to be as good as they are able or willing to be. He will not, like the Platonist, confine himself to consideration only of the best bodies and to the construction only of regimens for the most eager wills. Likewise with the lawgiver.[9]

What principles, then, will the lawgiver follow, and what structures and laws will he institute? He will follow the principles of virtue, for only virtue is the good, and only this good is the aim of life in the city. But he will not follow perfect virtue. He will follow the sort of virtue and the sort of lessening of vice that imperfect men in large numbers admit of (*Politics* 6(4).11.1295a25–96b12). The virtue such men admit of is sociological virtue, and the lessening of vice they admit of is enlightened self-interest, or what we might call Aristotle's theory of rational choice.

By sociological virtue is meant the virtue that is automatically generated in masses of men by class differences. Some classes are naturally vicious, says Aristotle, but some are naturally virtuous. The vicious classes are the very rich and the very poor, of whom the very rich, for Aristotle, are undoubtedly the worse. The virtuous class is those in the middle who are neither very rich nor very poor. They are the middle class or perhaps the bourgeoisie. The middle class, however, are not virtuous by education or firmly instilled habit as are kings and aristocrats. They are virtuous by sociological condition. Because they are in the middle, they are most obedient to reason (for the very rich and the very poor are driven either by their superiority into insolent wickedness or by their poverty into knavish villainy). They are least desirous of rule when they do not have it and least tenacious of it when they do. They are not tyrannous and contemptuous like the rich, or slavish and envious like the poor. They are the most fit for the friendship and community that make the city, because they are the most equal and similar, being similar and equal not only among themselves, as even the poor and rich might be, but to the extremes too, since the middle are closer to the rich and to the poor than the rich or the poor are to each other.

These differences are moral, but they are effects of class and not of true virtue. Hence they are unstable in the sense that someone from the middle who rises or falls into rich or poor will also likely rise into insolence or fall into villainy, whereas someone truly virtuous will remain virtuous however good or ill his fortune (*Nicomachean Ethics* 1.10.1100b18–33). Aristotle's preference for the middle class is reserved and discriminating. There is baseness in every man, he opines, and he opines at the same time that men need to be made subject to others to keep that baseness in check. "The freedom to do whatever one wishes is incapable of providing defense against the base element in each man" (*Politics* 8(6).4.1318b39–19a1).

Legislative Contrivance and Political Institutions

The checks and balances, as we might call them, that Aristotle thinks of are that the officeholders be subject to the mass of the citizens and that the mass of the citizens be subject to the officeholders (*Politics* 3.11.1281b21–38). The officeholders hold office by the suffrage and sufferance of the mass, for the mass not only votes for the officeholders but also subjects them to scrutiny and the giving of accounts. The officeholders exercise certain functions of deliberation and judgment for the mass. The whole is bound together and supported by the law, the constitutional law that says that the officeholders judge and deliberate and that the mass elects and holds them to account. The rule of law is the rule of such constitutional restraints. Law is only needed where the people subject to it lack perfect virtue. Had they perfect virtue, they would need no restraints, because perfect virtue would be their restraint. Virtue is imperfect in the middle class; it is nonexistent in the classes of the rich and the poor. A government of the middle class, a polity, will be a correct government, for it will be of and for the virtuous. A government of the class of the rich (oligarchy) or of the poor (democracy) will be a deviation, for it will not be of or for the virtuous. Aristotle's discussion of these governments, the imperfectly virtuous and the vicious governments, is a discussion of institutions. The books he devotes to them [6(4)–8(6)] are all about numbers and kinds of offices and about the manner and length of appointments. The books he devotes to the best government of virtue [4(7)–5(8)], to kingship and aristocracy, are all about education. What true virtue achieves by formation of the soul in the latter, political construction achieves by contrivance of the law in the former.

The contrivance in the case of polity is to put the middle class in control and make the rich and the poor subject to them. The devices are many, and Aristotle describes more their principle than their number (*Politics* 6(4).9.1294a30–b14). One such device is limitation of the franchise. Only give the vote and participation in juries and the assembly to those with a certain minimum of wealth. Do not put this minimum too high, lest the rich be too strong for the middle; nor put it too low, lest the poor be too numerous for both middle and rich. When elections or jury service take place, fine the rich if they do not take part, and pay the poorer if they do. The same goes for arms and training in their use: pay the poor to arm and train, and fine the rich for failing to do either. The idea is clear; the details indefinite. Prudence, the prudence of the wise legislator, must decide, by direct experience of the facts on the ground, what is best where, when, and how.

Formed by prudence and experience as well as by the principles of political science, the legislator will know how to devise laws and structures to set up and preserve any government. He will aim at a virtuous government, but he will recognize, like the gymnastic trainer, that he cannot do more with the people he has in front of him than those people want or are capable of. In many cases he will have no choice but to set up a deviant government, such as an oligarchy or a democracy or even a tyranny. For the people and their circumstances will not permit him to do anything else, and if he tries anything else, he will make things worse. Fortunately, oligarchies, democracies, tyrannies, and even polities are not one but many (*Politics* 6(4).3–9.1289b27–94a29). Each includes several varieties under it. Fortunately too, these varieties differ according to better and worse. The legislator always has some choice whereby to make things better or to stop them from getting worse. He can always aim at good and always achieve good, if only a little good.

More important will be moral sociology, or knowledge of how, for most people, their moral character is a function of their class. Aristotle would have no problem with modern class analysis. He would just complain that the analysis does not go far enough. Not only are there the broad economic classes of lower, middle, and upper, there are also classes within these classes, and these classes are not only economic or even socioeconomic; they are moral. Some poor are poorer and their character worse than other poor, and some rich are richer and their character worse than other rich. Oligarchies and democracies not only differ in kind from each other but also within each other, as some are worse or better because they are composed of worse or better classes of rich and poor. The trick is to see where in any given city the weight lies. Are the rich, and which rich, so superior to the poor and the middle that nothing but an oligarchy could survive for very long, and if so, which oligarchy? Or are the poor, and which poor, thus superior? Is the middle strong enough, if not to form the government, then at least, by addition to rich or poor, to balance the two and mitigate their excesses?

Only the lawgiver on the spot can decide these questions. But he can decide them. And he can exploit them. He will need data and guidance, and Aristotle provides both, in the collections of governments and of customs produced by his school and in the joint treatises of the *Politics* and *Nicomachean Ethics*. The collections and the treatises are needed, because politics is a moral phenomenon reflecting the character of the people involved. The devices and structures of governments may be impersonal and mechanical, but the way they are put together is moral. They should be put together to make the government as morally good as the people who are its material admit of. One cannot know what is morally good or bad if one does not know what the standard of moral goodness is. That standard is virtue, the perfect virtue of the perfect man. The *Nicomachean Ethics* gives the standard. The *Politics* explains, in its books on the best government, the government and the education in which the standard is reached and preserved. The *Politics* explains, in its other books, the governments where the standard is not reached but where it is more or less approached. These other books are about the sociological virtue or vice of most men that mimics or mocks the true virtue of the perfected man.

Governments and Socio-Moral Classes

Aristotle's analysis of sociological virtue, or his analysis of the ways in which socioeconomic factors form the habitual behaviors of those who, because they lack true virtue, are under the predominating influence of such factors, is a systematic relating of behavioristic morals to classes. We today might call his reflections ideology or prejudice. He himself would regard them as observational common sense. The dispute is not worth debating in the abstract. It will be settled, if it is settled, by empirical data, and to such data we may dismiss it. The principle behind Aristotle's analysis is nevertheless worth noting: if socioeconomic factors determine behavioral habits, and if behavioral habits determine how those with the habit will exercise rule, and if rule is exercised well when it is exercised according to justice and virtue and not when it is not, then the rule of those whose behavioral habits come closer to justice and virtue will be better than the rule of those whose behavioral habits depart from them. Good and bad governments will reflect the good and bad moral effects of socioeconomic conditions. Aristotle's analysis of different kinds of government follows accordingly.

To take democracy first, then, or rule by the mass of the poor, the forms of democracy reflect the political sociology of the poor (*Politics* 6(4).4.1291b14–92a38, 6.1292b22–93a12). So the farmers among the class of the poor are the best, and the democracy based on them is also the best. Such a democracy is not a virtuous government, for only the middle with its imitation of virtue is that. But it is not a very vicious government. It rules for its own advantage and not for the promotion and cultivation of virtue (which alone is the common good of the city), but its own advantage is not so depraved. The farmers will keep final power in their own hands, but they will put the daily administration of affairs in better and wealthier hands. They will meet as a body rarely and only on important matters affecting the government. They will insist, and have the power to ensure, that each officeholder rule subject to their own periodic review and approval, serving but for fixed terms and over such matters as are deputed to each office and not over others. Farmers are on the whole a good class of poor, not because they would exercise office well if they had it, but because they do not have leisure to exercise it. They will also elect a better class of wealthy to office, a class as moderate in instincts as themselves. Also, because of their distance from the urban center, farmers will be able to attend but few meetings of the assembly, the necessary ones. They will confine the franchise to people like themselves who have enough property to own small farms. Others will be excluded.

Artisans and traders are a worse class of poor. They will not own land that they farm, and they will spend their time in or near the urban center. They will be less moderate, and they will also be able to attend more meetings of the assembly and to decide directly on more issues of policy. They will choose others to exercise office, for they do not have enough leisure to exercise office themselves. But they will give these offices less power and be more subject to the wiles of clever speakers playing on their passions, because they will be more often together in the popular assembly. Nevertheless, they will not be too extreme, for they have property, and their livelihood depends on things staying generally the same. The franchise they will limit to those like themselves, who have some minimal property.

Unskilled workers and day laborers are a worse class of poor still. They have no property, they gather about the urban center, and their livelihood is basic and precarious. They have little attachment to things as they are and are easy prey to clever speakers who counsel radical change. They can do little, nevertheless, because they do not have leisure to attend many assemblies and to decide directly issues of policy or principle. They will not limit the franchise, save perhaps to those who are full citizens.

The worst class of the poor is dominated by these last two groups that crowd the urban center, especially if immigrants or those of doubtful citizenship are added to their number. They are least attached to things as they are and would change both law and policy if they could or if clever speakers catch their ear. All that prevents them from realizing their power is leisure to attend the assembly. Such leisure is secured when the city has an abundance of revenues, whether from trade or war or despoiling the rich through taxation or the courts. The poor can then be paid when they attend the assembly or serve on juries and can make a living, not in grinding labor, but in the excitement of public speeches and disputed votes. Such as these will overthrow the law that limits the direct control of the assembly and puts office and daily management in the hands of the stable rich. They will take power into their own hands through frequent popular assemblies. Rule will cease to be that of law and become, in principle if not always in practice, the tyranny of the mob, which will care nothing for virtue, not even as sociological imitation, but only for the satisfaction of its passions. Something approaching such a sociological "rake's progress" of democracy is described in the first part of the *Regime of the Athenians* (the only one of the collections of regimes put together by Aristotle and his school that has come down to us), where the democracy of Athens' heyday at the end of the fifth century, and as restored in the fourth, represents the last and worst of democracy's kinds.[10] Similar declines of democracy, and their eventual overthrow into oligarchy or tyranny, are recorded for Cos, Rhodes, Megara, Cyme, and Syracuse (*Politics* 7(5).5.1304b19–05a36).

As for oligarchies, the *Politics* at any rate makes clear that these are similar to democracies in their kinds, save that they deviate in the opposite direction, getting worse as they are narrowed down to fewer and richer rulers (*Politics* 6(4).5.1292a39–b11, 5.1293a12–34). Where the rulers are of moderate wealth and anyone who meets the required property qualification shares in rule, the oligarchy is moderate and rule is by law, the law that says all who meet the qualification rule. In this case the rulers are not so rich that they can always be at leisure to rule, and they are many in number, so that none can be arbitrarily excluded to make the opinions or wishes of some small group of rich prevail. The oligarchy becomes worse when the qualification is set high and not all those who meet it rule but only those who are elected by those already ruling. Here the arrogance and insolence of great wealth, combined with the ability of the ruling group not to elect to their number any they do not wish, make the oligarchy freer to pursue the passions and self-interest of that group. It is checked nevertheless by the law that requires the rulers always to elect new members. The oligarchy becomes worse when membership is confined to certain rich families and sons succeed to fathers. It is worst when these families, being rich enough to rule all things on their own, even refuse to allow son to succeed to father but instead choose only those they want. Here rule of law has wholly broken down (for even the law that bids son succeed to father has gone), and the passion and self-interest of the ruling elite is without check. This rule is called dynasty and is equivalent to tyranny.

Examples of oligarchies and of their decline into dynasty, or of their overthrow, because of their extreme narrowness, into tyranny or democracy or even into a more moderate form of oligarchy, are given in the *Politics* (7(5).6.1305a37–06b17). The oligarchy on the island of Naxos, for instance, because of its ill treatment of the populace, was overthrown with popular support by the tyrant Lygdamis; the oligarchy in Massilia (the modern Marseilles), which was an extreme dynasty, was resented by the excluded oligarchs, who changed it to a more moderate form; the oligarchy at Elis went the other way when the few oligarchs who held the highest offices secured a dynasty for themselves; a similar extreme narrowing down of rulers took place at Athens in the oligarchies of 411 and 404 before each was overthrown and the democracy restored.

Tyranny itself, the worst of all governments and hardly even a government, also has kinds, according to the slavishness of the ruled and the vice of the ruler (*Politics* 6(4).10.1295a1–24). Tyrannies among barbarians often have kingly elements to them, such as being according to law and over subjects who willingly submit (as in parts of Asia, *Politics* 3.14.1285a16–24), but the reason lies in the natural slavishness of the barbarians in question, who are fit only to rule and be ruled like slaves (*Politics* 1.2.1252b5–7, 4(7).7.1327b37–29). The worst tyranny is that over unwilling subjects who are the equals or betters of the tyrant and must be coerced into submission. Examples would include the notorious Periander in Corinth and Dionysius I and II in Syracuse (*Politics* 7(5).11.1313a34–37). All tyrannies are rule without law, and the worst kinds of democracy and oligarchy are tyrannies for this same reason. Tyrannies are lawless because tyrants are not a law themselves, as the perfectly virtuous are, but pursue against reason and without check their depraved and self-interested passions (*Politics* 7(5).11.1313a39–14a29).

Polities too have kinds, but these are kinds within sociological virtue. Those where the middle is large are more like democracies, while those where the middle is small, or combined with elements of the rich, are more like oligarchies. Such governments are correct in aiming for the common good of virtue. Solon's moderate democracy in Athens, for instance, was really a democratic polity. It became a democracy, and an extreme one, because of things Solon could not foresee or control. The populace became strong through being the cause of naval empire in the Persian Wars, and chose for themselves base demagogues, like Ephialtes and Pericles, who gave them complete control of the government (*Politics* 2.12.1274a7–21, 3.11). Polities may also become aristocracies. Or elements of virtue may be combined with elements of wealth and the people to form aristocracies. These aristocracies are not the true aristocracies of perfect virtue, but the virtuous among them will have achieved a degree of true virtue and not just be sociologically virtuous. The Spartans, Cretans, and Carthaginians all seem to be instances of such lesser aristocracies. The Cretans had an oligarchic aristocracy and one that could at times collapse into dynasty (*Politics* 2.10.1271b20–72b23); the Carthaginians managed a government that was a mixed aristocracy but with tendencies to oligarchy (*Politics* 2.11.1272b24–73b26); the Spartans had a mix of aristocracy and democracy but with strong oligarchic deviations (*Politics* 2.9.1269a29–71b19). A combination, indeed, of democracy and aristocracy can be achieved if the poor elect to office, but those they elect from are the virtuous (*Politics* 7(5).8.1308b38–9a9). A democratic aristocracy or aristocratic democracy will be a correct government and fall under the heading of polity or mixed government. It is of and for the virtuous, albeit not the perfectly virtuous.

In a polity, or in any of the moderate oligarchies and democracies, rule will be variously shared between the offices and those who elect to office. Other devices, of which Aristotle lists many (in particular the mixing of election with lottery in choosing to office), will be judiciously employed to ensure as balanced and moderate a government as the people and the circumstances permit (*Politics* 6(4).14–16.1297b35–01a15). In such governments, where none are so virtuous as to deserve always to rule, there will be alternation in ruling and being ruled. But Aristotle understands alternation in several ways. One way is that parts of rule are shared by different parts of the city, such as that the offices are occupied by the wealthier, but elections and audits and control of the assembly belong to the poorer. This sort of thing happens in polities of a democratic caste. Day-to-day control and decisions of policy and management are in the hands of the offices, but ultimate oversight—major questions of law, of appointment to office, of war and peace, and the like—are in the hands of the populace through the assembly and the jury courts (*Politics* 6(4).14.1298b5–11). Another way is when different persons from the same part of the city alternate in ruling, as happens especially in democracies where terms of office are short and the same person cannot be reelected or reappointed often or at all to the same office (*Politics* 8(6).2.1317a23–25). A third way is mentioned as holding of true aristocracies where no individual or family stands out so much from all others as to deserve to be king. Here all share in ruling, but they are ruled when young and rule when older and properly educated (*Politics* 4(7).14.1332b16–33a3). Of these ways, Aristotle evidently thinks the third is best, for it is what happens in the best government of true aristocracy. The first way, if not best, is yet a good way, and is the way that a government both democratic and aristocratic would function, with the aristocrats occupying the offices and the populace electing them to office. The second way is worst and really a form of tyranny by the populace, for control is in the hands of the popular assembly, while the offices, where alone alternation takes place, are subject in all things to the assembly. In addition, those who alternate in the offices, being chosen by lot, will come predominantly from the populace. The populace will thus always rule, even if the individuals in the offices are always different.

In some cases a decent or moderate government will not be possible, and the legislator will have to settle for oligarchy or democracy or perhaps even tyranny. But oligarchs and democrats and tyrants have conflicting desires. They want to rule for their own advantage, and they also want to go on ruling; they do not want their enemies to take over. Aristotle counsels the legislator to enlighten the rulers' self-interest by appeal to the latter wish to counter the evils of the former (*Politics* 7(5).9.1309b18–37, 8(6).5.1319b33–21b3). To rule long, one must rule moderately and not exasperate one's enemies. The poor must not attack the rich, and the rich must not abuse the poor. Each side should open to the other shares in the lesser offices, not provoke by extravagant or insolent behavior, keep rights to private property secure, and give opportunities to all for improving and maintaining their lot.

Regimes will thus vary from place to place, but some regimes are correct and others deviant. The correct regimes (kingship, aristocracy, polity) are correct because they pursue the common good, and they pursue the common good because the ruling body in each case is virtuous (with complete virtue in the case of kingship and aristocracy, with military virtue in the case of polity). The deviant regimes (tyranny, oligarchy, democracy) are deviant because they do not pursue the common good, and their ruling bodies are not virtuous (*Politics* 3.6–7). These rankings are everywhere the same, and among them kingship is always best. The regimes, however, that suit given cities are not everywhere the same, but for some kingship suits, for others aristocracy, for others polity; the deviant regimes may also suit some cities, not by nature (for no deviant regime accords with nature [*Politics* 3.17.1287b39–41]), but because the citizens can only be made to choose a deviant regime and not a correct one (*Politics* 6(4).12–13). In an extended sense, therefore, a deviant regime may be said to be natural for this or that city, if it will not tolerate a correct one.

A correct regime can, however, always in principle be set up, even in those cities that refuse a correct regime, for these cities will nevertheless have enough virtuous citizens in them to form the basis of a correct regime (whether a democratically leaning polity or an oligarchically leaning one [*Politics* 6(4).7–9, 11]). If they do not have enough virtuous citizens in them, then they are naturally slavish and may justly be subjected by force to a virtuous master (*Politics* 1.6–7), and under a master, if they do not have the political just, they will have the domestic just, for slaves share in the domestic just (earlier here, at 6.1134b8–17). Still, even where a correct regime can be set up, because the citizens are willing, the correct regime will not everywhere be the same. It will, however, everywhere be natural, for all correct regimes accord with nature.

Aristotle's position, then, on regimes and on the natural just steers a mean between the extremes of cultural imperialism and cultural relativism. It is not culturally imperialistic, because it does not say that if some city does not have the regime that my city has, therefore I should say or think that that city is unjust or unnatural (for, on the contrary, if it has a correct regime, it will not be). The position is not culturally relativist, because it does not say that all regimes everywhere are natural or just. On the contrary it says that some are natural and just and others unnatural and unjust. We are thus always able to rank all the regimes that we find in different times and places according to a standard that is everywhere the same: the standard of nature that ranks kingship best and the others after it, some as correct and others as deviant (and the deviant as some more and some less bad [*Politics* 6(4).4–6]).

Political Community and Happiness

Such is Aristotle's classification of governments and its immediate or proximate reasons. But Aristotle gives several accounts of differences among governments. These accounts are compatible and mutually reinforcing, but they are not all at the same level.[11] Differences in structure, for instance, such as choice of offices by lot rather than by election or from all rather than from some, are derivatives of the kinds of government. Democracies prefer lot to election and short terms of office to long (*Politics* 8(6).2.1317a40–b30). The reason Aristotle gives is the supposition of democracy or what it supposes justice to be, which is equality, and what its aim is, which is freedom. Why, however, do democrats aim at equality and freedom for all, while oligarchs aim at inequality and rule for the wealthy? Because these things give them what they most want. What do they most want? The same as everyone most wants: happiness. Differences in governments reflect differences in happiness (*Politics* 4(7).8.1328a35–b2). Democrats have one conception and oligarchs another, and different classes of democrats and oligarchs have different conceptions, and so on through all the classes and subclasses. But democrats have the conception of happiness they do because of their social condition of poverty and subordination to the rich. They want equality and freedom so that they will not be subject to the rich and can escape poverty. Oligarchs, likewise, having already the privileges of wealth, wish to keep and to enhance these privileges and not let others, particularly the poor or the less rich, take them away.

Democrats and oligarchs want the same thing, material sufficiency and freedom to do as they will, save that the oligarchs have these and want to keep them, and the democrats do not have them and want to get them. Hence arises the abiding hostility between rich and poor in cities. Wealth and freedom are goods of limitation that can be shared only by being lessened. The oligarchs lose wealth and freedom if the democrats gain in wealth and freedom, and vice versa. Happiness for each means wealth and freedom, because in wealth and freedom they can satisfy their wants, whatever these wants are. The kinds of happiness differ, because the wants to be satisfied differ. The differences that arise between governments arise because different groups in the city are differently disposed by their social status to the satisfaction of differing wants. The rich have satisfaction and will not share it. The poor lack satisfaction and will get it.

To arrange the city so that it is geared toward the satisfaction of the rulers, whether these are one or few or many, is to twist the city from the common good toward private advantage. The deviant governments are deviant because they have a deviant end, and they have a deviant end because those who form them, the rich and the poor, have a false view of happiness. The true view is that happiness is virtue or its exercise. The correct governments are correct because they have a correct end, and they have a correct end because those who form them, the virtuous, have a correct view of happiness. The correct governments are few or, in the end, only one, the government of perfect virtue, though the lesser government of lesser virtue may still qualify and may even, by some divine chance, make possible the emergence of a government of perfect virtue. The deviant governments, by contrast, are many, and more even than first appear, because vice is many and those who pursue the satisfying of vicious wants pursue it in as many ways as there are varying social conditions that determine the wants.

Happiness, in its forms of virtue and satisfaction of wants, and the several socially conditioned forms of wants, is what we would nowadays call a comprehensive vision of the good. Ancient political philosophy is the politics of comprehensive visions, and its aim is to find the true comprehensive vision and, by finding it, to work out what political arrangement or education will best secure it. The search for the best government is the search for that arrangement or education. Lesser governments are treated of as arrangements that do not secure the true comprehensive vision but that can be mitigated or moderated so that at least they do not obscure it and may even open the way to it. Because ancient politics is about the true comprehensive vision, it is about the city. Because modern politics is about neutralizing and pacifying the rivalry between comprehensive visions, it is about the state.

The city is not a state, and what the ancients meant by it is not what we mean by the state. Aristotle's classification of governments is a classification of communities devoted to the pursuit of comprehensive visions of the good. Our modern elaboration of legitimate and illegitimate states is an elaboration of fair terms of alliance between rival communities or visions of the good. The ancients wanted the big questions and the answers to them—the questions and answers about the good and human happiness—to fashion and structure their common life. Matters of defensive alliance, while they may be necessary, now as then, for securing peace, are too trivial to occupy the energy and attention that we devote to them under the title of politics. There are more important things to ponder and more worthy causes to live and die for.

In this regard, the ancients got the idea of politics right, as has been argued at length above. Accordingly the textbook, if there is one, that we should employ even today for the best guidance to organizing and understanding political life is not Rawls' *Theory of Justice* or *Political Liberalism* but Aristotle's *Politics*. Why we generally prefer Rawls and others instead has historically and politically, at least as regards the United States, a lot to do with the topic of the next chapter: the American counterrevolution.

Notes

1. Rawls (1971, §1).
2. Rawls (1971: §§1–6, 15, 85).
3. For the books after book three of the *Politics*, two book numbers are given, the second of which (in parentheses) is the manuscript numbering and the first of which is the logical numbering (books 7 and 8 in the manuscript ordering are logically books 4 and 5). In this practice the lead of Newman is being followed (1887–1902).
4. Women too fall under the heading of men, and not because "man" in English can also mean "human" and women are human (though that fact is linguistically true), but because women are perfected through men in the household, and because households and men are perfected through the city (*Politics* 1.2.1252b27–34, 13.1260a14–24).
5. Miller (1995) has argued, with no little success, that Aristotle's political theory can be cast in the form of a rights doctrine. But he has to admit, nevertheless, that Aristotle's notion of rights is not the same as ours, or as Rawls'. Hence his contentions do not show that it would be better to approach Aristotle on constitutions and governments from the notion of rights rather than from the notion of justice.
6. Rawls (1971: §§3–4, 11).
7. Actually what Aristotle is interested in is the *politeia*, which translators variously render as "government" or "constitution" or "regime." "Regime" is perhaps closest to the Greek word, but "government" and "constitution" are more familiar to us. Cf. Bates (2014).
8. Rawls (1971: chapters 7–9; especially chapter 7 on how the right defines the good).
9. The thesis, made popular by Jaeger (1923), that the *Politics* divides into "ideal" books dealing with the best constitution and "empirical" books dealing with concrete realities, is highly misleading. All the books of the *Politics* are ideal, if by "ideal" is meant moral, and empirical, if by "empirical" is meant responsive to the facts. For Aristotle's concern throughout, as the analogy of the gymnastic trainer makes clear, is with achieving the best moral results that the circumstances in any given case allow. That sometimes these circumstances will allow the best and at other times much less than the best is only to be expected and does not affect the unity of Aristotle's overall intention.
10. The details of this rake's progress are controversial; see Rhodes (1981: 5–15), along with *Politics* 2.12.1273b35–74a21. The *Athenaiōn Politeia* was just one of a collection of some 158 constitutions or governments of ancient cities put together by Aristotle and his school. The collection was part of a conscious program of gathering and organizing data. The data-gathering ranged over matters both human and nonhuman and included a collection

of customs and laws (Greek and non-Greek) as well as of constitutions; see Düring (1957). The *Constitution of the Athenians* was lost for centuries until it was recovered, from Egyptian papyrus rolls, in the late 1800s. Of the remaining constitutions, only fragments (often more tantalizing than informative) remain in other authors; see Rhodes (1981: 1–4), and the editions by Rose (1886) and Hose (2002).

11.   The matter is disputed. Schütrumpf has argued against unity of doctrine in the *Politics* on this and many other matters (1980 and 1991–2005); I have argued for such unity (1998). See also Pellegrin (1987: 129–59).

8

Devolved versus Centralized Rule

Anti-Federalists and Federalists on the US Articles of Confederation

Aristotle's analysis gives us a fairly comprehensive view of forms of government, save of course for the fact that he has no state in the modern sense. Or if he does, he would classify it as a tyranny, or a tyrannical empire (since the geographical range of its authority is typically very large). The fact that the state is essentially tyrannical in form was argued in the first chapters, so here this point will simply be assumed. One should add, however, that Aristotle is not opposed to empire as such, since he seems to allow that it might sometimes be just (*Politics* 4(7).6.1327a40–b6, 14.1333b38–34a2). He would distinguish just empire from tyrannical empire, of course, but he says little about the details. We can, however, ourselves develop the details, extending and adapting Aristotle's insights in view of later historical events, such as in particular the Roman Empire (in both its pagan and Christian forms). For this purpose, and because of the dominance today of the state, a useful beginning can be found in the rise of the state in the United States. This point was already briefly discussed earlier in the contrast between the original Articles of Federation and the US Constitution (in Chapter Two). More now needs to be said to extend and confirm what was said before, because the introduction of the US Constitution was fiercely debated at the time, and it is necessary to see something of the structure of that debate through the eyes of the rival sides. These sides are the Federalists on the one hand, who proposed and supported the Constitution, and the Anti-Federalists on the other, who opposed it. The Federalists have had by far the better reputation since that time, largely through the widespread influence of the Federalist Papers. The arguments of the Anti-Federalists, by contrast, have generally been ignored. To get a sense of the position of the Anti-Federalists, then, and of how they attacked the Constitution, the most truthful and effective method would be to give a series of quotations from them as juxtaposed with the opposing ones of the Federalists. What follows, next, is precisely such a series. The quotations are rather long, but so must they be to give a fair sense of the facts. So must they also be to show that the United States, which is regarded as an archetypal instance of a liberal state, is no exception to the claim that liberalism is despotism. As the Anti-Federalists well point out, the United States Constitution was despotic in spirit from the start, to say nothing of later political developments.

The first quotations are from Anti-Federalists arguing against the moves made by Federalists to introduce a new, and far more centralized, system of government such as was eventually achieved in the US Constitution. We may call these moves by the Federalists the American counterrevolution, since, as the Anti-Federalists often pointed out, it reversed the achievements of the revolution of 1776. The headings and emphases are added.

1. Federal Farmer (Richard Henry Lee):
   a. *Feelings of Dissatisfaction*: During the war the general confusion and the introduction of paper money infused in the minds of the people vague ideas respecting government and credit. We expected too much from the return of peace and of course we have been disappointed. Our governments have been new and unsettled and several legislatures by making tender, suspension, and paper money laws have given just cause of uneasiness to creditors. By these and other causes several orders of men in the community have been prepared by degrees for a *change of government*. And this very abuse of power in the legislatures, which in some cases has been *charged upon the democratic part of the community*, has furnished *aristocratical men* with those very weapons and those very means with which they are rapidly *effecting their favorite object*.
   b. *Effect and Exploitation of These Feelings*: [W]hen by the evils on the one hand and by *the secret instigations of artful men* on the other the minds of men were become sufficiently uneasy, *a bold step was taken*, which is usually followed by *a revolution or a civil war*. A general convention for mere commercial purposes was moved for. The authors of this measure saw that *the people's attention was turned solely to the amendment of the federal system* and that had the idea of a *total change* been started probably no state would have appointed members to the convention. The idea of *destroying ultimately the state government and forming one consolidated system* could not have been admitted.

c. *Background to the Convention of 1787*: In September 1786 *a few men* from the middle states met at Annapolis and hastily proposed a convention to be held in May 1787 for the purpose of amending the confederation. This was done before the delegates of Massachusetts and of the other states arrived. Still not a word was said about *destroying the old constitution. . . .* The states . . . appointed members to the new convention *for the sole and express purpose of revising and amending the confederation* and probably not one man in ten thousand in the United States, till within these ten or twelve days, had an idea that *the old ship was to be destroyed. . . .* The States, I believe, *universally supposed the convention would report alterations in the confederation* which would *pass an examination in congress* and after being agreed to there would *be confirmed by all the legislatures, or be rejected. . . .* Pennsylvania appointed principally those *men who are esteemed aristocratical.* Here the favorite moment for *changing the government* was evidently discerned by *a few men*, who seized it with address. Ten other states chose men principally connected with commerce and the judicial department yet they appointed many good republican characters. Had they all attended we should now see, I am persuaded, a better system presented; the result of the convention would not have had that *strong tendency to aristocracy* now discernible in every part of the plan. There would not have been *so great an accumulation of powers in a few hands.*[1]

2. <u>Patrick Henry</u>: Similar examples are to be found in ancient Greece and ancient Rome—instances of *the people losing their liberty* by their own carelessness and *the ambition of a few.*[2]

3. <u>A Federalist</u>: The Lawyers in particular, keep up an incessant declamation for its adoption; the numerous tribunals to be erected by *the new plan of consolidated empire* will find employment for ten times their present numbers.[3]

4. <u>Brutus Junior</u>: It is at the same time well known to every man, who is but moderately acquainted with the characters of the members, that many of them are possessed of *high aristocratic ideas and the most sovereign contempt of the common people.*[4]

5. <u>The Yeomanry of Massachusetts</u>: Notwithstanding [General Washington] wielded the sword in defense of American liberty, yet at the same time he was, and is to this day, *living upon the labors of several hundreds of miserable Africans as free born as himself* and some of them very likely descended from parents who might cope with any man in America.[5]

6. <u>A Farmer</u>: Another class of men wishes to have it adopted so that the *public chest might be furnished with money to pay the interest on their securities* which they *purchased of the poor soldiers at two shillings on the pound.* I wish the soldiers were now the holders of those securities they fought so hard for.[6]

7. <u>Cincinnatus</u>: If the new government raises this sum in specie [gold and silver] on the people *it will give immense fortunes to the speculators but it will grind the poor to dust.*[7]

No doubt one could dismiss these sentiments as prejudice or *parti pris*, but they sufficiently manifest what Anti-Federalists thought. Their sentiments are also, interestingly, confirmed by the French ambassador in the United States at the time in a letter he wrote to the foreign minister in France. A more percipient account of what the Federalists were really up to would be hard to find. For, speaking of the report filed by the few states that appeared at the first, and abortive, meeting in Annapolis, which preceded and prepared the way for the Constitutional Convention in Philadelphia, the ambassador writes:

> They [the commissioners at Annapolis] endeavored to give [their report] an obscurity that the people will see through with difficulty, but which the powerful and enlightened citizens will not fail to turn to account. For a very long time, my Lord, they have felt the necessity of giving the federal Government more energy and vigor, but they have also felt that the excessive independence accorded to the citizens with regard to the States, and to the States with regard to Congress, is too dear to individuals for them to be divested of it without great precautions. . . . It is in the interest of the people to preserve, as much as possible, the absolute liberty that was accorded to them . . . that all power should emanate only from the people, that everything be submitted to its supreme will, and that the magistrates be only its servants.
>
> Although there were no patricians in America, there is a class of men known under the denomination of "gentlemen," who by their wealth, by their talents, by their education, by their families, or by the positions that they fill, aspire to a preeminence that the people refuse to accord them. . . . The people, generally discontented with the difficulties of commerce, and little suspecting the secret motives of their antagonists . . . named commissioners who were supposed to meet at Annapolis [to discuss matters of commerce].
>
> [. . .]
>
> The authors [of the Annapolis meeting] had no hope or even any desire to see this assembly of commissioners . . . succeed. The measures were so well taken that . . . there were no more than five States represented at Annapolis, and the commissioners of the Northern States were held up for several days in New York in order to delay their arrival. . . . The assembled States . . . broke up on the pretext that they were not numerous enough to enter into the matter, and to justify this dissolution they sent a report. . . . In this document the commissioners make use of an infinity of circumlocutions and ambiguous phrases to explain to their constituents the impossibility of taking into consideration a general plan of commerce and the powers relative thereto without touching at the same time on other objects intimately connected with the prosperity and the national importance

of the United States. . . . You will perceive, my Lord, that the commissioners do not wish to take into consideration the grievances of commerce, infinitely interesting to the people, without perfecting at the same time the fundamental constitution of Congress.[8]

The next series of quotations are from both Federalists and Anti-Federalists, contrasting the charges leveled against the Articles by the former and the answer to these charges given by the latter. First the Federalists:

1. *Federalist Charges against the Articles.* <u>Hamilton</u> *Federalist* 15:
   We have reached almost the last stage of national humiliation.
   a. Do we owe debts to foreigners and to our own citizens contracted in a time of imminent peril for the preservation of our political existence? These remain without any proper or satisfactory provision for their discharge. . . . Is respectability in the eyes of foreign powers a safeguard against foreign encroachments? The imbecility of our government even forbids them to treat with us. Our ambassadors abroad are the mere pageants of mimic sovereignty.
   b. Have we valuable territories and important posts in the possession of a foreign power which, by express stipulations, ought long since to have been surrendered? These are still retained, to the prejudice of our interests, not less than of our rights.
   c. Are we in a condition to resent or to repel the aggression? We have neither troops, nor treasury, nor government. Are we even in a condition to remonstrate with dignity? The just imputations on our own faith, in respect to the same treaty, ought first to be removed.
   d. Are we entitled by nature and compact to a free participation in the navigation of the Mississippi? Spain excludes us from it.
   e. Is public credit an indispensable resource in time of public danger? We seem to have abandoned its cause as desperate and irretrievable. . . . Is private credit the friend and patron of industry? That most useful kind which relates to borrowing and lending is reduced within the narrowest limits, and this still more from an opinion of insecurity than from the scarcity of money.
   f. Is commerce of importance to national wealth? Ours is at the lowest point of declension. Is a violent and unnatural decrease in the value of land a symptom of national distress? The price of improved land in most parts of the country is much lower than can be accounted for by the quantity of waste land at market, and can only be fully explained by that want of private and public confidence, which are so alarmingly prevalent among all ranks, and which have a direct tendency to depreciate property of every kind.
   g. What indication is there of national disorder, poverty, and insignificance that could befall a community so peculiarly blessed with natural advantages as we are, which does not form a part of the dark catalogue

of our public misfortunes? This is the melancholy situation to which we have been brought by those very maxims and councils which would now deter us from adopting the proposed Constitution.

2. *Falsity of Charges against the Articles,* from Various Anti-Federalist Writers. These quotations respond to each of the above charges in order.

   a. William Grayson: As to the foreign debt, they have the promise of more interest from us than they can get anywhere else. But it is said they will declare war against us if we don't pay them immediately. Common sense will teach them better. We live at too great a distance, and are too hardy and robust a people, for them to make money out of us in that way. . . . Mr. Adams applied to the Dutch for a new loan to the poor, despised Confederation. They readily granted it. . . . The loan of a million of Holland gilders, a sum equal to 250,000 Spanish Dollars, and all this done by the procurement of that very Congress whose insignificancy and want of power had been constantly proclaimed for two or three years before. . . . I believe the money which the Dutch borrowed of Henry IV is not yet paid.[9]

   b. A Newport Man: The British will never relinquish the posts in question until compelled by force, because no nation pays less regard to the faith of treaties than the British.[10]

   c. Patrick Henry: The Confederation, this despised government, carried us through a long and dangerous war; it rendered us victorious in that bloody conflict with a powerful nation; it has secured us a territory greater than any European monarch possesses; and shall a government which has been thus strong and vigorous be accused of imbecility, and abandoned for want of energy?[11] Candidus: This government, in particular, has produced an instance of ENERGY in suppressing a late rebellion [*Shays' Rebellion*] which no absolute monarchy can boast.[12]

[N.B. Shays' Rebellion was used by Federalists as an excuse for introducing a more powerful federal government, but scandalously because the rebellion was put down in a short time and with little bloodshed by Massachusetts alone, without any help from other states or from Congress. Contrast this rebellion with the Whiskey Rebellion, which was put down by President George Washington after he summoned federal troops for the purpose. The response was wholly out of proportion to the rebellion.]

   d. Candidus: What motive would induce Britain to repeal the duties on our oil, or France on our fish, if we should adopt the proposed Constitution? Those nations laid these duties to promote their own fishery etc. and let us adopt what mode of government we please they will pursue their own politics respecting our imports and exports.[13]

   e. Centinel: The history of mankind does not furnish a similar instance of an attempt to levy such enormous taxes at once nor of a people so wholly unprepared and uninured to them—the lamp of sacred liberty must indeed have burned with unsullied luster, every sordid principle of the mind must have been then extinct, when the people not only submitted to the grievous impositions, but cheerfully exerted themselves to comply with the calls of their country. Their abilities, however, were not equal to furnish the necessary sums—indeed, the requisition of the year 1782 amounted to the whole income of their farms and other property, including the means of their subsistence.[14] A Farmer: Requisitions were made which every body knew it was impossible to comply with. In 1782 or 1783 ten millions of hard dollars, if not thirteen, were called into the continental treasury, when there could not be half that sum in the whole tract of territory between Nova Scotia and Florida.[15] Centinel: How then can we impute the difficulties of the people, to a due compliance with the requisitions of Congress, to a defect in the confederation? Any government however energetic would have experienced the same fate.[16]

f. A Plebian: The merchant drives his commerce and none can deprive him of the gain he honestly acquires; all classes and callings of men amongst us are protected in their various pursuits and secured by the laws in the possession and enjoyment of the property obtained in those pursuits. . . . The farmer cultivates his land, and reaps the fruit which the bounty of heaven bestows on his honest toil. The mechanic is exercised in his art and receives the reward of his labor.[17]

g. A Plebian: Does not every man sit under his own vine and under his own fig-tree having none to make him afraid? Does not every one follow his calling without impediments and receive the reward of his well-earned industry? . . . The laws are as well executed as they ever were, in this or any other country. Neither the hand of private violence nor the more to be dreaded hand of legal oppression are reached out to distress us.[18]

These juxtaposed quotations show very clearly that the arguments of the Federalists are largely self-serving, and indeed deceitful, propaganda, and do not represent a fair description of the situation at the time.

Federalists and Anti-Federalists on the US Constitution

The next set of quotations contrasts the way the new US Constitution was defended by the Federalists and how the Anti-Federalists responded to this defense.

1. *Defense of the Constitution.* Hamilton, *Federalist* 23 and 31.
   a. The principal purposes to be answered by union are these: the common defense of the members; the preservation of the public peace as well against internal convulsions as external attacks; the regulation of commerce with other nations and between the States; the superintendence of our intercourse, political and commercial, with foreign countries.

b. The authorities essential to the common defense are these: to raise armies; to build and equip fleets; to prescribe rules for the government of both; to direct their operations; to provide for their support. These powers ought to exist without limitation, because it is impossible to foresee or define the extent and variety of national exigencies, or the correspondent extent and variety of the means which may be necessary to satisfy them. For the means ought to be proportioned to the end and the persons from whose agency the attainment of any end is expected ought to possess the *means* by which it is to be attained.

c. As revenue is the essential engine by which the means of answering the national exigencies must be procured, the power of procuring that article in its full extent must necessarily be comprehended in that of providing for those exigencies. As theory and practice conspire to prove that the power of procuring revenue is unavailing when exercised over the States in their collective capacities, the federal government must of necessity be invested with an unqualified power of taxation in the ordinary modes. . . . We must abandon the vain project of legislating upon the States in their collective capacities; we must extend the laws of the federal government to the individual citizens of America.

d. Hamilton or Madison, *Federalist* 51: In republican government the legislative authority necessarily predominates. The remedy for this inconveniency is to divide the legislature into different branches and to render them, by different modes of election and different principles of action, as little connected with each other as the nature of their common functions and their common dependence on the society will admit.

e. Whilst all authority in [the United States] will be derived from and dependent on the society, the society itself will be broken into so many parts, interests, and classes of citizens, that the rights of individuals, or of the minority, will be in little danger from interested combinations of the majority. . . . In the extended republic of the United States, and among the great variety of interests, parties, and sects which it embraces, a coalition of a majority of the whole society could seldom take place on any other principles than those of justice and the general good.

2. *Charges against the Constitution and Central Government* from Various Anti-Federalist Writers:
   a. Connecticut Journal: It is now almost five years since the peace. Congress has employed thirteen commissioners at 1500 dollars per annum, as I am informed, to settle the public accounts, and we know now no more what the national debt is than at the first moment of their appointment.[19] A Farmer: All human authority, however organized, must have confined limits, or insolence and oppression will prove the offspring of its grandeur, and the difficulty or rather impossibility of escape prevents resistance . . . In small independent States contiguous to each other, the people run away and leave despotism to reek its vengeance on itself.[20]

b. <u>A Democratic Federalist</u>: I need only adduce the example of Switzerland which, like us, is a republic under a federal government and which besides is surrounded by the most powerful nations in Europe, all jealous of its liberty and prosperity. And yet that nation has preserved its freedom for many ages with the sole help of a militia and has never been known to have a standing army, except when in actual war.[21]

c. <u>Federal Farmer</u>: It has long been thought to be a well founded position that the purse and sword ought not to be placed in the same hands in a free government.[22]

d. <u>Federal Farmer</u>: To produce a balance and checks the constitution proposes two branches in the legislature. But they are so formed that the members of both must generally be the same kind of men, having similar interests and views, feelings and connections, men of the same grade in society, and who associate on all occasions. . . . The partitions between the two branches will be merely those of the building in which they fit. There will not be found in them any of those genuine balances and checks among the real different interests and efforts of the several classes of men.[23]

e. <u>Federal Farmer</u>: We talk of balances in the legislature and among the departments of government. We ought to carry them to the body of the people. . . . Each order must have a share in the business of legislation actually and efficiently.[24] <u>Federal Farmer</u>: The republican principle is to diffuse the power of making the laws among the people and so to modify the forms of the government as to draw in turn the well informed of every class into the legislature.[25] <u>Cato</u>: It is remarked by Montesquieu in treating of republics that in all magistracies the greatness of the power must be compensated by the brevity of the duration and that a longer time than a year would be dangerous.[26]

One might think these responses by the Anti-Federalists are again prejudiced and mistaken, but a striking proof that they are not is given by the predictions that Anti-Federalist writers made about the effects of the US Constitution. All these predictions are striking in their prescience. They show that the Anti-Federalists knew far more about political realities and about the real aim and function of the US Constitution than the Federalists did, or at least than the Federalists admitted (for one may suspect that the actual results that the Anti-Federalists foresaw and feared were foreseen and perhaps in part welcomed by the Federalists).

3. *Anti-Federalist Predictions* from Various Anti-Federalist Writers:
   a. *Consolidation of Power at the Center and the Proliferation of Laws and Bureaucracies.* (i) <u>Federal Farmer</u>: Should the general government think it politic, as some administration (if not all) probably will, to look for a support in a system of influence, the government will

take every occasion to multiply laws and officers to execute them, considering these as so many necessary props for its own support.[27] ...
(ii) <u>Federal Farmer</u>: If, on a fair calculation, a man will gain more by measures oppressive to others than he will lose by them, he is interested in their adoption. It is true that those who govern generally by increasing the public burdens increase their own share of them; but by this increase they may, and often do, increase their salaries, fees, and emoluments in a tenfold proportion by increasing salaries and by making offices.[28]

b. *The Federal Debt.* <u>Brutus</u>: I can scarcely contemplate a greater calamity that could befall this country than to be loaded with a debt exceeding our ability ever to discharge. It is unwise and improvident to vest in the general government a power to borrow at discretion without any limitation or restriction.[29]

c. *Suppression of Dissent* [the Whiskey Rebellion; Fries' Rebellion]. <u>Federal Republican</u>: Congress will have the power of leading troops among you in order to suppress those struggles which may sometimes happen among a free people, and which tyranny will impiously brand with the name of sedition.[30]

d. *Tariffs.* <u>Cato</u>: Is human nature above self interest? If the Northern States do not burden the Southern in taxation it would appear that they are more disinterested men than we know of.[31]

e. *Nullification Crisis.* <u>Federal Farmer</u>: Does the constitution provide a single check for a single measure by which the State governments can constitutionally and regularly check the arbitrary measures of Congress? Congress may arm on every point and the State governments can do no more than, by petition to congress, suggest their measures are alarming and not right.[32] <u>Brutus</u>: If then the State legislatures check the general legislature it must be by exciting the people to resist constitutional laws. But such kinds of checks as these, though they sometimes correct the abuses of government, more often destroy all government.[33]

f. *Civil War.* <u>A Farmer</u>: Our State disputes in a Confederacy would be disputes of levity and passion which would subside before injury. The people being free, government having no right to them but they to government, they would separate and divide as interest or inclination prompted—as they do at this day, and always have done, in Switzerland. In a National government the disputes will be the deep-rooted differences of interest, where parts of the empire must be injured by the operation of general law; and then should the sword of government be once drawn (which Heaven avert) I fear it will not be sheathed until we have waded through that series of desolation which France, Spain, and the other great kingdoms of the world have suffered, in order to bring so many separate States into uniformity of government and law.[34]

The accuracy of these predictions is remarkable, and a brief summary of the history of the United States after the acceptance of the Constitution will make the fact very plain.

1. Concentration of power at the center by Federalists; increasing factional strife
   a. Hamilton institutes "the American System," 1790
   b. Adams and the Alien and Sedition Acts, 1798
   c. Jefferson and Madison and the Virginia and Kentucky Resolutions ("Doctrine of Nullification"), 1798
2. Culmination of factional strife during the presidential election of 1800; Federalists lose
3. Jefferson dismantles Hamilton's American System, 1801–1809
4. Defeated Northern Federalists talk and threaten secession, 1804 on
5. Attempts to reinstate the American System by Henry Clay and the Whigs (including the young Lincoln), such as tariffs on the South to support Northern industry; the "Tariff of Abominations," 1828, 1832; the Morrill Tariff, 1861
6. Secessionist arguments adopted by the South from the old Northern Federalists ("Nullification Crisis"), 1828 on
7. South secedes; Lincoln declares war on the South over tariffs, and restores the American System by force, 1861–1865; Lincoln's *First Inaugural*: "The power confided to me will be used to hold, occupy, and possess the property and places belonging to the Government [e.g., Fort Sumter in Charleston Harbor] and to collect the duties and imposts [Fort Sumter was an armed customs post suitable for collecting "duties and imposts"]; but beyond what may be necessary for these objects, there will be no invasion, no using of force against or among the people anywhere" [For Lincoln, ending slavery was always secondary to saving the Union and therewith his favored American System]
8. An alleged deal with the South by Hayes to get the presidency ends emancipation ("Reconstruction") but saves the American System, 1877 on
9. Federal debt increases enormously, reaching now unimaginable proportions

Melanchthon Smith's Protest

An excellent summary of the Anti-Federalist position and of the brazen effrontery of the Federalists is given by Melanchthon Smith. His remarks are quoted below, with divisions and headings added for ease of comprehension.

Melanchthon Smith: "Evils under Confederation Exaggerated; Constitution Must Be Drastically Revised before Adoption."[35]

1. *Review of Objections to the Articles.* It is insisted that the present situation of our country is such as not to admit of a delay in forming a new government. On this head all the powers of rhetoric and arts of description are employed to paint the condition of this country in the most hideous and frightful colors. We are told that agriculture is without encouragement and trade is languishing; private faith and credit are disregarded and public credit is prostrate; that the laws and magistrates are condemned and set at naught; that a spirit of licentiousness is rampant and ready to break over every bound set to it by the government; that private embarrassments and distresses invade the house of every man of middling property and insecurity threatens every man in affluent circumstances: in short, that we are in a state of the most grievous calamity at home and that we are contemptible abroad, the scorn of foreign nations and the ridicule of the world.

2. *Answer to the Objections.* But suffer me, my countrymen, to call your attention to a serious and sober estimate of the situation in which you are placed. . . . All classes and callings of men amongst us are protected in their pursuits and secured by the laws in the possession and enjoyment of the property obtained in those pursuits. . . . Neither the hand of private violence nor the more to be dreaded hand of legal oppression are reached out to distress us.

   It is true many individuals labor under embarrassments, but these are to be imputed to the unavoidable circumstances of things rather than to any defect in our governments. We have just emerged from a long and expensive war. During its existence few people were in a situation to increase their fortunes but many to diminish them. Debts contracted before the war were left unpaid. . . . Add to these that when the war was over too many of us, instead of reassuming our old habits of frugality and industry, took up the profuse use of foreign commodities. The country was deluged with articles imported from abroad and the cash of the country has been sent to pay for them, and still left us laboring under the weight of a huge debt to persons abroad. But will a new government relieve you from these? Your present condition is such as is common to take place after the conclusion of a war. Those who can remember our situation after the termination of the war [the French and Indian War, 1754–1763] preceding the last will recollect that our condition was similar to the present but time and industry soon recovered us from it. Money was scarce, the produce of the country much lower than it has been since the peace, and many individuals were extremely embarrassed with debts; and this happened although we did not experience the ravages, desolations, and loss of property that were suffered during the late war.

   With regard to our public and national concerns, what is there in our condition that threatens us with any immediate danger? We are at peace with all the world; no nation menaces us with war; nor are we called upon by any cause of sufficient importance to attack any nation. The state governments answer the purposes of preserving the peace and providing for present exigencies. Our condition as a nation is in no respect worse than it has been for several years past. Our public debt has been lessened in various ways and the western territory, which has been relied upon as a productive fund to discharge the national debt, has at length been brought to market and a considerable part actually applied to its reduction. I mention these things to show that there is nothing special in our present situation, as it respects our national affairs, that should induce us to accept the proffered system without taking sufficient time to consider and amend it.

3. *Review of and Answer to Reasons for Immediate Adoption of the Constitution.* But it is said that if we postpone the ratification of this system until the necessary amendments are first incorporated the consequence will be a civil war among the states. The idea of [New York] being attacked by the other states will appear visionary and chimerical if we consider that though several of them have adopted the new constitution yet the opposition to it has been numerous and formidable. The eastern states from whom we are told we have most to fear should a civil war be blown up would have full employ to keep in awe those who are opposed to it in their own governments. Massachusetts, after a long and dubious contest in their convention, has adopted it by an inconsiderable majority and in the very act has marked it with a stigma in its present form. No man of candor, judging from their public proceedings, will undertake to say on which side the majority of the people are. Connecticut, it is true, have acceded to it by a large majority of their convention, but it is a fact well known that a large proportion of the yeomanry of the country are against it. And it is equally true that a considerable part of those who voted for it in the convention wish to see it altered. In both these states the body of the common people, who always do the fighting of a country, would be more likely to fight against than for it. Can it then be presumed that a country divided among themselves upon a question where even the advocates for it admit the system they contend for needs amendments would make war upon a sister state? The idea is preposterous.

4. *Review of and Answer to Reasons for Delaying Amendments until after Adoption.* The reasonings made use of to persuade us that no alterations can be agreed upon previous to the adoption of the system are as curious as they are futile. It is alleged that there was great diversity of sentiments in forming the proposed constitution, that it was the effect of mutual concessions and a spirit of accommodation, and from hence it is inferred that further changes cannot be hoped for. I should suppose that the contrary inference was the fair one. If the convention who framed this plan were possessed of such a spirit of moderation and condescension as to be induced to yield to each other certain points and to accommodate themselves to each other's opinions and even prejudices, there is reason to expect that this same spirit will continue and prevail in a future convention and produce an union of sentiments on the points objected to.

There is more reason to hope for this because the subject has received a full discussion. . . . Previous to the meeting of the convention the subject of a new form of government had been little thought of and scarcely written upon at all. . . . It was never in the contemplation of one in a thousand of those who had reflected on the matter to have an entire change in the nature of our federal government. . . . I will venture to say that the idea of a government similar to the one proposed never entered the minds of the legislatures who appointed the convention and of but very few of the members who composed it until they had assembled and heard it proposed in that body; much less had the people any conception of such a plan until after it was promulgated. While it was agitated, the debates of the convention were kept an impenetrable secret and no opportunity was given for well informed men to offer their sentiments upon the subject.

The system was therefore never publicly discussed, nor indeed could be, because it was not known to the people until after it was proposed. Since then it has been the object of universal attention; it has been thought of by every reflecting man; it has been discussed in a public and private manner in conversation and in print; its defects have been pointed out and every objection to it stated; able advocates have written in its favor and able opponents have written against it. And what is the result? It cannot be denied but that the general opinion is that it contains material errors and requires important amendments.

5. *Uniformity of the Objections to the Constitution.* But it is further said that there can be no prospect of procuring alterations before it is acceded to, because those who oppose it do not agree among themselves with respect to the amendments that are necessary. To this I reply that this may be urged against attempting alterations after it is received with as much force as before, and therefore, if it concludes anything, it is that we must receive any system of government proposed to us because those who object to it do not entirely concur in their objections. But the assertion is not true to any considerable extent. There is a remarkable uniformity in the objections made to the constitution on the most important points. It is also worthy of notice that very few of the matters found fault with in it are of a local nature or such as affect any particular state; on the contrary, they are such as concern the principles of general liberty in which the people of New Hampshire, New York and Georgia are equally interested.

   a. It has been objected that the new system is calculated to and will effect such a consolidation of the states as to supplant and overturn the state governments.
   b. It has been said that the representation in the general legislature is too small to secure liberty or to answer the intention of representation.
   c. The constitution has been opposed because it gives to the legislature an unlimited power of taxation . . . a right to lay and collect taxes, duties, imposts and excises of every kind and description, and to any amount.
   d. The opposers to the constitution have said that it is dangerous because the judicial power may extend to many cases which ought to be reserved to the decision of the state courts, and because the right of trial by jury is not secured in the judicial courts of the general government in civil cases.
   e. The power of the general legislature to alter and regulate the time, place and manner of holding elections has been stated as an argument against the adoption of the system.

    f. The mixture of legislative, judicial, and executive powers in the Senate, the little degree of responsibility under which the great officers of government will be held, and the liberty granted by the system to establish and maintain a standing army without any limitation or restriction are also objected to the constitution.

    g. The opposers to the constitution universally agree in these objections.

6. *Appeal against Adoption. Untrustworthy Character of the Constitution's Supporters.* You have heard that both sides on this great question agree, that there are in it great defects; yet the one side tell you, choose such men as will adopt it and then amend it; while the other say, amend previous to its adoption. I have stated to you my reasons for the latter and I think they are unanswerable. Consider, you the common people, the yeomanry of the country, for to such I principally address myself, you are to be the principal losers if the constitution should prove oppressive. Attempts have been made and will be repeated to alarm you with the fear of consequences; but reflect there are consequences on both sides and none can be apprehended more dreadful than entailing on ourselves and posterity a government which will raise a few to the height of human greatness and wealth while it will depress the many to the extreme of poverty and wretchedness. [. . .]

The path in which you should walk is plain and open before you; be united . . . and direct your choice to such men as have been uniform in their opposition to the proposed system in its present form, or without proper alterations. In men of this description you have reason to place confidence, while on the other hand you have just cause to distrust those who urge the adoption of a bad constitution under the delusive expectation of making amendments after it is acceded to. Your jealousy of such characters should be the more excited when you consider that the advocates for the constitution have shifted their ground. When men are uniform in their opinions it affords evidence that they are sincere. When they are shifting it gives reason to believe they do not change from conviction. It must be recollected that when this plan was first announced to the public its supporters cried it up as the most perfect production of human wisdom, It was represented either as having no defects, or if it had, they were so trifling and inconsiderable that they served only as the shades in a fine picture to set off the piece to the greater advantage. One gentleman in Philadelphia went so far in the ardor of his enthusiasm in its favor as to pronounce that the men who formed it were as really under the guidance of Divine Revelation as was Moses, the Jewish lawgiver. Their language is now changed; the question has been discussed; the objections to the plan ably stated, and they are admitted to be unanswerable. The same men who held it almost perfect now admit it is very imperfect; that it is necessary it should be amended. The only question between us is simply this: shall we accede to a bad constitution under the uncertain prospect of getting it amended after we have received it, or shall we amend it before we adopt it? Common sense will point out which is the most rational, which is the most secure line of conduct.

Federalist High Crimes

A final point very much worth drawing attention to, though surprisingly not noted by Smith,[36] is that the US Constitution in its very wording does direct violence to the oath that all the states had made in the Articles. For the final article, number thirteen, reads as follows:

> Every State shall abide by the determination of the United States in Congress assembled, on all questions which by this confederation are submitted to them. And the Articles of this Confederation shall be inviolably observed by every State, and the Union shall be perpetual; nor shall any alteration at any time hereafter be made in any of them; unless such alteration be agreed to in a Congress of the United States, and be afterwards confirmed by the legislatures of every State.
>
> And Whereas it hath pleased the Great Governor of the World to incline the hearts of the legislatures we respectively represent in Congress, to approve of, and to authorize us to ratify the said Articles of Confederation and perpetual Union. Know Ye that we the undersigned delegates, by virtue of the power and authority to us given for that purpose, do by these presents, in the name and in behalf of our respective constituents, fully and entirely ratify and confirm each and every of the said Articles of Confederation and perpetual Union, and all and singular the matters and things therein contained: And we do further solemnly plight and engage the faith of our respective constituents, that they shall abide by the determinations of the United States in Congress assembled, on all questions, which by the said Confederation are submitted to them. And that the Articles thereof shall be inviolably observed by the States we respectively represent, and that the Union shall be perpetual.

Note here especially two things. First, the Articles are to be "inviolably observed" and will be "perpetual" unless alteration is agreed to by Congress and then confirmed by the legislature of every state. Second, the signers appeal to God for their acts and "plight and engage" the faith of their constituents to the determinations of Congress, and of their States to the observation of the Articles. Nothing, one would think, could be plainer, and yet Article Seven of the Constitution expressly violates the last part of the Articles and the plighted oath it contains. For Article Seven reads:

> The ratification of the conventions of nine states shall be sufficient for the establishment of this Constitution between the states so ratifying the same.

In other words, the Constitution simply dismisses the provision of the Articles that the Articles cannot be altered unless confirmed by the legislatures of all the states. Without even a word of excuse, the Constitution changes "legislatures" to "conventions" and "all" to "nine," and thereby treats the oath given in the Articles as so much empty air. The contempt that the framers of the Constitution thus showed not only to their fellows and their oath but also to God (for God is invoked as approving what the states did) is astonishing, and yet it has gone almost wholly unremarked by generations of Americans and historians. Recall too that the Constitution was put into effect in 1788, even though, first, Congress had not agreed to it (no agreement could be reached, and the document containing the Constitution was sent to the states without comment); and second, two of the states, North Carolina and Rhode Island, had refused to ratify it and did not ratify it until late 1789 in the case of North Carolina and mid-1790 in the case of Rhode Island. That the Constitution was established by oath-breaking and impiety is not the least sign of the reprehensible behavior of its founders and propagandists.

No doubt the Articles were not perfect and required some emendation, at least in certain matters, such as commerce for instance (though Smith suggests that no change was needed there either). What they did not require was wholesale abolition and replacement by a centralized system that was designed to increase centralization from the beginning. The fact was proved by the presidency of John Adams (if not already by that of Washington) and the outrageous way he attacked people in the United States through his Alien and Sedition Acts. These acts were famously repudiated by Jefferson and Madison in the Kentucky and Virginia resolutions, which roundly declared the acts to be unconstitutional (and remember that Jefferson was vice president at the time). Adams was not prepared to give way, and neither was Jefferson. Jefferson, however, won the fiercely contested presidential election of 1800 and then used his presidency to dismantle what Hamilton had done under Washington and what Adams did as president. Had Jefferson lost, it is a nice question whether civil war might not have broken out already under a second term of Adams. Indeed the Northern Federalists were threatening secession almost as soon as Jefferson was elected. They never finally acted on those threats, but their arguments became fodder for the Southern secessionists, and these latter did act on them in 1861, precipitating the civil war that the Anti-Federalists had predicted. Lincoln's aim in the civil war was what it had been throughout his political career, namely a huge increase in centralized power. He achieved it, and the Southerners who might otherwise have been expected to oppose it were happier to regain control over their former slave population through Reconstruction than to resist the encroachments of the federal government almost everywhere else.

Still, even Adams and Lincoln would be surprised at the encroachments that have been made in the United States in the twentieth and twenty-first centuries. The ability of the federal government to ignore constitutional provisions and to run up debts of mind-boggling proportions, without any serious resistance from either Congress or the states, is something that the founders of the Constitution would have been astonished to see. But this ability was arguably present from the beginning, as the Adams presidency proves, and was firmly cemented in place without risk of further serious opposition by Lincoln and his war. No president arose after Lincoln to undo his centralizing of federal power as Jefferson had done after Adams. Our present plight is a natural, if not entirely inevitable, development of what the US Constitution had set in place from the beginning, and that Adams and, more so, Lincoln did most to realize in their own time, and that Lincoln did most to enable the expansion of afterward. The fault, to quote Brutus in Shakespeare's *Julius Caesar* (Act 1, Scene 2) is not in our stars, but in ourselves, that we are underlings. Or, to be more precise, the fault is in the Founding Fathers.

A final quote, then, is worth adding here, from what Jefferson wrote about Adams and his Alien and Sedition Acts in the Kentucky Resolution of 1798.

> If the acts before specified should stand, these conclusions would flow from them—that the general government may place any act they think proper on the list of crimes, and punish it themselves, whether enumerated or not enumerated by the Constitution as cognizable by them; that they may transfer its cognizance to the President, or any other person, who may himself be the accuser, counsel, judge, and jury, whose suspicions may be the evidence, his order the sentence, his officer the executioner, and his breast the sole record of the transaction; that a very numerous and valuable description of the inhabitants of these states, being, by this precedent, reduced, as outlaws, to absolute dominion of one man, and the barriers of the Constitution thus swept from us all, no rampart now remains against the passions and the power of a majority of Congress, to protect from a like exportation, or other grievous punishment, the minority of the same body, the legislatures, judges, governors, and

counsellors of the states, nor their other peaceable inhabitants, who may venture to reclaim the constitutional rights and liberties of the states and people, or who for other causes, good or bad, may be obnoxious to the view, or marked by the suspicions, of the President, or be thought dangerous to his or their elections, or other interests, public or personal; that the friendless alien has been selected as the safest subject of a first experiment; but the citizen will soon follow, or rather has already followed; for already has a Sedition Act marked him as a prey: That these and successive acts of the same character, unless arrested on the threshold, may tend to drive these states into revolution and blood, and will furnish new calumnies against republican governments, and new pretexts for those who wish it to be believed that man cannot be governed but by a rod of iron; that it would be a dangerous delusion were a confidence in the men of our choice to silence our fears for the safety of our rights; that confidence is every where the parent of despotism; free government is founded in jealousy, and not in confidence; it is jealousy, and not confidence, which prescribes limited constitutions to bind down those whom we are obliged to trust with power; that our Constitution has accordingly fixed the limits to which, and no farther, our confidence may go; and let the honest advocate of confidence read the Alien and Sedition Acts, and say if the Constitution has not been wise in fixing limits to the government it created, and whether we should be wise in destroying those limits; let him say what the government is, if it be not a tyranny, which the men of our choice have conferred on the President, and the President of our choice has assented to and accepted, over the friendly strangers, to whom the mild spirit of our country and its laws had pledged hospitality and protection; that the men of our choice have more respected the bare suspicions of the President than the solid rights of innocence, the claims of justification, the sacred force of truth, and the forms and substance of law and justice.

Notes

1. These first three quotations are in Borden (1965: document #37).
2. Borden (1965: #4).
3. Borden (1965: #1).
4. Borden (1965: #38).
5. Borden (1965: #40).
6. Borden (1965: #13).
7. Borden (1965: #12).
8. Louis Guillaume Otto to Comte de Vergennes, New York, October 10, 1786, in Kaminski and Leffler (1998: 180–183).
9. Borden (1965: #2).
10. Borden (1965: ##18–20B).
11. Borden (1965: #4).
12. Borden (1965: #22).

13. Borden (1965: #22).
14. Borden (1965: #21).
15. Borden (1965: #10).
16. Borden (1965: #21).
17. Borden (1965: #85).
18. Borden (1965: #85).
19. Borden (1965: #13).
20. Borden (1965: #3).
21. Borden (1965: #29).
22. Borden (1965: #41–43p1).
23. Borden (1965: #63).
24. Borden (1965: #55).
25. Borden (1965: #63).
26. Borden (1965: #67).
27. Borden (1965: #36).
28. Borden (1965: #57).
29. Borden (1965: #23).
30. Borden (1965: #8).
31. Borden (1965: #54).
32. Borden (1965: #58).
33. Borden (1965: #25).
34. Borden (1965: #3).
35. Borden (1965: #85).
36. It is noted in passing by the anonymous author of document #2 in Borden (1965) and by the Federal Farmer in item 1.c in the first quotations from the Anti-Federalists at the beginning of this chapter.

9

Temporal and Spiritual Empire

Combining Solidarity and Subsidiarity

The previous chapter illustrated, with respect to the US experience, how centralization replaced, by systematic structural changes, the preexisting devolution of the Articles. These changes were consolidated by the civil war that subordinated the states to the federal government in a way that had not been realized before. The states had retained considerable ability to resist the federal government, and had done so through arguments and acts of nullification and secession. Both nullification and secession have been off the table since the Civil War (save for some rumblings in recent years). Another, and in some ways more significant, structural change was the Seventeenth Amendment to the Constitution, which required senators to be elected by the people of their state and not appointed by the state government itself. The amendment was justified on the grounds of eliminating corruption (since senators were often buying their seats through influence-peddling with state-based legislators), and perhaps rightly, but it had other and worse effects. When senators were appointed by state legislatures, they were beholden to those legislatures and to their interests, which were of course all toward keeping power in the hands of the states (where the state legislatures had authority) and out of the hands of the federal government (where state legislatures had no authority). But when senators were elected directly by the people, they were beholden to the people and had to find ways to satisfy popular demands, and the only way that federal senators can satisfy popular demands is by using the powers of the federal government (such as by bringing home federal funding or federally funded projects for local benefit). So the interest of senators now was not to maintain or increase state control but instead to maintain

171

and increase federal control. Their interest was centralization, not devolution. It is hard to overestimate the effects of this change, for they are clearly considerable. Whether the proponents of the Seventeenth Amendment, or some of them, intended this result or not is unclear, but it was the result all the same, and a worse result in terms of the balance of power between the federal and the local than was the corruption in senatorial appointments that the amendment was officially introduced to stop.

The solution cannot be simply to repeal the Seventeenth Amendment, for such a repeal will not go far enough. In fact the best way forward would seem to be some sort of return to the original Articles of Confederation. That these Articles were not at all defective in the way Federalist propagandists said was made clear in the previous chapter. That they might need to be changed in certain ways is perhaps also clear. But the overall structure of government contained in the Articles is sound and needs no change. The reason is the principles of subsidiarity and solidarity discussed before. What the United States has promoted under the Constitution is solidarity at the expense of subsidiarity, since states have lost power and are now beholden in many ways to the federal government and the largesse that the federal government dispenses (using, be it noted, the introduction of an income tax made constitutional by the Sixteenth Amendment, which is from the same period as the Seventeenth Amendment). But solidarity without subsidiarity is not really solidarity either, for since it removes or debilitates the intermediate authorities and structures between the individual and the federal government, it reduces political life to a single central authority on the one hand and uncoordinated and unconnected individuals on the other. So there is not so much solidarity here (which betokens union and support between individuals) as a single force of coercion on the one hand and isolated individuals on the other. Such a single force working on individuals is the very idea of the modern state, which, as argued before, is indistinguishable in form from despotism. The Articles, by contrast, had solidarity with subsidiarity, first because federal authority operated on the states and not on individuals (and so operated on structures that were uniting individuals and not isolating them), and second because it left many things in the hands of the states, such as defense, the militia, the army, commerce, and so forth, that have now been monopolized by the federal government.

Roman Empires

The Articles, however, are not the only example of solidarity combined with subsidiarity that theorists and historians can appeal to. As good if not a better example would be diffuse empires where subordinate authorities have real and independent control over local areas but subject to a central authority that has some but not absolute powers of intervention and arbitration and, where necessary, coercion. The Hellenistic world had some of these features,[1] as did also the old pagan Roman Empire, though in fact Rome, and later Constantinople, had larger powers of intervention and control than is desirable. The way, in fact, in which governors appointed by Rome to the provinces used their authority to fleece the provinces is well known and is painfully illustrated by the case of Verres, against whom Cicero wrote his famous Verrine orations. Verres, however, was only one of many, if lesser, instances. The provinces directly under the control of the emperor during the imperial period seem on the whole to have been better managed, in part because the governors, being servants of the emperor and not appointees of the Senate and being required often to engage in military actions to preserve the empire's frontiers, had to be competent and responsible to be effective. It was in the emperor's interest as emperor to make sure the provinces were well ruled, since bad rule would likely precipitate inroads from hostile tribes, if nothing else.[2]

However, perhaps the most extensive and, ultimately, most successful instance of the combination of subsidiarity and solidarity is the Holy Roman Empire, as it is now called, though it referred to itself as the Roman Empire simply, for it understood itself to be a continuation or transfer of the pagan empire (*translatio imperii*). Relations with the eastern emperor at Constantinople were sometimes rocky but on the whole peaceful. At all events, it is less relations with the East than certain structures in the West that matter for the present analysis. The structures in question have been given the general name of feudalism, though the accuracy of the term is disputed and anyway carries a negative connotation. Perhaps it is better to talk simply of the medieval settlement, without further specification. No doubt there were imperfections and problems with the medieval settlement as actually lived (as is true of any human institution), but the idea, and sometimes the practice, can be used at least for example's sake.[3]

The essence of the medieval settlement may be said to be the mutual bonding between persons through a mutual exchange of rights and duties. Vassals, for instance, had possession, even hereditary possession, of some part of a lord's land, and this land the vassal was to care for, providing sustenance from it to the lord and to himself, such as through the so-called manorial system of peasants and serfs who, while tied to the land and to service, had rights too that could be enforced in manorial courts. The vassal, and even peasants, would also have duties of military service when called on and also of giving advice in councils summoned by the lord. Thus vassals and peasants had to have and be practiced in the use of weapons, for they were the lord's army and indeed his police force to keep the peace. There was no independent army or police separate from the people themselves and the leadership of the lord. The lord in turn had duties to protect the vassal and peasants and preserve them in possession and use of the land. There could be, and were, several levels of vassalage and lordship, since lesser lords were in a sense vassals of lords above them. This relation of vassal and lord extended in principle up to the emperor, who was the chief lord and of whom kings could be vassals, as the lords were vassals of the kings. The position of emperor, in the case of the Holy Roman Empire, was elected not inherited, but elected only by certain princes or kings (known as electors). The emperor was, therefore, not popularly elected and did not engage in expensive election campaigns as modern candidates for president or prime minister do. He also served for life, unless he resigned or was formally deposed. Nevertheless, in all cases and at all levels of the feudal system, the idea and practice was the mutual giving and receiving of rights and duties. The system was naturally rather static, since the rights and duties were inherited and sons succeeded to fathers in the exercise of them. But it was also very stable and effective.

In addition to these relations of peasants, vassals, and lords, there were towns whose inhabitants were not directly part of the agricultural system, for many towns enjoyed a certain independence from lordly oversight and authority. The towns were where the arts and commerce flourished and so where lords and vassals could receive the benefits of this art and commerce for the management and development of farming and pasturage and armaments. Rivalry naturally could emerge between town and country, but the mutual benefits (the fruits of the land for the town from the country, and the fruits of art and commerce for the country from the town) were considerably larger and, if left to work their effects, would no doubt moderate and mitigate the rivalry. Only as the towns and cities expanded and were able to take greater advantage of expanding foreign trade did the system begin to break down, and the country became more beholden to the town and less an independent authority. Nevertheless, in France the system lasted up to the French Revolution, and in Germany, rather longer.

Besides the towns and the vassals and lords in the country, there was also another class of persons who were in some ways outside the system of lords and vassals and operated as an independent check upon it. This class of persons was the clergy, or the bishops and priests and other clerics in the Church. The Church was the locus of the spiritual power, just as the lords and emperor were the locus of the temporal power. The two powers were distinct, and each had its own court and system of rule. Clerics, for instance, were subject to clerical courts and not temporal ones, and clerical lands were not subject to taxation or control by temporal lords. These lands could sometimes be extensive, as they were in the case of the great monasteries, but almost always as a result of gifts to the Church by lay lords and owners. The Church, of course, had great authority in all people's lives, since it taught the truths of the faith, suppressed theological errors, dispensed the sacraments, inculcated the duties of faith and morals, arbitrated in secular disputes (at the request of temporal princes), imposed the peace and truce of God, and the like. As a result the medieval system, as actually lived, was subject to a host of checks and balances founded on reciprocal rights and duties that extended through the whole of society. At the same time, it had multiple levels of appeal in cases of disputes, from peasants to manorial courts, from vassals to lords, from lords to the emperor, and also, where necessary, from these temporal rulers to the spiritual power of the Church. The whole was a complex and multilayered network of subsidiary powers related to higher powers, and of solidarity within and between its different parts, for peasants, serfs, and vassals were in solidarity by common class with each other respectively, by rights and duties with lords and emperor, bishops and pope, and by common faith with everyone through the Church.

The actual practice of the medieval system should not be idealized. It had its defects, as do all human institutions. But it should not be dismissed. In particular the idea of it should not be dismissed, and the idea rather than the practice is what is of relevance. For the aim here is to lay out a system of human relations in community that manifests the principles of subsidiarity and solidarity. Other and different systems could doubtless be worked out, but an actual example, however imperfect, helps more to make the idea real and show its concrete possibility.

There is one matter, however, that needs repeat discussion and emphasis, and this matter is the separation of the temporal and spiritual powers. To follow prior argument (in Chapters Four and Five), that there are such powers and that they are in principle distinct, even if the same persons may exercise both, is entailed by the very idea of human community and of its striving for the comprehensive good. Human community, if it is to work, needs to satisfy both the needs of the body and the needs of the soul. The body and its needs, which include peace and physical safety as well as sustenance and shelter, fall under the temporal power and are strictly within human competence to determine and regulate. The need or striving for the comprehensive good will fall under the same human competence, provided there is no superhuman revelation and authority given in addition. Without such revelation and authority, while there will be those in society deputed to the care of the soul (educators, priests, seers, prophets, and the like), those so deputed will have no authority that does not itself arise from human nature and its principles. So they will have no authority that transcends the competence of the temporal power. In point of fact, however, almost all priestly classes have claimed authority from revelation, for they have claimed to be in direct contact with the gods and to be able to convey the commands and wishes of the gods to men. The history and literature of the old Greek and Roman worlds furnish rich examples of these facts.

Consequently there have been in every society some members of it whose authority and power is claimed not from man but from the gods. This power is thus distinct and separate in its kind from the power that does come from man. Even if kings claimed to possess both powers, as they often did, this claim did not deny but instead emphasized the difference in the powers. For the king did not wield spiritual power because he was king but because he was also priest, or even the highest priest, through whom the gods were pleased to convey their will.

This state of affairs was not changed in idea but was changed in fact by the advent of a single revelation authoritative for all men. As stated before (in Chapter Four), if a revelation is given, it must not only come from God but also be guaranteed and preserved in its integrity by God. If God himself does not directly exercise this guarantee, it has to be exercised by people deputed by God for the purpose. These people will, as such, be a separate body exercising a separate power within society. But they must be united in some way, so that the one revelation is everywhere taught and practiced the same, and they must in the last instance be endowed with infallibility in their teaching.

A body of men charged with the deposit of revelation and of handing it on without corruption to others must be infallible, as already argued, or else no one can ever be sure that the teaching is indeed uncorrupted. There can be no right of private interpretation, therefore, unless there is also a right of private infallibility. But who has the infallibility and in what way is not for men to determine but instead for God, since it is only God who can confer such infallibility. So it is evident that a book, even if it contains the revelation, can never be the infallible authority. A book needs authentication, so that all know that the book does indeed contain the revelation and not something else; and it needs interpretation, because no book fully explains itself. It must be read and correctly understood, which is to say that it must be correctly interpreted. The infallible authority, therefore, can only be God himself or those persons he has expressly deputed to the task.

The persons so deputed would, of necessity, have to make public claim for themselves of such a grant of infallibility, for the grant would only have been made, if it was made, so as to be used publicly, for the benefit of all. They would also have to give some coherent account, backed up by revealed evidence, of how and to what sort of persons God made such a grant. For only God is naturally infallible, and others are so, if they are, only by divine decree, and divine decree can only be known, if it is known, by revelation. Accordingly only those who make these claims can, even in principle, also make a rational claim to teach religious truth authoritatively for all men. Others who claim such authority but do not claim infallibility, or can give no coherent account of how they were granted it, refute themselves. For they openly confess that they do not meet the conditions on which alone could rest the right to teach revealed truth authoritatively. They are claiming, then, an authority and a right that they cannot possibly have, and so they are claiming an authority and a right that they can be denied, and forcibly denied, if need be. The spiritual authority, since it is charged with guarding the truth of religion, would certainly have the duty to deny them this right; and by the same token, the temporal authority would have the duty to carry out the decisions of the spiritual authority where the spiritual authority was unable to carry them out on its own. This conclusion follows from the idea of community often repeated above, namely that it is a striving for the comprehensive truth and that this comprehensive truth can, in the last resort, only be vouchsafed by God. So the temporal authority, since it rules the community for the common good of the community, must act for the good of this striving, and so must act to preserve, protect, and enforce the spiritual authority and its decrees where this authority can be definitely known (as it can be so known, above all, through miracles and the like).

The spiritual authority can, in turn, act to support the temporal authority, above all through the teaching of morals and of obedience to legitimate temporal rulers. But it can also, to some extent, guard against despotism or tyranny by teaching the justice of rule, the necessity of not obeying immoral commands, and, even in extreme but carefully defined cases, the necessity of using force against tyrants and unjust rulers, either to expel them or make them desist from their tyranny.[4] It can also serve as an accepted and impartial arbiter in the case of disputes between rulers and countries. Clerics, and notably Bartolomé de las Casas, were instrumental in mitigating some of the savagery and injustice of the conquerors in the New World and in ensuring fair treatment of the indigenous peoples.[5] The role of the king of Spain in promulgating and upholding these laws (not entirely successfully, but nevertheless really) and in serving as a court of appeal against the conquerors, who acknowledged the king of Spain as overlord, seems to have been of no little value to the indigenous peoples while the king of Spain retained authority. When Spanish authority was overthrown by the various liberation movements, so called, in South and Central America, this protection and appeal for the indigenous peoples was removed, and not, it seems, to their advantage.

But however it may be with the truth of these claims (subject naturally to historical dispute), the idea they illustrate, at least in theory, is plain. For the feudal system, with its clear but in principle cooperative division between the temporal and spiritual authorities, shows how subsidiarity and solidarity can be jointly observed over large tracts of territory and between rulers of greatly varying secular interests and ambitions. It can serve, if only in idealized form, as a model for similar practices, even in our own day.

If we return, then, to the example of the United States and the unjustly maligned Articles of Confederation, we can see how the system set up by the Articles, or some analogous system, can serve even now for combining subsidiarity with solidarity to the benefit of all. There will be some overarching temporal and moral authority, operating not directly or immediately on lesser authorities but instead indirectly and by appeal and moral suasion and, if necessary, the marshaling of other forces to ensure compliance. This authority was well exercised by kings and emperors, but it need not be. Collective councils and judges (of the sort envisaged by the Articles for arbitrating disputes between the states) could serve the same purpose. But these councils would need to possess moral and not just coercive authority, so that their decisions would naturally command respect, even before any resort to armed force. Of course there is never any guarantee here. Human beings and human affairs, whether temporal or spiritual, are forever threatened by the passions for fame and money and power, and holding these passions in proper check is an endless and always necessary task. The point, nevertheless, is to set up some system that at least in principle will perform the needed role of solidarity without destroying subsidiarity. The US Constitution signally failed to perform the needed role.

Modern Unions

One might say that this sort of authority can be supplied in our times by international bodies like the United Nations, and the European Union in Europe or the fledgling African Union in Africa. It would be nice if things were so, but these bodies lack much in the way of moral check and often become tools for ambition and greater centralized control, thus destroying subsidiarity in almost all its forms, replacing a measured and human government with thinly disguised autocracies and lusts for wealth and power. The losses have been greater than the gains, despite the hopes with which these bodies were first introduced. Part of the problem, if not the main problem, is the introduction of the modern idea of representation (which, as noted before in Chapter Two, is really a clash of conflicting wills and not a moral check) and the worldwide phenomenon of elections and election campaigns. What is needed is not representation of clashing interests but representation of wisdom and moral authority. Such representation can as easily be provided by hereditary monarchs as by elected leaders, if not better. A monarch's interest is more likely to be the interest of the country, not personal success in elections. Monarchs serve for life, are not subject to the corrupting pressures of election campaigns, and win honor and renown for the goodness of their rule, not their electoral success or their satisfying of special and partial interests through their continuing need to win votes and financial support. Still, the same effect secured by hereditary or elected kings can perhaps be secured by other institutional structures, such as bodies of arbiters and judges. The trick here is to endow these arbiters and judges with moral authority and not just coercive authority. A good king who serves for life can more easily win such authority, because he can also more easily win affection and honor from the people. Provided kings themselves exist in systems of subsidiarity with higher kings or emperors, they can be a welcome safeguard for both subsidiarity and solidarity to the benefit of all, especially of the weak and poor. The system altogether failed to hold, for example, in the case of Henry VIII in England because of his overthrow of subsidiarity or limited subordination to emperor and pope (for Henry made himself head of the Church as well as head of state). It also failed to hold in the case of the United States after the overthrow of the Articles and their replacement by the Constitution.

One might also say in response to the line of argument here that a political arrangement that gives special authority to the spiritual power, and in particular to something like the Catholic Church, will just regenerate the wars of religion precipitated by the Protestant revolt from Rome (from both emperor and pope), so we must have an arrangement where such wars can be prevented as far as possible. The only plausible such arrangement, and the one that did actually succeed in the end, was the modern liberal state, where the spiritual authority exists but is confined to the private sphere, and all have liberty to accept it or not.

First, however, the wars of religion were not principally caused by religion, or not by religious heterodox opinions. For such opinions had long existed previously but had not caused anything like the wars of religion. The main change at the time of Protestantism seems to have been that various princes and lords joined, and supported with armed force, the Protestant religious leaders. The wars of religion were thus political wars and wars for power, rather than religious wars. Second, the liberal arrangement, even if it stopped the wars of religion (which is anyway questionable), has brought with it something worse, namely universal despotic power (as argued in Chapter One above). Third, the liberal arrangement is false in its understanding of the point and purpose of human community, since it relegates to the private sphere what should be at the center of public life, namely the striving for the comprehensive truth. Fourth, while anyone is of course free to reject the authority of the proclaimed religious power in spiritual matters, one should do so for good reasons. But there are no good reasons to reject an infallible revelation infallibly taught (if there is one) and proved to be so by innumerable miracles and other supernatural acts. If there is an infallible teacher of an infallible revelation, and if the fact can be proved by miracles and the like, it is irrational to reject that teacher from playing a chief, or the chiefest, role in community life. Certainly it is irrational to reject such a thing as a matter of principle, in the way liberalism does, rather than as a matter of fact. For since the thing is, in principle, possible (it can hardly be ruled out *a priori*, if only because the existence of a god who reveals cannot be ruled out *a priori*), no political arrangement may rationally be adopted that prevents the thing, even when fully authenticated by miracles, from playing the role in community that is proper to it.

It may be said in response to these considerations that whether the Protestants had right on their side or not in the wars of religion, those wars did tear Europe apart and did break the unity of Christendom under the one pope and the one emperor. Once this break had happened, only something like the liberal arrangement of political community was likely to ensure a lasting peace. The claim is doubtful, if only because, as facts show, the state created by liberalism has been the cause of equally destructive wars, if not of worse wars. The state, because of its monopoly of coercion over the whole of society, has introduced the phenomenon of total war, where everyone and everything are at stake. Wars may be unavoidable in human life, but total war is avoidable and will be avoided, or more likely avoided, if there is no state. Besides, as noted before, if there are causes worth dying for or wars worth fighting, religious ones would seem the chiefest, since God's cause (if it really is his cause) must be greater than any merely human one. Finally, even if we allow that liberal theory and the state it creates are now the condition for peace, they are the condition only relative to existing circumstances, or only *faute de mieux*. If the conditions change, there will be no need for the state to keep the peace. To make the state and liberalism the condition *in principle* has no warrant either in fact or in theory.

What human community needs is an arrangement that systematically introduces and preserves the principles of subsidiarity and solidarity. Liberal theory and practice do neither but in the end destroy both principles. The medieval arrangement, for all its faults, did do much to preserve both principles, through a host of varying differences in social existence: differences of rights and privileges and duties; an ultimate court of appeal in politics and morals and religion; freedom for subordinate communities to manage their own affairs as they wished, subject to the differentiation of rights and privileges long hallowed by tradition and particular preference; civil order and peace preserved by these communities within themselves and between others, as arbitrated and enforced by clear ultimate authorities; the conscious orientation of all community life to striving for the comprehensive truth; and a political liberty governed and preserved by overarching moral teaching and suasion and not first, or at all, by the overarching, coercive surveillance and intrusion of despotic power. The medieval arrangement put character and not structure first, focused society on concern with humanity's striving and supreme goal, emphasized moral teaching over sheer force, permitted the diffusion of power and authority through all ranks, and did not concentrate it all in the despotism, always incipient and increasingly realized, of the one monopolistic state.

This appeal to the medieval arrangement, or to other arrangements of loose empire with strong local differences and independence as opposed to the despotic liberal state, is not put forward as nostalgia for a lost past. It is put forward as a way of stimulating a more imaginative and free-ranging approach to the treatment of contemporary political questions. In fact, the past combination of extensive empire with the multiplication of local differences could be imitated today precisely by a rethinking of the notion of the liberal state. For the state of nature doctrine (whence the notion of the liberal state principally derives) can be reformed into an argument for loose empire combined with strong communities. All one needs to do is to make the state of nature doctrine apply not to individuals (the way Hobbes and Locke and others did), but rather to communities. So instead of individuals forming a state by means of a social contract, let communities form a federation or league by means of defensive alliances, not unlike the way the former colonies in the United States did by means of the Articles of Confederation. Such alliances may differ in many ways and embrace more or fewer things, and the alliances might depend on a superior power as well as on member communities (the way the medieval arrangement depended on the emperor, or the way the settlement in Greece after the battle of Chaeronea depended on Philip of Macedon and then on his son Alexander the Great[6]). No matter. The basic idea remains the same, and it is the idea that is important, rather than the details.

Such a way of applying the state of nature doctrine would be not only better but also more historically accurate. For it is manifest that men do not exist first, or at all, as individuals but rather as belonging to communities. Not only are we all born into some community, such as the family or the equivalent, but with few and largely irrelevant exceptions, we all remain and function as parts of one or more communities for the whole of life. It is as such parts of communities that we live and act, that we form visions of the good and pursue them, and that, in the service of these visions, we love and hate, fight and die. Community is too large a fact in human life and too intimately bound up with every individual's sense of being and well-being to be set aside in the discussion of politics. The error in the state of nature doctrine (and the error too in the theory of the liberal state, or of the state generally) lies as much in the object the doctrine is made to work on as in the doctrine itself. Shift this object from individual to community, and the doctrine can be shifted to an argument for a loose or federated empire of communities and not an argument for the modern state.

The shift does not entirely preserve the state of nature doctrine, for it does not entirely preserve the idea that the comprehensive good is one thing and political rule another. The comprehensive good may indeed now find its place in communities as opposed to individuals, but the overarching imperial authority will not be or necessarily aim to be neutral with respect to rival comprehensive visions of the good. For, at least the comprehensive good of a public divine revelation would make legitimate claim to support and protection from the imperial authority, over and against concerted or organized opposition, whether from communities or individuals. But the idea that the imperial authority should be loose or minimal because it is directed at communities rather than individuals—and so at communities where local rule would decide local problems—would prevent the emergence of the tyranny and despotism of liberalism and the state. It would foster instead precisely the combination of solidarity and subsidiarity that has been argued for above. Solidarity would be realized through the imperial authority and subsidiarity through the constituent communities. The goods of both principles, so necessary for a genuinely human politics, would thus more surely and fully be realized.[7]

War and Peace: A Modern Spiritual Authority in Practice

There is no need, however, to leave this series of contentions, or their historical illustrations, at the level of theory or the distant past. The ancient and medieval Roman empires may have long disappeared, but not everything from them has been lost. In particular the papacy remains. It lacks now much independent power of coercion, but its moral authority has surprisingly remained intact and is now in some ways greater than it was before. The fact was made especially manifest under Pope St. John Paul II.[8] It is arguable that his influence, especially in Poland, and his global status as pope were decisive in the downfall of communism in Eastern Europe. His teaching and counsel were not always followed (such as, in particular, over the Iraq War under

President George Bush, which the pope opposed), but if that teaching is carefully studied, it lays out, in clear and comprehensive terms, compelling solutions to a whole host of modern problems related to war and peace. If peoples and politicians were to imitate their medieval counterparts and pay heed to what he said, they would win both lasting peace and lasting honor. An analysis of John Paul's teaching, first in relation to the Iraq War and then more generally, will amply illustrate the fact.

In the run-up to this war, the position taken against it by the hierarchy of the Catholic Church had become a matter of much debate. The debate was only in part about the Iraq War itself. A deeper question concerned the principles of just war and whether what Church leaders were saying about a possible invasion of Iraq was or was not compatible with those principles. But while it is clear that some bishops opposed the war because they thought it would fail to meet the conditions of just war,[9] it is far from clear that the pope was moved by the same reason. In January of 2003, in an address to the diplomatic corps, he said the following:

> "*NO TO WAR!*" War is not always inevitable. It is always a defeat for humanity. International law, honest dialogue, solidarity between States, the noble exercise of diplomacy: these are methods worthy of individuals and nations in resolving their differences. I say this as I think of those who still place their trust in nuclear weapons and of the all-too-numerous conflicts which continue to hold hostage our brothers and sisters in humanity. . . . And what are we to say of the threat of a war which could strike the people of Iraq, the land of the Prophets, a people already sorely tried by more than twelve years of embargo? War is never just another means that one can choose to employ for settling differences between nations. As the Charter of the United Nations Organization and international law itself remind us, war cannot be decided upon, even when it is a matter of ensuring the common good, except as the very last option and in accordance with very strict conditions, without ignoring the consequences for the civilian population both during and after the military operations [2003b].

On March 16 of the same year, he spoke as follows:

> I would also like to remind the member countries of the United Nations, and especially those who make up the Security Council, that the use of force represents the last recourse, after having exhausted every other peaceful solution, in keeping with the well-known principles of the UN Charter. That is why, in the face of the

> *tremendous consequences* that an international military operation would have for the population of Iraq and for the balance of the Middle East region, already sorely tried, and for the extremisms that could stem from it, I say to all: There is still time to negotiate; there is still room for peace, it is never too late to come to an understanding and to continue discussions [2003c].

Reflecting on the war in subsequent years, he said, "In recent months peace has been overwhelmed by the events in the *Middle East* that appears once again as a region of disputes and wars. The many attempts made by the Holy See to avoid the grievous war in Iraq are already known" (2004b, emphasis in original). And again:

> As a supreme good and the condition for attaining many other essential goods, peace is the dream of every generation. Yet how many wars and armed conflicts continue to take place—between States, ethnic groups, peoples and groups living in the same territory! From one end of the world to the other, they are claiming countless innocent victims and spawning so many other evils! Our thoughts naturally turn to different countries in the Middle East, Africa, Asia, and Latin America, where recourse to arms and violence has not only led to incalculable material damage, but also fomented hatred and increased the causes of tension, thereby adding to the difficulty of finding and implementing solutions capable of reconciling the legitimate interests of all the parties involved [2005b].

These remarks make clear the pope's opposition to the war, but they do not openly say that the war was unjust or failed to meet the conditions of just war. The pope adverts, to be sure, to elements of just war theory (such as that war is always a last resort), yet he refers, in support, to the UN Charter and to international law, not to that theory. Further, if we look at what he did expressly say, we will be inclined to conclude that just war theory was secondary or even irrelevant to his thinking. Just war theory does not say *no* to war, as the pope did, nor does it say that war is always a defeat for humanity. On the contrary, it says *yes* to war, namely when the conditions for a just war are met. By the same token, it also says, or at any rate implies, that a just war, justly waged, can be a victory and not a defeat for humanity, insofar as it can rid humanity of the crimes and tyranny of evil men.

We should not press these remarks of the pope too far. He was doubtless speaking pastorally rather than doctrinally, and appealing to what he thought his audience might more readily respond to rather than making a contribution to Church teaching. However, even pastoral remarks are supposed to cohere with such teaching. Presumably, too, his pastoral duty is not only to urge peace but also to guide thinking, and he would fail to do the latter if he urged peace at the cost of confusing minds. Now, in fact, his appeals for peace were giving guidance to thought, though not in ways that fit neatly into traditional just war theory. His thinking was neither pacifist—as some hoped and others feared at the time—nor the opposite, but instead it was transcendent to both. Indeed here, as throughout his life, John Paul II was initiating ways of dealing with contemporary problems that altogether escaped the terms of the debates that raged around him.

That John Paul II was, first, not a pacifist is evident from what he said on the topic of war over the long years of his papacy. We can begin with the quotation just given about the Iraq War, namely that a war can rightly be decided on when it is the last resort and meets the requisite conditions, for this manifestly implies that a war can be necessary and just. But lest this concession seem to be merely theoretical, not to be regarded as a live option, consider next remarks he made in his message for the 33rd World Day of Peace. Speaking of the horrors of the century then ending, he declared, "At times brutal and systematic violence, aimed at the very extermination or enslavement of entire peoples and regions, has had to be countered by armed resistance" (2000a). That the pope considered such resistance not only necessary, as this quotation indicates, but also *just* is shown by what he said in his message for the fiftieth anniversary of victory of the Allies over the Germans at Monte Cassino. This victory clearly stirred deep emotions in the Polish pope, since many of his countrymen had fought and died there on the side of the Allies. He much lauded the sacrifice of these Poles, described the battle they engaged in as a defense of the Christian tradition of Europe and of the European spirit, hailed the dead as martyrs of freedom, pronounced the cause for which they died holy, and declared the decision of these and all Poles back in 1939 to fight Hitler right (1994b). These are not the words and sentiments of a pacifist; they are the words and sentiments of a militant Polish patriot.

But what, we may ask, were Polish troops doing in Italy, where, far from their native land, they were helping to expel the forces of a nation with which the Italian government had but lately had a military compact, and with which, but for the Allied invasion some months earlier, it would still have had? If the Poles could justly fight to expel the Germans from Italy, and fight moreover, as the war progressed, to overthrow the German government in Germany, then if John Paul II thought there was something wrong about the Americans, along with other foreigners, fighting to expel Iraqis from Kuwait and, later, to overthrow the Iraqi government in Iraq, his thought could not have been that it is wrong to use force to overthrow governments in foreign lands. The comparison is of small things with great, to be sure, but the point of the comparison is to show that if John Paul II opposed the Iraq wars, as he did, the ground of his opposition could in no wise be that he thought wars, even wars of invasion and government overthrow, are never just or never necessary.

Other quotations prove the same. In his Angelus for March 16, he said, "We know well that peace is not possible at any price" (2003c). In his message for the 35th World Day of Peace, he said of terrorism that it was "a true crime against humanity," and that there exists therefore "a right to defend oneself against terrorism" (2002a). In a homily for the jubilee of the armed forces and the police, he said that the duty of these forces to build justice and peace sometimes involves "concrete initiatives to disarm the aggressor," and he referred to the idea of humanitarian interference, which, he said, "after the failure of efforts by politics and the instruments of non-violent defense, is a last resort in order to stay the hand of the unjust aggressor" (2000b). Again, in his message for the 37th World Day of Peace, when he said of the fight against terrorism that it could not be limited "solely to repressive and punitive operations" and insisted that "the use of force, even when necessary, be accompanied by . . . analysis of the reasons behind terrorist attacks" (2004a), he was clearly allowing that repressive and punitive measures were permissible and that the use of force could indeed be necessary. John Paul II's credentials, therefore, as a believer in and exponent of just war seem unimpeachable.

What, then, are we to make of his oft-repeated cries of "no to war" and "war never again," and of his oft-repeated assertion that "war is a defeat for humanity" (1995b; 2000a; 2002b; 2003b; 2004c; 2004d)? How could he set himself against all future wars if he believed that wars can be, and that some wars have been, both necessary and just?

The answer would seem to be, paradoxically enough, that he set himself against all future wars precisely *because* they can be necessary and just. Hints of this paradox, and of its meaning, can already be found in the last quotations given above, but others make both points more clearly. Take his message for the 37thWorld Day of Peace, when he declared:

> By itself, justice is not enough. . . . [F]or the establishment of true peace in the world, *justice must find its fulfillment in charity.* . . . [J]ustice is frequently unable to free itself from rancor, hatred and even cruelty. . . . Indeed, it can even betray itself, unless it is open

187

to that deeper power which is love. . . . For this reason I have often reminded Christians and all people of good will that *forgiveness is needed* for solving the problems of individuals and peoples. . . . [A] solution to the grave problems which for too long have caused suffering for the peoples of [the Middle East] will not be found until a decision is made to transcend the logic of simple *justice* and to be open also to the logic of *forgiveness* [2004a, emphasis in original].

These statements are again, no doubt, pastoral ones, and not, or not primarily, doctrinal, but they do help to unravel the above paradox, whose meaning will thus be that even just wars must, for John Paul II, be opposed because, or insofar as, they are *simply* just. *Simple* justice never goes far enough, and so while a just war (the invasion of Iraq, let us suppose) may solve the immediate problem (removal of a dangerous tyranny), it can never solve the larger and more pervasive problems (ambition among the few, poverty and ignorance among the many, hatred and fear among both) that made a war just and necessary in the first place. But of course all wars, insofar as they are actual fighting or actual military engagements, can never be more than cases of *simple* justice. Wars, qua military engagements, are acts of killing and destruction, even if, in accord with the principles of justice, they are kept in due measure and proportioned to subsequent peace. Moreover, such acts, while they can remove a military threat or repel or punish an invader, can never repair damage or comfort the bereaved or supply the needs of the wounded, starving, and homeless. These things belong not to the fighting, but instead to what follows or accompanies the fighting, whether as done by the soldiers themselves or by others specially deputed to the task. If these things are not done, or not done well, or if the fighting has made them incurably worse, then the war has ended only to be followed, sooner or later, by another war that may be no less just, and no more capable of solving the underlying problems, than the first one was.

In fact, John Paul II's views about the first and second world wars were exactly along these lines. In his message for the fiftieth anniversary of the end of World War II in Europe, he said:

We can still appreciate the stern warning which Pope Pius XII of venerable memory voiced in August 1939, on the very eve of that tragic conflict, in a last-minute attempt to prevent recourse to arms: "The danger is imminent, but there is yet time. Nothing is lost with peace; all may be lost with war. Let men return to mutual understanding. Let them begin negotiations anew." Pius XII was here following in the footsteps of Pope Benedict XV who, after making every effort to prevent the First World War, did not hesitate to brand it "a useless slaughter." I myself reaffirmed these principles when on 20 January 1991, on the eve of the Gulf War, I observed that "the tragic situation of recent days makes it even more evident that problems are not resolved with arms, but that new and greater tensions among peoples are thus created" [1995b].

Again, in his message for the 33rd World Day of Peace, he said:

> The twentieth century bequeaths to us above all else a warning: *wars are often the cause of further wars* because they fuel deep hatreds, create situations of injustice and trample upon people's dignity and rights. Wars generally do not resolve the problems for which they are fought and therefore, in addition to causing horrendous damage, they prove ultimately futile. *War is a defeat for humanity* [2000a, emphasis in original].

But if John Paul II applied these remarks also to World War II, which he judged to be a just war on the part of the Allies, then it is clear that he held the view that even just wars are defeats for humanity, that they often cause further wars, that they generally do not resolve the problems they are fought for, and that they prove ultimately futile. Lest this view appear an outrageous one to hold about World War II, let us recall (as John Paul II insisted on us recalling) that, as far as Poland and Eastern Europe were concerned, World War II did not end in 1945 but in 1989, with the fall of communism, and that 1945 was, for them, indeed futile and a defeat.

What we might say, then, is that in John Paul II's eyes, even just and necessary wars always come too late. If a situation has arisen where a war is necessary and just, the reason can only be that not enough was being done beforehand to stop that situation from arising. Moreover, while in the situation recourse to arms has become the right response, it can never be a sufficient response. It cannot, for instance, solve the problems that made the enemy an enemy or that brought him to arms in the first place. Moreover, if the only problem solved is the immediate one that fighting by itself can solve, and if the others are left untouched or even exacerbated, as they almost always are, then the war, however just, has but prepared the way for a further war, which may also, when it comes, be just. Surely, pleads John Paul II, the twentieth century has provided enough evidence for that proposition. If so, then the only rational response to the threat of war, even a just war, is that taken to World War I by Pope Benedict XV, to World War II by Pope Pius XII, and to the Iraq War by Pope John Paul II—namely to go on pleading right up to the last minute, and even perhaps beyond the last minute, that negotiations are still possible, that peace can still be kept, that the war, if started, will be but another defeat for humanity.

Well, one might say, such ideas sound rather splendid in theory, but how are they going to work in practice? Did John Paul II believe, like Neville Chamberlain perhaps, that Hitler could have been stopped by negotiations? Or did he believe that Saddam Hussein could have been thus induced to fulfill his international obligations or to give up his tyranny? Surprisingly, he does seem to have believed something of this sort, although he had in mind means more penetrating and far-reaching than mere negotiations.

In order to find and apply a cure for something, one must first identify its causes. Now, all of us could perhaps come up with some sort of list of the causes of war, but one doubts if anyone could come up with as probing and as comprehensive a list as John Paul II did over the course of his pontificate. Listed here are only certain key points:[10]

> Extreme kinds of poverty; allowing, with sinful disregard, irresponsibility, injustice, and inequality to thrive on the planet; excessive economic or social inequalities, envy, distrust, and pride raging among men and nations; abortion, divorce, and all that destroys the family; doctrines of national or cultural supremacy; totalitarian tyranny; powerful and deceitful propaganda; the culture of war and its contempt for man and violation of human rights; the practical disregard, in these conflicts, of both ordinary laws and of the laws of war; direct attacks on civilians, making them into victims and, in turn, assassins of others; the assertion of a pluralism that denies a universal and intelligible human nature; and the refusal to repent or to forgive.

It is enough to read through this list and the other statements of John Paul II to see that he went far beyond what others were saying within the confines of the debate that raged about just war and the invasion of Iraq. The immediate situation and the limited range of facts that, by the nature of just war theory, were alone relevant to that narrow debate, are transcended in John Paul II's globalized vision. Others saw a particular problem and a particular war; he saw a whole nexus of problems and a proliferation of wars after wars, long into the future. Others were concerned about securing a particular peace at a particular time and in a particular place; he was concerned about securing a universal peace for everyone, always and everywhere.

But lest so grand a vision and so extensive a hope seem naïve and utopian, let another list, culled again from the same sources, be given of the very concrete and eminently achievable means that John Paul II had thought out as the way to achieve his goal. Again, only certain key points are listed, but for ease of grasp, they are divided into three general groupings:

(1) *Political and Institutional*—commitment to a fair distribution of resources; rethinking cooperation in terms of a new culture of solidarity, which, for instance, makes the poor the agents of their own development; democracy and a market economy that give all a legitimate share of well-being and growth; political leaders who put at the heart of their political activity the promotion of peace and justice, have respect for law, and are honest and selfless; media devoted to truth and to the duty to foster justice and solidarity at all levels; the UN to respond fully to the breadth and height of its universal mission of peace; honest dialogue between peoples and nations

(2) *Legal and Juridical*—need for a vision of man as a creature of intelligence and free will, immersed in a mystery that transcends his own being; defense of the dignity of the person; respect for rights, as inalienably given by God, that transcend national sovereignty; every culture to be respected as a way of giving expression to the transcendent dimension of human life, or the mystery of God; development of a comprehensible and common language of dialogue based on the universal moral law, the "grammar" of the spirit, written on the human heart; the paramount value of the natural law, of the universal common good; full use of the UN declaration of human rights as the highest expression of the human conscience of our time; education of the young, especially by women, making the family a school of peace; equal respect for women and girls

(3) *Moral and Religious*—necessary role of religion in fostering peace and universal brotherhood and solidarity; total gift of self to God and neighbor; shared prayer, fasting, and dialogue between religions; pilgrimages of penance and reconciliation; conversion of heart; moderation and simplicity in daily life; healing of memories, or learning to replace revenge with a newfound liberty of forgiveness and love; formation of the consciences of the young in the integral and fraternal humanism of equal rights and dignity; religion not to be considered authentic if it advocates terrorism or violence or does not seek to promote the unity and peace of the whole human family[11]

A summation of this list, and certainly an expression of its spirit, is contained in the ten rules for peace proclaimed by the assembled religious representatives, including John Paul II, at the end of the Day of Prayer for Peace held at Assisi. Among the pledges made are:

> We commit ourselves to proclaiming our firm conviction that violence and terrorism are incompatible with the authentic spirit of religion; we commit ourselves to defending the right of everyone to live a decent life in accordance with their own cultural identity; we commit ourselves to forgiving one another for past and present errors and prejudices; we commit ourselves to encouraging all efforts to promote friendship between peoples [2002c].

That all these proposals, taken together in their totality, constitute a comprehensive program of peace that transcends (though it also embraces) the limits and the goals of just war theory is evident. They show how far John Paul II had taken his vision of peace and how deeply and carefully he had developed a practical plan of action. He left no one and nothing out of his grasp but instead outlined for everyone, from the highest to the lowest, and for every level of community, from the family to the United Nations, how each could and must contribute to the building up of a culture of peace, fit for a world of peace. Notice, therefore, just how concretely practical and achievable his proposals were and are. All that could stand in the way of their implementation is not any impossibility in the acts to be done but only a refusal in our will to do them. There can be little doubt that John Paul II was aware that the only problem here could lie in our will. That is why he placed conversion of heart and appeals to divine aid at the center of his teaching. That is also why, in the service of such conversion, he spoke so often and so forcefully on the subject and went on insisting that, however bad things seemed to be or indeed were, if his proposals were sincerely put into practice, peace could always actually be achieved, even at or beyond the last minute.

Such was the message he was urging in his remarks about the Iraq War. He was not trying to enter, or enter very seriously, into the details or the development of just war theory. His vision was grander and his goal more comprehensive. He wanted to subsume the principles of war under the principles of peace and to do so not by ignoring or denying justice, but instead by transcending it with charity. The law of the one was to yield to the higher law of the other. We should not, then, in our thinking about the Iraq War (or any other war), remain at the level of just war technicalities. These have their place, to be sure, but it is a low place. We should instead follow John Paul II's example and set our sights on things that are higher.

Notes

1. See the essays by Strootman and Wiemer in Beck (2013: 38–53, 54–69).
2. One useful example here is the letters of the Younger Pliny, especially those he exchanged with the Emperor Trajan.
3. For some details see the Carlyles (1903–1936), Dawson (1932, 1954), Heer (1968).
4. This whole question is nicely discussed by Francisco Suarez in Book Six of his *Defense of the Catholic and Apostolic Faith* (translation, 2012).
5. See Hanke (1959).
6. The battle of Chaeronea took place in 338 BC, and Philip's settlement was accepted by the Greeks at the Congress of Corinth, the text of which can be found in Defourny (1932): 536–37 n1; see also Simpson (1990) and (1998): 216.
7. For a more extended discussion of this idea than is needed here, see Simpson (1990, 1994, 1995, 2012).
8. But see also Pope St. John XXIII and his encyclical *Pacem in Terris.*
9. For instance Cardinal Martino, who opined that in present circumstances, "with modern weaponry, there is no proportionality between the offense and the reply.... War is so destructive now. It is not just a fight between one person and another." He said further that the proposed intervention in Iraq would be a "crime against peace that cries out for vengeance before God" (Martino 2003). Note that these remarks were not based on the revelations, which came later, about the falsity of the Bush administration's charge that Iraq had weapons of mass destruction. The present discussion abstracts from such revelations and their truth or accuracy.
10. This list is culled, as are the subsequent lists, from the writings and talks of John Paul II listed in the references, but in particular from his *Messages for the Annual World Day of Peace* of 1993; 1994; 1995; 1997; 2000; 2002; 2003; 2004; 2005. Other causes of wars listed in these documents (the list does not pretend to be complete) include denial to individuals and groups of their freedom and dignity; the crushing foreign debt of developing countries; drugs and the drug trade; the frenzied race for possessing material goods; the idolatrous cult of the nation; the invention and use of biological, chemical, and nuclear weapons; the arms trade; misery, desperation, emptiness of heart; squandering enormous wealth to develop merely private interests; the scandal of division and lack of dialogue between religions and cultures; armed conflicts within, and not just between, states; an insidious terrorism capable of striking at any time and anywhere; unresolved problems in the Middle East, South America, Africa, and elsewhere; diseases spreading contagion and death; irresponsible behavior contributing to the depletion of the planet's resources; fear and hatred of the "other"; the fundamentalism of religiously based nationalisms; ways of disseminating information that violate the principles of truth and justice, injure the reputation of nations and individuals, and serve narrow interests, national, ethnic, racial, and religious prejudices, material greed, and false ideologies; the lack of an attitude of sincere forgiveness, which makes wounds fester and fuels in the younger generation endless resentment and the desire for revenge; loss of any sense of respect for human life; and the assertion of a pluralism that denies a universal and intelligible human nature.

11.   Other proposals, despite their multiplicity, are worth noting:

   (1) *Political and Institutional*—the harmonious and united promotion of a
   society in which everyone feels welcomed and loved; subordination of the
   good of single nations to the common good of humanity; new and deeper
   reflection on the nature of the economy and its purposes; developing
   countries to guarantee proper management of aid received and replace
   corruption and tyranny with participatory democracy; all members of the
   UN to have equal opportunity to be part of the decision-making process,
   eliminating privilege and discrimination that weaken the UN's role and
   credibility; effectiveness of the UN depends on its embracing an international culture and ethic, on its being a moral center for all nations as a
   family of nations, on its fostering values of solidarity, of living for others,
   and of fruitful exchange of gifts, as a common effort to build the civilization of love, justice, solidarity, peace, and liberty; building up the UN as
   a solid structure capable of withstanding the uncertainties of politics and
   guaranteeing everyone freedom and security in every circumstance

   (2) *Legal and Juridical*— true and lasting peace not a matter of balanced
   forces or reprisals or hateful propaganda or terrorism, but instead moral
   and juridical action; respect for life (the right to abortion, for instance, is
   only thinkable when freedom is separated from truth and democracy from
   transcendent values); respect for the rights and freedom of individuals and
   groups, cultures and peoples; recognition of rights of nations, rights to one's
   own language and culture, duty to live in peace, and respect and solidarity
   with other and diverse nations; the right to integral development born of
   solidarity; law to be understood as a real juridical corpus of international
   humanitarian law, drawing on traditional *jus gentium*, expressing universal
   principles prior to and superior to the internal law of states; international
   law not to be the law of the stronger or the majority or a single international
   organization, but instead to be based on principles of natural and moral law
   binding on all; a need not for new legal texts but for the will to put existing
   ones into practice; the UN to function as an international legal authority,
   recognized by universal consent as advancing common good; recognition
   of the global character of the *UN Universal Declaration of Human Rights*,
   of universal human rights as rooted in the nature of the person, rights that
   reflect the objective and inviolable demands of a universal moral law; full use
   of the provisions of the UN Charter; international politics to be governed
   by international law; respect for international agreements; respect for the
   right of civilians to safety in war; respect for the family as the fundamental
   unit of society; the family to be fully protected and fostered by the state, as
   active agent of peace and as able to transmit peace to the whole society

   (3) *Moral and Religious*—love of other peoples as one loves one's own; aware-
   ness that humanity is a single family and called to be such; total gift of self to
   God and neighbor; personal commitment to the cause of peace; parents who
   are examples of peace in their families and who educate their children for
   peace; teachers who pass on genuine values; working men and women who
   bring the dignity of work where it is most needed; young people committed
   to peace always and with and for everyone; discovering beyond all frontiers
   the faces of brothers, sisters, friends; embracing peace as a lifestyle based
   on the four pillars of truth, justice, love, and freedom; universal pilgrimage
   of peace, beginning with an attitude of sincere forgiveness in human hearts;
   everyone consciously to take responsibility for building peace, beginning

from the family and in the thousand little acts of daily life; cultivation of charity, the queen of the virtues; the church as everyone's family; peace a gift from God to be prayed for and built up through profound inner conversion; a culture and ethics of forgiveness to precede a politics of forgiveness; peace to rest on justice, and justice to rest on the love that is forgiveness, which, beginning in people's hearts, heals and rebuilds troubled human relations from their foundations in all circumstances, great and small; fighting the evil of war at its roots by each and all building a culture of peace together, from the family to the nation to the UN; Jewish, Christian, and Islamic leaders to take the lead in publicly condemning terrorism and denying terrorists religious or moral legitimacy; violence never to be legitimated in God's name; Christians everywhere to witness that peace is always possible; Christians to overcome their divisions and give united witness and increase solidarity

10

Illiberal Morals

Acquiring Virtue

Morals are an important part of any community life, since morals concern the way we behave, and we need to behave morally if we are to live well. Living well means living to the fullest of our powers, and our powers are at their fullest when they are exercised with excellence. Another word for excellence is virtue, for by virtue is meant not some narrow attention to sexual purity but excellent exercise of power. Excellent exercise of power, in the human case, is rational exercise. The reason is plain. We are by nature rational beings, and the good of any being is the completion of its nature, so our good is to exercise all our powers rationally. But it is rational to treat all things according to what they are, both in themselves and relative to us. Animals, for instance, should be treated as animals, not as stones, but since animals are subordinate relative to us, they may be used for our needs, as horses and oxen are for riding and hauling and dogs for hunting and companionship. Animals may be eaten for our needs too, but only for our needs and not for our indulgence. The same goes for plants, which we grow to eat as well as for adornment and beauty.

Human beings, by contrast, are not as such subordinate to human beings, or only so for the sake of all involved, as children are subject to parents and slaves to masters, for both are preserved and enhanced by such subjection. Reason itself teaches that children should be treated as children, slaves as slaves, parents as parents, and so on, provided the respective parties truly are as they are named. Indeed, as a general rule, one may say that rational behavior, and therefore virtuous behavior, is understood from the several roles and functions occupied by human beings in their relations with each other. So a soldier is a good soldier if he behaves as a soldier, a sailor if he behaves as a sailor, a teacher as a teacher, and so on. What this "behaving as" means in particular cases and on particular occasions will need particular decision by the reason of those directly involved, although some general points may be laid down (such as that a soldier must be skilled in the use of weapons, a sailor in managing a ship, a teacher in imparting knowledge). The "behaving as," wherever it is and whomever it concerns, will typically involve both skills (such as shooting and sailing) and virtues (such as courage and patience). The virtues in fact are qualities of behavior that are very general in kind. All of us need courage in facing fears and dangers, so that we confront those it is rational to confront and retreat from those it is irrational to confront. All of us need temperance, too, in taking pleasures and pains, so that we take those that are rational to take and avoid those that are irrational to take. The like holds of generosity in the rational gaining and using of money and resources, of mildness in the rational showing or resisting of anger, and of magnanimity in the rational pursuit or avoidance of honors. How rationality is to be determined in all these cases will need, of course, particular perception in particular cases, but the general outlines are clear enough in advance.[1]

Music

Such moral virtues, however, are not automatic but must be taught and learned from youth up, so that we learn first from elders what rational behavior is and then, by repeated practice, are able to discern rational behavior directly ourselves. What form this training must take is a large question (dealt with at length by many ancient and medieval philosophers), though the coercive sanction of physical punishment, suited of course to the person and the case, will play a role. But physical punishment is a blunt instrument and too easily overdone or underdone. Different instruments are needed. The example of others, real or imagined, who lived exemplary lives or performed outstanding deeds and are celebrated in song and story will be particularly valuable, especially for the young. But there is one tool of education in virtue that has generally been ignored, though its effect, for good or ill, is profound. This tool is music, which nowadays goes almost entirely unregulated, whether by parents or teachers or rulers. Music directly affects the emotions, exciting them, softening them, indulging them, or affronting them, and since emotions figure so largely in the virtues as their primary object (for fear and daring are the object of courage, sensual pleasure and pain of temperance, anger and careless indifference of mildness), whatever affects them as directly as music does should not be left unregulated by educators or left to the hazard and whim of the young.

Unfortunately modern music presents us in this regard with a severe problem. The music that now dominates our culture is a recent Western phenomenon, and yet it presents itself as the only music, or at least as providing the only true measure for all music. The point can be explained by reference to a story taken from India about the king of the apes, Hanuman, who happened to be very proud of his musical attainments.

> Rama, the hero of the Ramayana epos, devised a plan to humble him. In the jungles there dwelt a noble Rishi who caused the Seven Notes to become embodied in seven lovely nymphs. Rama took Hanuman into the vicinity of the abode of the Rishi, and Hanuman, wanting to show off his qualifications, proudly took up the *vina* and began to play. Just then the seven lovely nymphs or notes passed by; they were going to fetch water. Hearing the music, one stopped, swayed and fell dead. Hanuman had sung that note incorrectly. The sister notes were comfortless and moaned and lamented her death piteously; the Rishi, seeing all this, smiled, took up the *vina* and struck the notes loudly. As soon as the dead note was played correctly it revived and gaily rejoined its sister notes and there was much rejoicing. Hanuman, thoroughly ashamed of himself, hung his head and performed penance for his silly vanities (From Curt Sachs, *The Rise of Music in the Ancient World*, Norton, New York, 1943: 173–174).

If one were now to listen to an excerpt from the music, say, of J. S. Bach, orchestral or keyboard or other solo instrument, and were to subject the Rishi's notes to this excerpt, most of these notes would be dead, and a great deal of retuning and replaying would be needed to revive them. But why should the music of Bach constitute such a mortal blow? First and principally because few of the intervals in Bach's music are pure (in a sense to be explained shortly). The scale he uses is the so-called well-tempered scale (his celebrated 48 Preludes and Fugues are, one recalls, entitled *The Well-Tempered Clavier*). The well-tempered scale is an anticipation of and preparation for the modern equal-tempered scale. In the equal-tempered scale, the intervals between each of the twelve notes of the octave (the interval of the semitone) are fixed at an equal distance (that of 100 cents, to use the standard way of measuring musical intervals). Thus the interval of a fourth (from C to F, say) is measured at 500 cents (or five semitones), and that of a fifth (from C to G, say) is measured at 700 cents (or seven semitones), and the difference between these two intervals (from F to G) is measured at 200 cents (or two semitones). If, however, these intervals were to be measured accurately or according to purity of musical consonance, the intervals would in fact be different.

By purity of consonance is meant purity of the ratio between the notes constituting the interval. For instance, the interval of an octave sounds at a ratio of 2:1. To use the modern theory of sound waves, the higher note is resonating twice as fast as the lower one, in the sense that the peak of every wave of sound of the lower note coincides with the peak of every second wave of sound of the higher note. The ear accordingly hears the octave as a harmony, because it hears the notes resonating together. The interval of the fifth resonates at the ratio of 3:2, in the sense that the peak of every second wave of sound of the lower note coincides with the peak of every third wave of sound of the higher note. The interval of the fourth resonates at the ratio of 4:3, in the sense that the peak of every third wave of sound of the lower note coincides with the peak of every fourth wave of sound of the higher note. The octave, fifth, and fourth are the most readily detectable harmonies, closely followed by the major and minor third, which have ratios of 5:4 and 6:5 respectively. As so calculated, they constitute the natural harmonies (for they constitute the coincidence of the natural phenomenon of sound waves detectable to the human ear).

However, it so turns out that, when translated into cents, these intervals do not constitute a tempered scale. The natural interval of the fourth, for instance, is 498 cents and not 500, of the fifth 702 cents and not 700, and of the interval between them 204 cents and not 200 (or near enough for present purposes). These discrepancies are, to be sure, too small to be noticeable to the human ear, but when they get repeated often enough, they soon do become noticeable. Now, such repetition is actually what happens if one constructs or tunes all the notes of one's scale using the natural intervals and not the tempered intervals (that is to say, if one tunes all notes using some such method as the so-called up and down method: up a fifth from one's first chosen note, say C to G, then down a fourth from G to D, up a fifth from D to A, down a fourth from A to E, and so on). The upshot is, to cut a long story short, that while one will thus get natural harmonies in one key (the key of C), one will not get harmonies (whether natural or tempered) in other keys, but the intervals will sound more and more out of tune. To get natural intervals in other keys, one has to start afresh by tuning or constructing one's notes in that key. But then, of course, one will lose the natural harmonies in one's original key, and so on, and so on. The only way to keep tolerable harmonies among intervals across all scales (without having laboriously to retune one's instrument each time one changes key) is to fudge or temper each note so that they are all slightly out of tune with respect to each other, but not so out of tune as to sound harsh to the ear. In this way one can move freely from one key to another without losing too much harmony in the process. This fudging is what we call temperament, and the resultant fudged keys are what we call equal-tempered.

It is for this reason that Bach's music and all Western music since then would kill the Rishi's notes; because the Rishi's notes are in pure intervals, and Bach's are not. Bach, of course, is just one of many composers of modern Western music, but he is chosen as representative here because he is one of the first to popularize well temperament. Experiments had, indeed, been going on before Bach's time to achieve a tempered scale, and the experiments have continued after Bach as well. But Bach represents a sort of beginning of what we now know in the West as music, for later developments have followed his lead.

There are, however, other features of Bach's music, related to that of temperament, that also need noting and that are equally part of its impurity. For one might wonder why there should be so much interest in having a well-tempered scale if music before Bach's time had managed, for so many centuries, to get by pretty much without it. Partly, or perhaps mainly, it is because of the desire to have a multiplicity and a variety of notes all sounding together. For a feature of Bach's music (and even more a feature of music after Bach) is the piling up of notes to produce chords of multiple notes and chordal progressions. But because of what has just been explained above, it is hard to have much harmonious piling up of notes, or chordal progressions, without a tempered scale. The purer one's notes, in other words, the more one is forced to play few notes separately instead of many notes together.

Yet the piling up of notes and sounds in modern Western music is not just a matter of having many sounds coming from one and the same instrument, but also of having many sounds coming from many instruments. For another feature of Western music is the large orchestra, which got much larger after Bach, indeed, than it did during his lifetime. But how is one to get many instruments playing many notes all at the same time and preserve some sort of musical harmony? The only solution is to make all instruments conform to some common measure or standard, so that despite differences of quality and timbre, they all do play the same notes or notes conforming to the same intervals. Now, it is a feature of many instruments that they have few, if any, fixed intervals. Stringed and wind instruments, for instance, have in principle the potential to play an infinite number of notes at an infinite variety of intervals. A violin string can be stopped at any point and notes can be played not only a tone or a semitone apart, but also a quarter tone or an eighth tone apart. Indeed even these intervals themselves can be varied infinitely, and a given tone can be played now higher and now lower, or now sharper and now flatter, entirely as one wills. But since instruments have this capability, getting them all to keep sounding tolerably in tune when played together requires fixing on them all a common set of notes and intervals. This requirement is best met by having an instrument with fixed notes at fixed intervals from which all other instruments are made to take their cue, as it were. Here enters the keyboard, or more particularly the piano. For the very idea of a keyboard is fixed notes at fixed intervals (the guitar, of course, has the same character because of its frets, and the guitar has, interestingly enough, achieved the same dominance in what we nowadays call pop music as the piano has in what we nowadays call classical music). Hence the dominance of the piano in Western music has come hand in hand with the dominance of the equal-tempered scale. Both are connected with the desire to have a multiplicity and a variety of notes from a multiplicity and variety of instruments sounding all at once.

The dominance of the piano in Western music is not just evident from the fact that all musicians, whatever other instrument they may play, are required to be at least minimally familiar with how to play the piano, but above all and much more from the fact that all music is taught and all music composed using a system of notation that fits the tempered keyboard (and also the guitar, to some extent). The reference here is to the standard five-bar staff that we use to write music. For this five-bar staff allows one only happily to write twelve notes to an octave at evenly fixed intervals. Systems of notation designed for instruments and music played with an infinite variety of notes at an infinite variety of intervals (such as in non-Western and non-modern music, at least as regards notes played between the pure and fixed intervals of fourth and fifth) do and must look very different. Indeed the one notation will hardly be intelligible in terms of the other.

Now, these features of modern Western music, which are very much distinctive of it, namely the well-tempered scale and the dominance of the keyboard, are related to the desire for variety and multiplicity of sounds. But one might well be puzzled or intrigued by this desire itself. For it manifests itself also in Western music in another way, namely in the love of novelty and the desire for ever different sorts and styles of music. For it is not just variety of notes within a musical piece that is desired, but novelty of pieces too, and this love of novelty, once let loose, knows few bounds. Western music presents us with such a rapid succession of periods and styles of music that have come and gone since the days of Bach. For from Bach's period of the baroque, we pass in a matter of decades to the classical and then to the romantic, ending in what we now call the modern period (of the twentieth and twenty-first centuries). This last period is marked by such a dizzying succession of novelties that it defies any definite single characterization. The passion for novelty means, indeed, that each new generation of composers has to do something different from its predecessor to gain attention and have its music played or recorded. All the better, therefore, if the novelty is not only new but even goes out of its way to shock, for what shocks gets more attention. Hence the fact that the development of Western music is often marked by shocks (such as Stravinsky's *Rite of Spring*), which, however, after a while cease to be shocking, because the novelty wears off. Hence also the premium placed on new and more sophisticated instruments and on highly developed technical skill among players.

The effect of this sort of music on the passions and emotions seems evident. These will tend toward the new, the shocking, or the violent; they will not tend toward the peaceful, the moderated, or the controlled. But since moral character or virtue is so much a function of the emotions and how we are disposed with respect to them, the fact that our music favors the new and shocking, and not the settled and tried, must inevitably generate characters and behaviors that are similar. Certainly a human community that cares, as it should, for moral character and its growth, especially in the young, cannot be indifferent to or cavalier about the sort of music that proliferates within it. Some sort of discipline and control over music and musicians, so as to make both serve moral virtue and not the opposite, are clearly needed. Indeed, since music has power to make character good or bad, to leave it alone is almost inevitably to leave it to be exploited by the ill-intentioned, so that through its morally destructive effects, they can take advantage of others for their own gain. Slavish characters in particular, those subject to passion rather than in control of passion, are dear to tyrants and lovers of tyranny, because they can be used to shore up tyranny as well as to commit crimes in its service.

The chances, however, of reversing the parlous effects of temperament in modern music, are very low in the West. They are greater perhaps in the East, as in particular India, where the old traditions still flourish. If one compares and contrasts the traditional music of India—such as, for instance, the ragas, as they are called—one will find that its features are virtually all opposite to those of Western music, including Bach. It does not use the tempered scale; it is not based on or tied to the keyboard; it is not marked by a multitude of notes or by chords and chordal progressions; it is relatively spare and unadorned; further, one raga compared with another will seem, at least initially, very similar and lacking in novelty and variety. But what traditional Indian ragas thus lack in the obvious or immediate impression they create, they make up for in their depth and penetration. Such features of Indian music are hard or impossible to reduplicate in modern Western music, and largely if not wholly because of the tempered scale. Doubtless, the subtleties of non-modern and non-Western music need to be discovered by much learning and meditation and are not open to immediate view. Doubtless, their ethical power too is equally hard to appreciate. Indeed, even proponents of this music openly declared that not everyone could appreciate every type of music, but that some music was fit only for the wise and the virtuous, while other music was fit only for the vulgar, the crude, and the uneducated.[2] We are dealing here with things that defy and even affront standard Western prejudices. But there is no reason to ignore or dismiss them, for suppose that such music does have the powers attributed to it. Suppose indeed that all music, including Western music, has some such power, more or less. Suppose, in other words, that the lives we lead, the cosmos we live in, are affected, for better or worse, by the kind of music we enjoy and give ourselves to. Could we then remain so complacent in our preference for Western music?

Music is an art of life applied to sounds and is likely to reflect what we are doing with the rest of our life generally and to express the same attitudes and embody the same expectations and drives. A certain kind of fevered pursuit of pleasures, of fairly obvious pleasures, seems to characterize the life we make for ourselves within Western culture. Western music, as described above, has much of the same character, for the love of many and varied sounds, all present together, is a love of obvious pleasures. The subtler pleasures of non-Western music require time and meditation to appreciate. Of course there is a place for obvious pleasures, just as there is for subtle ones. But we in the West would seem to have an abundance of the first and a dearth of the second.

The human striving for the comprehensive good, which is the mark of all authentic human community, since it requires passions that serve thought and do not disrupt or distort it, requires too the moral virtues that modern Western music seems capable now only of marginalizing or destroying and not of generating or enhancing.

Marriage

If music is a chief tool of moral education, the family is its chief locus. Attacks on the family and the conditions for its flourishing are proliferating, and proliferating absurdly in the name of freedom. Two such attacks are same-sex marriage and abortion. There is some suitability, therefore, in ending this book, because of its emphasis on the comprehensive good and on virtue, with a discussion of these two issues.

Human beings begin, as a matter of biological necessity, in the union of male and female and, since human young need many years of care and education before they mature, in a union that is itself long-lasting. Such a union has long been dignified with the name of marriage. The name is now contested, since same-sex marriages have been legalized in many places. But names are one thing and realities are another, and even if the name remains identical, the corresponding realities need not. Consider first, then, what has traditionally been called marriage, namely the lifelong union of male and female for the sake of children. That there is such a thing, and that it is rational and natural, follows from the following facts:

1. The sexual difference between male and female is a procreative difference. The two sexes differ as they do for sake of the procuring of offspring.
2. The sexual act between male and female is a unitive one. It brings the two together in the most intimate of physical unions.
3. Male and female are equal in this act and this function. They have equal dignity.
4. The offspring born as a result of sexual union derive their physical origin from both their parents equally and are in need of long education from both of them equally.
5. The physical derivation of offspring in this way ties people together in a multitude of family relationships: parent, child, grandparent, uncle, aunt, cousin, and so forth. These relationships are of a unique kind and tie definite people to definite people in a way that is of immeasurable value throughout life, from cradle to grave.
6. As physical beings, people mark significant events in their lives and significant moments of commitment in physically manifest ways, using elaborate ceremonies to fix and display settled acts of intention and choice.

From these facts, one can deduce that there is a kind of personal union of male and female that has these necessary characteristics:

1. It is heterosexual (from 1).
2. It is exclusive (from 1 and 2).
3. It is lifelong (from 2 to 5).
4. It is communal or has a recognized social status (from 6).
5. Hence, by all the same tokens, it is not homosexual, not promiscuous, not contraceptive, and not isolated or solitary.

Such a union may rightly be called natural marriage, or what marriage is by nature, because it is a union whose distinctive characteristics follow from the natural facts about human beings and how they come to be and to flourish.

On the other hand, marriage as it is now actually practiced, or the sort of unions that nowadays get called marriages and are given legal sanction as marriages, even when such marriages are confined to heterosexual unions, do not correspond to natural marriage as above described.

They are not for life, but instead can end in divorce and be replaced by second or third or more marriages; they permit the use of artificial contraceptives to prevent childbirth; they permit promiscuity, or sexual intercourse with persons other than the spouse; they permit abortion. Such unions, while they may be called marriages, are not natural marriages. That they are heterosexual unions makes no difference. Natural marriage is characterized by several features. Heterosexuality is only one of these features. The other features must be present too, and if only one of them is lacking, there is no natural marriage.

So suppose that, instead of taking away, say, the features of permanence and exclusivity, as these so-called or merely civil marriages do, we were to leave these features and take away the feature of heterosexuality. Would the resulting union be any less a marriage? Of course it would not be a natural marriage. But the other is not a natural marriage either. So if we are appealing to the natural notion of marriage to rule out same-sex marriages, we must, to be consistent, rule out impermanent and promiscuous heterosexual marriages too. Such heterosexual unions are no more natural marriages than homosexual unions are. Both fail to reach that measure, if for different reasons.

There is, therefore, a certain inconsistency, not to say hypocrisy, involved in trying to outlaw homosexual marriage while not also outlawing impermanent or promiscuous or contraceptive heterosexual marriage. We cannot outlaw one without outlawing the other, or allow one without allowing the other. Such, however, is what popular opinion wants to do. Popular opinion, therefore, is inconsistent if not hypocritical.

What should be done, then? There are, it seems, only two serious options here: either return to natural marriage, and refuse to allow any union the name or privileges or duties of marriage that is not a natural marriage, or abandon natural marriage altogether, and allow people to call marriage any sexual union that takes their fancy. Thus not only could members of the same sex claim to be married, but so could members of different maturity or species. There could, therefore, be pederastic marriages, or marriages between adults and children. There could, in addition, be polygamous marriages (whether heterosexual, homosexual, or pederastic).

These solutions are, admittedly, not desirable, but they are solutions that no one can consistently object to who wants to describe modern civil unions between heterosexuals as marriage. Moreover, they are perhaps solutions worth adopting in the immediate and short term, because they will have the beneficial effect of shocking people into realizing how far they have departed from natural marriage in the unions they now call marriages. For if the idea of natural marriage is ever to be restored in the popular mind, the inconsistency that now infects the same-sex marriage debate, and that vitiates the arguments of most of those who oppose it, need to be exposed.

What solution would, however, be better in the long term instead? Well, ideally no union should be dignified with the name of marriage, whether civilly sanctioned or not, that is not also a natural marriage. But if legislation to this effect would be impossible to implement (as seems likely), then abandoning the institution of civil marriage altogether would likely be a better path. Let those who really want to get married—that is, who want a natural marriage—have recourse to some other social body, such as the several religions, to sanction and ceremonially solemnize their marriage. This solution would have the additional advantages of strengthening marriage. Religious vows would endow the marriage bond with divine awe and reverence and make the breach of the bond an offense not only against man but also against God. That local religious authorities would officiate and solemnize the marriage would cohere with the principle of subsidiarity as well as with the principle of the difference between the temporal and the spiritual powers. In both respects family life, which is so vital to the pursuit of the comprehensive human good, would be empowered, enhanced, and elevated.

As for civil marriage, if it is to be retained at all, it should ideally follow and support the religious marriage, so that civil and religious power both work for the same end. Otherwise it should be simply a legal contract guaranteeing to the relevant parties certain legally enforceable rights for as long as the contract is in force. What these legal rights are should be left to the parties themselves. Perhaps there could be a standard civil contract that contained what most people would want from such a contract. But variations to the contract, or special versions of it made to order, should be available. These contracts should, of course, be available also to those who want and have contracted a natural marriage. For there are certain legal or civil obligations that any union of persons will naturally bring with it, and there is no reason that those with natural marriages should be prevented from receiving the benefits of the civil law.

The only point left, and it is one of the most important, is what to do about names. Which union, the natural or the civil, should be called marriage? Well, in justice, only the natural one should be so called, because the civil sanctions for marriage were introduced for natural marriage so as to foster and protect it. But this name has become so divorced from its origin that there is doubt whether it can, in present circumstances, be restored to its natural meaning. Perhaps it should simply be abandoned, for to allow the word to apply to so called civil marriages, when such marriages are so far from being natural marriages, is more likely to obscure the truth about marriage than to reveal it. Let civil marriages then be called partner contracts or same domicile contracts or the like. As for natural marriage, let it be called natural marriage. Or if that name lacks rhetorical force, one could adopt some other existing name, such as matrimony or wedlock. Or one could invent a new name, such as "familliage," perhaps. In any event, since there are two distinct realities here—natural marriage and what nowadays gets called marriage—some difference of names is desirable for describing and referring to them.

Abortion

Abortion has become commonplace almost everywhere in the modern world and is widely regarded as a basic right of choice for women. That such a right is claimed in the name of liberal freedom is of course not at all in its favor, for liberal freedom, as has been argued above, is very far from being freedom. There can be little doubt, indeed, that abortion attacks the family at its heart, since the production of children through the sexual union of married persons is that heart. The health of the family is crucial to the achievement and retention of freedom, for the young are introduced to freedom as to everything else through the family. Still the question of abortion can be dealt with by itself even in a certain abstraction from the family, for it raises puzzles in its own right: These puzzles deserve a separate treatment for precision's sake as well as for how they can, once properly analyzed, shore up the status and foster the health of the family.

A first problem concerns whether abortion is ever morally good or permissible. A second concerns what laws, if any, should be made about abortion and its regulation. These two issues are not necessarily connected. If abortion is shown to be immoral, it has not yet been shown to be deserving of legal prohibition. Not everything immoral can or should be prohibited by law. Hatred and malice are morally evil, but legally prohibiting them would be impossible, for unless they issue in some discernible action, they cannot be fairly judged by human courts of justice. In what follows, the moral issue will be discussed first, followed by the legal issue.

The basic argument against the morality of abortion goes roughly as follows: (1) abortion is the direct killing of an innocent human being; (2) the direct killing of an innocent human being is murder; (3) murder is morally wrong; (4) therefore, abortion is morally wrong.

The logic of this argument is simple and straightforward enough, and it is clearly valid, for the conclusion does indeed follow from the premises. What has excited opposition, of course, and provoked all the controversy is the truth of the premises themselves. Reasons for rejecting the truth of these premises are roughly as follows. As regards premise one, that abortion is the direct killing of an innocent human being, some protest that what abortion kills is not human. It is just a collection of cells lacking the fully developed structure of a human being. Or if what abortion kills is human, then, at least in some cases, it is not innocent. It is, if only despite itself, threatening the life of the mother and may be opposed and removed as a matter of simple self-defense against an aggressor. As regards premise two, that the direct killing of an innocent human being is murder, some protest that murder is really the killing of *persons*, not the killing of human beings merely. To kill something that is biologically human but that lacks the characteristics of persons, as thought or self-consciousness and the like, is not murder.

The permanently comatose, for instance, are in this condition, and to end their lives by removing or withholding life support is not murder and is not regarded by us as such, even though we would all regard as murder the doing of the same thing to someone who was not comatose but in full possession of his faculties. The unborn are like the comatose, for as the latter are humans but *no longer* persons, so the former are humans but *not yet* persons. Hence aborting the unborn is no more murder than is removing life support from the comatose.

As regards premise three, that murder is wrong and not morally permissible, some protest that, to the contrary, certain murders are right and morally permissible, or even morally obligatory. A classic example is where some terrorist has kidnapped a number of innocent persons whom he intends to kill; however, he is prepared not to kill them if you agree to kill one of them. Then he will let the rest go free. In this case, so it is argued, it would be right for you to kill one to save the rest. Another example is where there is a conflict between rights, and one right trumps another, such as precisely in the case of the pregnant woman's right to choose, or her right to life, trumping the unborn's right to life. Here too, it is argued, to kill the unborn to save the mother is morally right or even morally obligatory.

These objections raise deep and interesting puzzles, and each needs to be dealt with fairly. Since they turn, however, either directly or indirectly, on the moral and ontological status of the unborn, the following discussion will first focus on what sort of being the unborn within the mother really is. Specific responses to the objections will be given later.

The first and most important point, then, concerns the status or being of the unborn in the womb. That the unborn is a human being and a person can be argued in two ways, the first from science and the second from ontology or metaphysics.

The scientific argument goes basically as follows: (1) the zygote, etc., is a distinct human life; (2) a distinct human life is a person; (3) therefore, the zygote, etc., is a person.

The premises here need defense. As regards the first premise, the defense is: (1a) the zygote is alive; (1b) it is not alive as an *organ* of the mother's body, or as living residue or tissue of the mother's or father's body; it is alive as a distinct *organism,* with its own genetic code and its own principle of life and development; (1c) it is alive with human life and not, say, feline or equine or avian life.

As regards the second premise, the defense is: (2a) "Person" is a generally accepted term for an individual human being. (2b) "Person" is a substance term and not a property term: a person is classically defined as an individual substance of a rational nature (Boethius). As regards putting the first and second premises together for the conclusion, the defense is: the zygote, being a living *organism*, is a living, substantial thing and, being human (and not feline or avian), has a rational nature, though not (yet) rational functions. The nature of a thing is not its functions but that which grounds its functions; so to object that the zygote does not have developed functions or organs (consciousness, arms, legs, etc.) is to confuse being a person with being a postnatal person (child, adult, etc.), or the genotype with the phenotype. The phenotype may be the *way* we recognize the natures of things, but it is not *what* we thus recognize. The conclusion (3) validly follows, but its meaning is not that the zygote behaves or looks like a postnatal person, or a child, or an adult. Its meaning is that since the life of the zygote is the life of a distinct individual thing that, like any such thing, has a nature, or some determinate structure that makes it to be this thing (a human being) and not that thing (a cat or a horse), the zygote satisfies all that is required for it to be a person.

So much for the scientific argument. The ontological or metaphysical argument goes basically as follows: (1) the zygote, etc., is a person *in statu fiendi* (in a state of becoming); (2) a person *in statu fiendi* has the being of a person; (3) what has the being of a person is a person; (4) therefore, the zygote, etc., is a person.

Premises (1) and (3) here are self-evident. The problematic premise is (2), and it needs some defense. The defense turns on what may be called the metaphysics of becoming.

The first point, then, is that becoming both is and is not: it is what has already come to be and is not what is still on the way to coming to be; it is what goes on *between* being and not-being. Take, for instance, a "becoming" from A to B. There is no becoming at A or B, nor at any point C between A and B, for a becoming thing qua becoming is not *at* any point of its becoming. No point is a place for it to stop at; all are places for it to pass through without stopping, for a becoming thing is a becoming thing only when it is becoming; that is, only when it is not *at* a place but *between* places. As soon as it can properly be said to be at a place, it is no longer becoming but stopped. For take the "becoming" from A to B, and interrupt it at C. There is no sense in saying here that the becoming was *interrupted* at C unless we can identify the end, B, toward which the "becoming" was tending, and can identify the actual end at C as intervening contrary to the tending that the thing had toward B. Interruption is a failure to get to the end aimed at. Interruption is a real failure, a failure in being. The thing that was becoming B really ceases, because of the interruption, to be becoming B and really loses its being as tending toward B. So, if we want to say what *being* a thing has that is *becoming* B from A, we will have to say that its being is its *tending* toward B. The tending of it to this end is an essential part of what it is; the end enters into it as determinative of what it is. To understand it in terms of what it is now, without reference to anything further, is to miss out the very fact of its becoming.

There is a common error that arises here, namely to identify becoming with the observable and measurable features that are manifest at some particular time-slice of the "becoming" and to exclude the features that will only be observable at some later date. So, for example, the zygote, etc., is said to be just a single cell of forty-six chromosomes, or a collection of such cells, and what these cells are becoming, since it is not yet present or observable, is not regarded as relevant to determining what the cells now are. Thus both the future condition of the cells and the present becoming-ness of these cells toward that future condition are denied to be part of what they now are; but this denial is false. It amounts to a reduction of the dynamic to the static.

Now, a "becoming" has thus not only an end but also some motive power driving the "becoming" to the end. In the zygote, this power is internal, for a zygote is a *self-moving* "becoming." It contains within itself, as actively aimed at, the end it is driving the "becoming" toward.

So from the fact that the zygote, as a becoming thing, has an end and an inner drive to that end, the result is that the end enters into the zygote as determinative of what it is, both actively and passively (both in its directing and its being directed). Consequently the fullness of human nature or of personhood enters into the analysis of the being of the zygote (for this fullness is its end and the object of its drive). Consequently, further, the zygote has the being of a person (the genetic structuring appealed to in the scientific argument may be viewed as the observable expression of this fact). Note, then, as an important corollary here, that the zygote is thus shown to be *actually* a person. What it is *potentially* is not a person but a newborn person, a teenage person, an adult person, etc.

So much, then, for the argument, scientific and metaphysical, that the unborn in the womb, from zygote on, is a human being and a person. What is required next is a reply to the objections given earlier to the basic argument against the morality of abortion. Note in the first

212

place, however, that none of the standard arguments in favor of abortion can stand up against the basic argument. Appeals, for instance, to the so-called right to choose, or to one's own body, or to privacy, beg the question by assuming that life in the womb is not human and that to kill it is not murder. But there is no right to commit murder, so if abortion is murder, no one's right to choose, or to their own body, or to privacy, whatever other rights they give, can give a right to abortion. Not even in a case of rape can these rights give a right to abortion. If abortion is murder, then to abort in a case of rape is still murder. (At least it is murder morally speaking; what laws, if any, there should be relative to abortion in the case of rape is a separate question and will be discussed later.)

The usual counters to this point, of course, are to say either that the life in the womb is not human or that, if it is human, it is not a person, and hence, further, that it is not protected by the prohibition on murder. These counters were the first in each case of the objections noted at the beginning to premises one and two of the basic argument. In answer, then, note that these objections misunderstand what murder is and what a person is. First, murder is, by its standard definition, the deliberate killing of innocent human life. So if the life in the womb is human, aborting it is murder. Second, those who say that life in the womb is human but not a person identify personhood, as already noted, with the manifesting of certain properties or activities, such as consciousness and reasoning in particular. But the falsehood of this supposition was argued above. The unborn is a person in the same way, and for the same reason, as it is human. It is a human person *in statu fiendi*. Hence it is of no consequence that it lacks thought or self-consciousness, for it possesses these too *in statu fiendi*. "Person," being a substance-term and not a property-term, refers not to certain properties but to a certain kind of thing. This thing is indeed the kind of thing that, under suitable conditions, manifests the properties in question. But it will still be that thing whether or not it is now manifesting the properties (as when it is asleep, for instance). Such is characteristic of a thing: that it remains what it is throughout changes of state and activity. Hence if "person," being a thing-term, refers to a thing that is human, then human beings, regardless of what properties they do or do not manifest, are *ipso facto* persons. Third, the unborn, despite manifesting none of the properties of persons, possess these properties substantially or in their root, as was said above. For these properties are rooted in human nature, and genetics and embryology, as well as the metaphysics of becoming, show the unborn to be radically human. Contrary, therefore, to what is often said, one does not, in the case of the unborn, discover if they are persons from whether they have the properties. Rather, one discovers if they have the properties from whether they are persons.

The second objection to premise one noted at the beginning was that even if the unborn is human, then, at least in some cases, it is not innocent (it is, if only despite itself, threatening the life of the mother and may be opposed and removed as a matter of simple self-defense against an aggressor). The answer to this second objection is as follows. First of all, on a practical point, self-defense could justify few, if any, of the abortions now actually performed. The number of pregnancies that pose a threat to the mother's physical life so great that killing the child is necessary to save her is virtually nil. Second, killing in self-defense is not justifiable if one can save oneself without killing, and one could save the mother's life by removing the child alive from the womb instead of by killing it, as abortion does (recent medical advances are now, in fact, making it possible to preserve and bring to term outside the womb a child at almost any stage of its development). Third, the relationship of mother to unborn child is not that of victim to attacker, which is what alone would justify killing in self-defense; rather is it the relationship of giver to gift. The mother is giver of life to her child, and the child is not only the receiver of that gift but is even the gift of new life in return to its mother. Such a relationship is perfected in the mother giving herself to her child to the uttermost, even unto death if need be, as comrades give themselves to each other unto death in danger and war. Certainly the mother must give herself wholly to her child after it is born, or else the child will not grow and flourish. How, then, can she do less while it is still within her? To construe abortion as killing in self-defense is to take a view of the relationship between mother and child that is inhuman and destructive of the notion of family. (Note again, however, by way of anticipation, that none of this entails anything about how the law should treat women who have abortions.)

The objections to premise two, that the direct killing of innocent human life is murder, were first, as just mentioned, that murder is really the killing of persons, not the killing of human beings merely; and consequently, second, that to kill the unborn is no different from removing life support from the comatose, which we do not regard as murder (the unborn are, it is said, like the permanently comatose in being only biologically human and lacking the thought and self-consciousness characteristic of persons).

Of these objections, the first, that the unborn are human but not persons, has just been responded to and needs no further comment. The second objection, the likening of killing the unborn to removing life support from the permanently comatose, is more complex because it labors under two errors. The first error is to suppose that the unborn are like the permanently comatose, at least if we mean by the latter those who are no longer persons. For if the latter have ceased to be persons, then they are not persons at all, but the unborn, because they are persons *in statu fiendi*, are persons and should be treated as such. After all, an oak tree that has decayed and, though still standing, is dead has ceased to be an oak tree (save in name), while an acorn just planted is an oak tree *in statu fiendi* and should be treated as such. Hence, if it is not murder to remove life support from the permanently comatose, it does not follow that to do the same to the unborn is also not murder. The second error is to suppose that removing life support is the same as killing. For there is, as has long been realized, a difference between killing and letting die, and removing life support is the latter, while abortion is the former. Thus the two cases are not the same. One must, nevertheless, be careful with this distinction, for though it is always an *act* distinction, it is not always a *moral* distinction.

An act of letting die can be as much a murder as a direct killing, if, say, there is some moral obligation not to let die, or if letting die amounts to criminal negligence or conspiracy or the like. There is, nevertheless, a moral point to the distinction, because at least sometimes, the fact that one's act was a "letting die" and not a killing absolves one from any moral guilt and may even confer merit. Let us suppose, then, as is indeed often the case, that there is no obligation to do more than one has already done to keep the permanently comatose alive. Let us even suppose that to do more to keep the comatose alive would prevent one from saving the life of someone else, even perhaps of someone whom one is under some obligation to save. Failing to remove the life support and going to the aid of this other person might thus be a moral wrong, while doing so would be morally praiseworthy. Certainly in cases of war, for instance, where triage is required and one must leave the very badly wounded to die in order to give scarce resources and time to the wounded who stand a good chance of living, there is no murder involved in the way one treats the former but much merit involved in the way one treats the latter. By going off to help these others, one does a good deed to them, while one simply lets the very badly wounded die. One does not murder the badly wounded. On the other hand, one would murder them, and could be rightly accused of so doing, if one took a gun in one's hand and shot them, for that would be a killing and not a "letting die." Here, then, is a clear case, one would think, of the distinction between killing and letting die being not only an *act* distinction but also a moral distinction.

The same is true in the case of the permanently comatose. It does not follow that just because one could morally remove life support from such patients, one could therefore morally kill them. For suppose that after the removal of life support, a given patient unexpectedly goes on living. Taking a gun and shooting him through the head does not thereby become the moral thing to do. Nor does some less bloody means of killing him become the moral thing to do. On the other hand, it might turn out to be true (though there is plenty of room for doubt here) that one could dispose of the living remains without moral fault. For if the permanently comatose have indeed ceased to be persons and are, shall we say, just artificially preserved human tissue, then disposing of this tissue would not count as murder (though it might be wrong in some other way). Nevertheless, the fact that this tissue was a human person, and was the relative or friend of someone still living, does give one plenty of reason to treat it with a due of respect that one does not give, say, to pieces of discarded fingernail or hair or surgically removed tonsils and appendices. Certainly the tissue, like any corpse, should be given proper funeral rites. Perhaps, therefore, it ought not to be directly disposed of either. But whatever the truth here may be, abortion is not at all like killing artificially preserved human tissue or removing life support from the permanently comatose. Abortion is, first, not a "letting die" but a direct killing, and second it is the killing of a person *in statu fiendi*. Hence it is murder, as already argued. Hence, further, the assimilation of abortion to the letting die of the permanently comatose is false.

The objection to premise three, that murder is wrong and not morally permissible, was that certain murders are right and morally permissible, or even morally obligatory. The examples were, first, deliberately killing one innocent person in order to save a greater number of other innocent persons from being deliberately killed, and, second, where there is a conflict of rights, such as precisely in the case of abortion itself, where the mother's rights trump those of the child and permit the child to be directly killed for the sake of the mother.

The first example assumes the correctness of a consequentialist theory of ethics, namely that acts are right or wrong according to their consequences. So it has no force against non-consequentialist theories of ethics. In the latter kind of theories, such as are deontological and rights theories, acts are wrong or not independently of their consequences; or, if consequences do play a role, they do so only in the sense that bad consequences can make a permissible act wrong, not in the sense that good consequences can make a wrong act permissible. For instance, it is morally permissible to drink alcohol. But it is not morally permissible to drink alcohol and then drive on the highway. The reason is not, of course, that there is anything wrong with drinking alcohol; it is that the foreseeable consequences of drinking alcohol when driving on the highway are very bad, namely the injury or death of oneself and others. On the other hand, it is always wrong to commit murder, and murder is wrong, in non-consequentialist theories, because of the nature of the act itself. Accordingly, even if a given act of murder happens to have good consequences (several other people are saved from being murdered), these consequences still do not make the act good. The reason is that the consequences do not change the nature of the act. So if the nature of the act stays the same, and if, because of this nature, the act is in itself wrong, the act will stay wrong regardless of how many good consequences it also happens to have.

Now all these points, while sufficient to show that the first example will cause no problems for non-consequentialist theories of ethics, do nevertheless raise puzzles about the coherence of such theories. For if murder is so wrong that it should be prohibited, then a situation where more murders are committed would seem to be morally worse than a situation where fewer murders are committed; and if the aim of the moral injunction not to commit murder is to prevent murders, then to do what will make more murders come about would seem to be more opposed to morality than to do what will make fewer murders come about (even if, in order to do the latter, one must oneself commit murder). Since non-consequentialist theories accept the antecedents of these conditionals, they ought to accept the consequents as well. But they do not. In fact, they would seem to fall into a self-refuting paradox. For to refuse to commit any violations against a certain moral injunction, even when committing a violation would reduce the number of violations, involves these theories in setting up some goal or end of pursuit, the good of not committing violations, and then refusing to do the action that will realize that end better than any other possible action.[3]

Plausible though this reasoning appears, it is nevertheless fallacious. It misidentifies the wrongness of murder and so misidentifies what the goal of non-consequentialist morality is. As regards the wrongness of murder, two points need to be made. First, what makes murder wrong is not the mere fact that death is a harm, or that it frustrates someone's interest or desire to live. Any death is a harm and a frustration in this sense, even a death that happens accidentally or because of some natural disaster or disease. Such deaths might be called sad and tragic, but they cannot be called wrong. Death and other harms are only wrong when they are inflicted deliberately by another rational being and contrary to what is due; that is, when an undue death or harm is expressly chosen by someone as the direct object of his act. But death is not due to the innocent; rather help and mutual regard are. So deliberately inflicting death on the innocent is an undue harm. It is a particular kind of injustice, since justice consists, in its most general idea, in giving each his due. Hence deliberately killing the innocent is wrong, and wrong in its very nature, regardless of the consequences.

Second, one must distinguish between a just agent, a just act, and a just state of affairs. A just state of affairs cannot exist in abstraction from just acts and just agents. A greater number of deaths, for instance, is not more unjust than a lesser number of deaths merely because more people are dead. It is more unjust, if it is more unjust, because more people are *unjustly* dead, and more people can only be unjustly dead if they died because of some agent's unjust act. Of course, it is better to have a more just state of affairs than a less just one. But it does not thereby follow that a state of affairs where one murder is committed is better than a state of affairs where several murders are committed. For the term "murder" is ambiguous. On the one hand, the term can be used to mean the state of affairs where someone is dead through murder. On the other hand, it can be used to mean the agent's act itself of murder and its wrongness. If, when judging the relative moral worth of states of affairs, one uses "murder" only in the first way and ignores or forgets the second way, one can easily err in one's judgment. So, for instance, in the state of affairs where one commits a murder oneself to prevent someone else committing more murders, there are indeed fewer murders in the sense of fewer people dead through murder, but this resulting state of affairs is not thereby morally better. In fact, properly considered, it is morally worse.

The reason is that, from the point of view of acts and agents, this state of affairs is more murderous and more unjust. For in the state of affairs where, as in the example given earlier, one commits murder oneself to prevent the terrorist committing several murders, both are equally murderers and both treat murderously everyone involved. One is oneself, by actually committing the murder, clearly a murderer, and one performs an unjust act. But the terrorist whom one thereby prevents from committing murders is no less a murderer and performs no less an unjust act. For he is party to that one murder, since he has induced another to commit it, and he intends to commit several murders directly himself should that other refuse to comply. As regards everyone else involved, or those not murdered, both are again murderers and unjust. For the terrorist obviously retains a murderous intention in their regard (for this intention is what gets the other to comply with his wishes); and while that other may owe it to them to do what he can to save them, he does not owe it to them to kill another to save them. By doing so he is effectively making them accomplices to his own act of murder. He sullies the life he wins for them with innocent blood and requires them to accept it as the price of innocent blood. No just man could accept such an offer. To wish for life as a result of injustice is itself unjust, since it is, in desire, to be party to that injustice. The just man would prefer death to life on these terms. The case is similar to being offered a gift by a friend who has stolen money in order to buy that gift. No just man would want such a gift, however desirable the gift might be. On the contrary, he would be offended by it.

In short, where someone commits murder to prevent another from committing more murders, the result is murderous and unjust in every way. There is no redeeming moral feature about it at all. No just man, therefore, could possibly prefer it, either as an abstract state of affairs or as himself being active in it. Nor is any non-consequentialist theory of ethics logically committed to preferring it. Such theories counsel the goal of justice, in the sense of all agents living lives of just acts. But this goal, as shown, cannot be achieved by performing unjust acts, no matter what the circumstances may be. It can only be achieved by performing just acts always and everywhere. *Fiat iustitia, ruat caelum*: let justice be, though the heavens fall. Or rather, *fiat iustitia ne ruat caelum*: let justice be, *lest* the heavens fall. For it is absurd to think that anything really worthwhile could get worse by the performance of justice. Only those, like consequentialists, who prefer lesser things to justice, or things like physical life and satisfaction of interests, could think that the heavens were more important than justice, or could think that the heavens that may fall because of justice are better than the heavens that can only stand if there is justice.

The second example used against premise three to show that some murders are right and morally permissible was where one right, that of the pregnant woman, trumps another, that of the child. This example is easier to dismiss than the first. It is sufficient to note that there can be no rights against justice. Rights are part of and flow from justice, or else they could not be rights. Hence whenever a presumed right is found to be against justice, it is not a right after all, or not a right in this case. For instance, everyone, we say, has a right to life, liberty, property, and happiness. So everyone has a right to choose how to live, earn money, buy a house, raise a family, and so on. But no one has a right to do these things in any way at all. No one has a right to live by stealing others' earnings, robbing their houses, seducing their spouses, or kidnapping their children. For all these things are unjust, and no one has a right to be unjust. Consequently no pregnant woman has a right to life or health or choice that could extend to include the right to abort the unborn within her. Abortion, as already argued, is murder and so unjust. There can, therefore, be no right to abortion, and no woman's right to life or choice can give her such a right. Thus there can be no trumping of rights here of the sort the example claims.

The objections, therefore, have clear answers, and the case against the morality of abortion can thus be seen to stand unrefuted. There remains the question of legality, which, in the case of abortion, raises special questions. For abortion, although it is murder, is a murder of a unique kind. The one murdered is not an individual extrinsic to the mother but an individual existing within her and depending on her. To bear new life within one's own body is a special privilege that brings with it many joys. But it also brings with it many difficulties and dangers, emotional and physical. These difficulties can sometimes reach extreme levels, especially if the child is defective in some way, or if the mother's health is seriously affected, or if the mother is not receiving support from the father or is even being pressured by the father and other relatives and friends to abort the child. In these kinds of conditions, it seems harsh or even inhuman to apply to abortion the same legal penalties as are applied to other murders. It is better in this sort of case to apply the principle of subsidiarity and leave things in the hands of the woman and local support and officials and not involve any laws of the larger community. Or if laws are applied, they should be laws that govern the abortion procedure and ensure that the procedure, if it is carried out, is carried out as safely as possible and above all with full explanation to the mother and relatives of all the risks involved. These risks will have to include especially those relating to the longer-term effects of abortion, such as in particular what is now called post-abortion syndrome, where mothers who have aborted their children suffer intense psychological distress and guilt.

This proposed absence of laws against abortion (and also of laws permitting abortion) will not entail any change or diminution in the claim and argument that abortion is a grave moral wrong. The moral case against abortion can and will remain as strong as before, and can still be publicly taught. The only difference will be that no laws are passed or enforced against this moral wrong. Family and friends alone, including, if need be, professionals of various sorts, will, according to the principle of subsidiarity, be the place where the question is faced and answered. Nothing further need be involved.

Notes

1. A useful summary of virtues and vices and the qualities of each is contained in Aristotle's brief treatise entitled *On Virtues and Vices*. For a translation, see Simpson (2013).
2. Sachs (1943: 105–106), and Aristotle, *Politics* 5(8).7.
3. See in particular Scheffler (1982) and Kagan (1989).

Bibliography

The Articles of Confederation and Perpetual Union, at Yale University's online Avalon Project, http://avalon.law.yale.edu/18th_century/artconf.asp.

Aristotle. *On Virtues and Vices*. Translation in Simpson, 2014. *The Great Ethics of Aristotle*. Rutgers: Transaction.

Barker, Sir Ernest. 1946. *The Politics of Aristotle*. Oxford: Oxford University Press.

Bates, C.A 2014. "The centrality of Politeia for Aristotle's Politics: Part II. The marginalization of Aristotle's Politeia in modern political thought." *Social Science Information* 53: 500–517.

Beck, H., ed. 2013. *Ancient Greek Government*. Oxford: Wiley-Blackwell.

Beckman, L. 2001. *The Liberal State and the Politics of Virtue*. New Brunswick, NJ: Transaction.

Bede. 2009. *Ecclesiastical History of the English People*. Oxford: Oxford World's Classics.

Berent, M. 1994. *The Stateless Polis: Towards a Re-evaluation of the Classical Greek Community*. Cambridge PhD thesis.

_____. 1996. "Hobbes and the 'Greek Tongues.'" *History of Political Thought* 17:36–59.

Bernard of Clairvaux, St. *De Consideratione*, in *Patrologia Latina* vol.182 ed. J-P Migne, Paris 1862–1865.

Blackstone, Sir William. 2002. *Commentaries on the Laws of England*, facsimile of the original edition (1765–69). Chicago: University of Chicago Press.

Boniface VIII, Pope. 1302. Bull *Unam Sanctam. Internet Medieval Sourcebook*, www.fordham.edu/halsall/sbook.asp.

Borden, M., ed. 1965. *Anti-Federalist Papers*. Michigan: Michigan State University Press.

Buber, M. 1923. *Ich und Du*, Leipzig: Insel-Verlag.

Burke, Edmund. 1987. *Reflections on the Revolution in France*. Indianapolis: Hackett.

_____. 1999. *Select Works of Edmund Burke: Miscellaneous Writings*, ed. Francis Canavan. Indianapolis: Liberty Fund.

Carlyle, R. W. and A. J. 1903–1936. *A History of Medieval Political Theory in the West*. 6 vols. London: Blackwood and Sons.

Collins, S. D. 2006. *Aristotle and the Recovery of Citizenship*. Cambridge: Cambridge University Press.

The Constitution of the United States of America, at Yale University's online Avalon Project, http://avalon.law.yale.edu/18th_century/usconst.asp.

Dawson, Christopher. 1932. *The Making of Europe*. London: Sheed and Ward.

_____. 1954. *Medieval Essays*. London: Sheed and Ward.

Declaration of the Rights of Man and of the Citizen, at the Center for History and New Media of George Mason University, http://chnm.gmu.edu/revolution/d/295/.

Defourny, M. 1932. *Etudes sur La Politique*. Paris: Beauchesne et Fils.

Den Uyl, D. and D. Rasmussen. 1991. *Liberty and Nature*. Open Court.

Dignitatis Humanae. 1965. Document of the Second Vatican Council, from the Vatican website: http://www.vatican.va/archive/hist_councils/ii_vatican_council/index.htm.

Düring, I. 1957. *Aristotle in the Ancient Biographical Tradition*. Göteborg.

The Federalist Papers, at Yale's Avalon Project, http://avalon.law.yale.edu/subject_menus/fed.asp.

Feinberg, J. 1987–1988. *The Moral Limits of the Criminal Law*. 4 vols. Oxford: Oxford University Press.

Flew, A. G. N. 1981. *Politics of Procrustes*. New York: Prometheus Books.

_____. 1989. *Equality in Liberty and Justice*. New York: Routledge.

Fortes, M. and E. E. Evans-Pritchard, eds. 1940. *African Political Systems*. London: Oxford University Press.

Furman, J. 1997. "Political Illiberalism: The Paradox of Disenfranchisement and the Ambivalences of Rawlsian Justice." *Yale Law Journal* 106: 1197–1231.

Galston, W. 1991. *Liberal Purposes*. Cambridge: Cambridge University Press.

Gauthier, D. 1986. *Morals by Agreement*. Oxford: Clarendon Press.

Gelasius, Pope. 494. *Duo Sunt*, letter to the emperor Athanasius. *Internet Medieval Sourcebook*, www.fordham.edu/halsall/sbook.asp.

George, R.P. 1995. *Making Men Moral*. Oxford: Clarendon Press.

Guttenplan, S., ed. 1975. *Mind and Language*. Oxford: Clarendon Press.

Hanke, L. 1959. *Aristotle and the American Indians*. Chicago: H. Regnery Co.

Hart, H. L. A. 1969. *Law, Liberty and Morality*. Stanford: Stanford University Press.

Heer, F. 1968. *The Holy Roman Empire*. Translated by Janet Sondheimer. New York: Praeger.

Hegel, G. W. F. 1991. *Philosophy of Right*, ed. A. W. Wood. Cambridge: Cambridge University Press.

Held, V. 2006. *The Ethics of Care*. Oxford: Oxford University Press.

Hobbes, T. 1994. *Leviathan*, ed. E. Curley. Indianapolis: Hackett Publishing Company.

Hose, M. 2002. *Aristoteles: Die historischen Fragmente*. Berlin: Akademie Verlag.

Hume, D. 1993. *An Enquiry concerning Human Understanding*. Indianapolis: Hackett Publishing Company.

Jaeger, W. 1923. *Aristoteles: Grundlegung einer Geschichte seiner Entwicklung*. Berlin: Weidmann.

John XXIII, Pope St. 1963 encyclical. *Pacem in Terris*.

John Paul II, Pope St. 1993. "If you want peace, reach out to the poor." *Message of His Holiness Pope John Paul II for the XXVI Annual World Day of Prayer for Peace* (January 1). http://www.vatican.va/holy_father/john_paul_ii/messages/peace/documents/hf_jp-ii_mes_08121992_xxvi-world-day-for-peace_en.html.

———. 1993 encyclical. *Veritatis Splendor.*

———. 1994a. "The family creates the peace of the human family." *Message of His Holiness Pope John Paul II for the XXVII Annual World Day of Prayer for Peace* (January 1). http://www.vatican.va/holy_father/john_paul_ii/messages/peace/documents/hf_jp-ii_mes_08121992_xxvi-world-day-for-peace_en.html.

———. 1994b. *Message of the Holy Father John Paul II for the Fiftieth Anniversary of Monte Cassino* (May 18). http://www.vatican.va/holy_father/john_paul_ii/messages/pont_messages/1994/documents/hf_jp-ii_mes_19940518_50th-montecassino_en.html.

———. 1995a. "Women: teachers of peace." *Message of His Holiness Pope John Paul II for the XXVIII Annual World Day of Prayer for Peace* (January 1). http://www.vatican.va/holy_father/john_paul_ii/messages/peace/documents/hf_jp-ii_mes_08121994_xxviii-world-day-for-peace_en.html.

———. 1995b. *Message of His Holiness Pope John Paul II on the Fiftieth Anniversary of the End of the Second World War in Europe* (May 8). http://www.vatican.va/holy_father/john_paul_ii/speeches/1995/may/documents/hf_jp-ii_mes_08051995_50th-end-war-europe_en.html.

———. 1997. "Offer forgiveness and receive peace." *Message of His Holiness Pope John Paul II for the XXX Annual World Day of Prayer for Peace* (January 1). http://www.vatican.va/holy_father/john_paul_ii/messages/peace/documents/hf_jp-ii_mes_08121996_xxx-world-day-for-peace_en.html.

———. 2000a. "Peace on earth to those whom God loves!" *Message of His Holiness Pope John Paul II for the XXXIII Annual World Day of Prayer for Peace* (January 1). http://www.vatican.va/holy_father/john_paul_ii/messages/peace/documents/hf_jp-ii_mes_08121999_xxxiii-world-day-for-peace_en.html.

———. 2000b. *Jubilee of the Armed Forces and the Police. Homily of John Paul II* (November 19). http://www.vatican.va/holy_father/john_paul_ii/homilies/2000/documents/hf_jp-ii_hom_20001119_jubilarmforces_en.html.

———. 2002a. "No peace without justice, no justice without forgiveness." *Message of His Holiness Pope John Paul II for the XXXV Annual World Day of Prayer for Peace* (January 1). http://www.vatican.va/holy_father/john_paul_ii/messages/peace/documents/hf_jp-ii_mes_20011211_xxxv-world-day-for-peace_en.html.

———. 2002b. *Angelus* (January 27). http://www.vatican.va/holy_father/john_paul_ii/angelus/2002/documents/hf_jp-ii_ang_20020127_en.html.

———. 2002c. *Letter of John Paul II to All the Heads of State and Government of the World and Decalogue of Assisi for Peace* (February 24). http://www.vatican.va/holy_father/john_paul_ii/letters/2002/documents/hf_jp-ii_let_20020304_capi-stato_en.html.

_____. 2003a. "Pacem in terris: a permanent commitment." *Message of His Holiness Pope John Paul II for the XXXVI Annual World Day of Prayer for Peace* (January 1). http://www.vatican.va/holy_father/john_paul_ii/ messages/peace/documents/hf_jp-ii_mes_20021217_xxxvi-world-day-for-peace_en.html.

_____. 2003b. *Address of His Holiness Pope John Paul II to the Diplomatic Corps* (January 13). http://www.vatican.va/holy_father/john_paul_ii/ speeches/2003/january/documents/hf_jp-ii_spe_20030113_diplomatic-corps_en.html.

_____. 2003c. *Angelus* (March 16). http://www.vatican.va/holy_father/ john_paul_ii/angelus/2003/documents/hf_jp-ii_ang_20030316_en.html.

_____. 2004a. "An ever timely commitment: teaching peace." *Message of His Holiness Pope John Paul II for the XXXVII Annual World Day of Prayer for Peace* (January 1). http://www.vatican.va/holy_father/john_paul_ii/ messages/peace/documents/hf_jp-ii_mes_20031216_xxxvii-world-day-for-peace_en.html.

_____. 2004b. *Address of His Holiness Pope John Paul II to the Diplomatic Corps* (January 12). http://www.vatican.va/holy_father/john_paul_ii/ speeches/2004/january/documents/hf_jp-ii_spe_20040112_diplomatic-corps_en.html.

_____. 2004c. *Letter of John Paul II to Cardinal Walter Kasper on the Occasion of the 18th International Meeting of "Peoples and Religions"* (September 3). http://www.vatican.va/holy_father/john_paul_ii/letters/2004/documents/ hf_jp-ii_let_20040903_card-kasper_en.html.

_____. 2004d. *Letter of John Paul II to Cardinal Roger Etchegaray Special Envoy to the Social Weeks of France* (September 20). http://www.vatican.va/ holy_father/john_paul_ii/letters/2004/documents/hf_jp-ii_let_20040920_ social-weeks-france_en.html.

_____. 2005a. "Do not be overcome by evil but overcome evil with good." *Message of His Holiness Pope John Paul II for the XXXVIII Annual World Day of Prayer for Peace* (January 1). http://www.vatican.va/holy_father/ john_paul_ii/messages/peace/documents/hf_jp-ii_mes_20041216_xxxviii-world-day-for-peace_en.html.

_____. 2005b. *Address of His Holiness Pope John Paul II to the Diplomatic Corps* (January 10). http://www.vatican.va/holy_father/john_paul_ii/ speeches/2005/january/documents/hf_jp-ii_spe_20050110_diplomatic-corps_en.html.

Jowett, B. 1871. *Dialogues of Plato*. Oxford: Clarendon Press.

Kagan, S. 1989. *The Limits of Morality*. Oxford: Clarendon Press.

Kalb, James. 2008. *The Tyranny of Liberalism*. Wilmington DE: Intercollegiate Studies Institute.

Kaminski, J. P. and R. Leffler, eds. 1998. *Federalists and Antifederalists: The Debate over the Ratification of the Constitution*. Madison: Madison House Publishers.

Kant, I. 1991. *Political Writings*, ed. H. Reiss and trans. H. B. Nisbet. Cambridge: Cambridge University Press.

Kymlicka, W. and W. Norman. 1994. "Return of the Citizen: A Survey of Recent Work on Citizenship Theory." *Ethics* 104:352–381.

Leo XIII, Pope. 1891 encyclical. *Rerum Novarum.*

Locke, J. 1980. *Second Treatise of Government.* Indianapolis: Hackett Publishing Company.

_____. 1983. *Letter Concerning Toleration.* Indianapolis: Hackett Publishing Company.

Martino, Cardinal Renato. 2003. Interview in the *National Catholic Register.* March 23–29. Also quoted by *Zenit News Agency,* March 17, 2003, at http://www.zenit.org/article-6804?l=english.

Mill, J. S. 1978. *On Liberty.* Indianapolis: Hackett Publishing Company.

Miller, F. D. Jr. 1995. *Nature, Justice and Rights in Aristotle's Politics.* Oxford: Clarendon Press.

Newman, W. L. 1887–1902. *The Politics of Aristotle.* Oxford: Clarendon Press.

Nielsen, T. H., ed. 2002. *Even More Studies in the Ancient Greek Polis.* Stuttgart: Franz Steiner.

Pellegrin, P. 1987. "La Politique d'Aristotle: Unité et Fractures." *Revue Philosophique de la France et de l'Etranger* 77:129–59.

Pinker, S. 2012. *The Better Angels of Our Nature: Why Violence has Declined.* New York: Penguin.

Plato. See Jowett.

Raz, J. 1986. *The Morality of Freedom.* Oxford: Clarendon Press.

Rawls, J. 1971. *A Theory of Justice.* Cambridge: Harvard University Press.

_____. 1993, 1996. *Political Liberalism.* New York: Columbia University Press.

Rhodes, P. J. 1981. *A Commentary on the Aristotelian Athenaiōn Politeia.* Oxford: Clarendon Press.

Rose, V. 1886. *Aristotelis Fragmenta.* Leipzig: Teubner.

Rousseau, J. 1988. *Social Contract.* Indianapolis: Hackett Publishing Company.

Sachs, C. 1943. *The Rise of Music in the Ancient World.* New York: Norton.

Sandel, M. 1984. *Liberalism and its Critics.* Cambridge: Cambridge University Press

Scheffler, S. 1982. *The Rejection of Consequentialism.* Oxford: Clarendon Press

Schooyans, M. 1997. *The Totalitarian Trend of Liberalism.* St. Louis, MO: Central Bureau, CCUA.

Schütrumpf, E. 1980. *Die Analyse der Polis durch Aristoteles.* Amsterdam: B. R. Grüner.

_____. 1991–2005. *Aristoteles: Politik.* Berlin: Akademie Verlag, Berlin-Darmstadt.

Simpson, P. L. P. 1990. "Making the Citizens Good: Aristotle's City and Its Contemporary Relevance."*Philosophical Forum* 22:149–166.

_____ 1994. "Liberalism, State, and Community."*Critical Review* 8:159–173.

_____. 1995. "Community in a New Libertarianism: Rejoinder to Legutko." *Critical Review* 9: 427–429.

_____. 1997. *The Politics of Aristotle.* Chapel Hill: University of North Carolina Press.

_____. 1998. *A Philosophical Commentary on the Politics of Aristotle.* Chapel Hill: University of North Carolina Press.

_____. 2001. *Karol Wojtyła.* Belmont: Wadsworth.

_____. 2006. "Aristotle's Defensible Defense of Slavery." *Polis* 23:95–115.

_____. 2011. *Goodness and Nature (with a Supplement on Historical Origins).* New York: Lucairos Occasio Press.

_____. 2012. "The Communitarian State."*Universitas* (Taiwan) 39:5–28.

_____. 2013. *The Eudemian Ethics of Aristotle.* New Brunswick: Transaction.

Stanford Online Encyclopedia of Philosophy. http://plato.stanford.edu.

Suarez, F., S. J. 2012. *Defense of the Catholic and Apostolic Faith against the Errors of Anglicanism,* trans. P. L. P. Simpson, 2 vols. New York: Lucairos Occasio Press.

Talisse, R. B. 2005. *Democracy After Liberalism.* New York: Routledge.

_____, 2007. *A Pragmatist Philosophy of Democracy.* New York: Routledge.

_____, 2009. *Democracy and Moral Conflict.* Cambridge: Cambridge University Press.

_____, 2012. *Pluralism and Liberal Politics.* New York: Routledge.

De Tocqueville, A. 2011. *The Ancien Régime and the French Revolution,* ed. J. Elster, trans. A. Goldhammer. Cambridge: Cambridge Texts in the History of Political Thought.

Weber, Max. 1965. *Politics As a Vocation,* trans. H. H. Gerth and C. Wright Mills. Philadelphia: Fortress Press.

Wojtyła, K. 1979. *The Acting Person.* Boston: Analecta Husserliana.

Index

burdens of judgment, 82–83, 109–10, 126, 128–29
bureaucracy, 99, 159
Burke, 37–38, 40, 47n
Bush, President, 184, 193n
Byzantine empire, 77

Caesar, 83, 109
campaign, *see* election
Carlyle, 47n, 193n
Carthaginians, 144
Catholic, Christianity, Church, 2, 81–82, 129, 180, 184
centralization, 36, 45, 151–69, 172
Chaeronea, 182, 193n
Chamberlain, 190
chance, 56–56, 66
character, 54–55, *see also* virtue
charity, 117, 187–88, 192, 195n
Charleston, 161
checks and balances, 40, 138, 159–60, 175
child, childhood, etc., 19, 53–55
Christ, 79, 81
Christendom, medieval, 11–12, 74, 77, 107, 181
Christian, 7, 11, 100–101, 151, 186, 188, 195n
Christianity, 73, 75, 79–82, 107
church, 11, 175, 185, 195n, state and, 12, 49
Cicero, 173
citizen, 4, definition of, 113–15
city, 18, 20
  nature and kinds of, 19, 26–27, 132, 148
civil war, 152, 160, 161, 163, 167–68, 171, the US Civil War, 120
civility, duty of, 126–27
class, analysis and kinds of, 25–26, 137–40
Clay, 161
coercion, 98
  and belief, 109–10
  and law, 60
  monopoly of, 4, 8, 11–13, 15, 46, 49, 98, 122, 172, 181
  see also force
Collins, 16n
comatose, permanently, 210, 214–15
commerce, 152–54, 157, 172, 174
common sense, 140, 156
communism, communist, 2, 24, 69, 74, 123, 183, 189

community, 15, 155
  authorities in, 72–83, 117–18
  and comprehensive good, truth, 13, 68, 73–74, 85–96, 109–110, 120, 126–28, 148, 176–77, 180, 183, 205, 208
  member of, 113–14
  men belong first to, 66–73, 182–83
  nature and function of, 56, 92, 94, 96, 104–105, 113–14
Comte de Vergennes, 169n
congress, 29–30, 153–58, 160, 166–68
Connecticut, 163
consciousness, 88–89, 211, 213
consensus, overlapping, 7, 101–102, 126–27
consequentialism in ethics, 216–19
consolidation, 164, 171
Constantinople, 173
contraception, 99
conversion, 192, 195n
Corinth, 143, 193n
corruption, 171-2, 194n
Cos, 142
counterrevolution, the American, 149, 152
courage, coward, 53, 55, 97, 117, 135, 198
courts, 175, 209
creation, ex nihilo, 89
credit, 144, 155, 162
Cretans, 144
crime, 166–68, 31, 106, 203
cultural imperialism and relativism, 146
Cyme, 142

David, king, 23, 28
Dawson, 47n, 193n
de las Casas, 102, 178
de Tocqueville, 47n
dead, death, 71–72, 98, 218–19
debt, 155–56, 158, 160–63, 193n
Declaration of Rights of Man and Citizen, 46n
Defourny, 193n
Delphic oracle, 87
demagoguery, 37–46
democracy, democratic, etc., 30, 44, 86, 133, 135, 143–47, 152, 191, 194n
  kinds of, 138–42
  modern, representative, 34, 46n, 93, 114–15
  and virtue, 140–41
demons, 129
Den Uyl, 62n, 130n

PGMO 04/24/2018